51, 52, 72, 109-11, 139.

THE THATCHER YEARS

THE THATCHER YEARS

A DECADE OF REVOLUTION IN BRITISH POLITICS

JOHN COLE

BBC BOOKS

For my wife, Madge

Published by BBC Books
A division of BBC Enterprises Ltd
Woodlands, 80 Wood Lane, London W12 0TT

First published 1987
© John Cole 1987

ISBN 0 563 20573 3

Typeset by Phoenix Photosetting, Chatham, Kent
Printed in England by Mackays of Chatham, Kent

CONTENTS

PREFACE

Politics is not simply a clash of ideologies or a continuous battle for power. It is also the story of a wide variety of human beings, most of whom have a sincere wish to serve the people they represent. The fact that their judgement of how life in Britain can be improved differs not only from one party to another, but even among political colleagues, must not blind us to their merits. Our politicians are a bewildering mixture of passion, talent, wit and wisdom, though with occasional lapses into humbug and folly. They are often convinced – even convincing – sometimes bigoted, often funny people. The best of them, if asked what on earth they think they are doing, would give Damon Runyon's ambiguous answer: 'The best I can.' It is an epitaph most of us might envy.

This is not a formal history of the Thatcher years, much less a biography of the Prime Minister. Indeed, her own characteristically combative view is that 'it is *much* too soon for that'. Rather it is an attempt to take a sceptical, though affectionate look at all the leading political figures of the eighties, and to extract from their actions and reactions the essence of this revolutionary decade.

During the eighties, Britain's domestic politics are 'a world turned upside down', to borrow a phrase used about such diverse events as the Acts of the Apostles and the American Revolution. It is a decade in which Margaret Thatcher, supported by a group with economic views further to the Right than Conservatives have espoused since the second world war, seized the helm of their party and changed its policies and image; and in which an equally determined group on the Left – symbolised, though not wholly controlled by, Tony Benn – tried to revolutionise the Labour Party by altering its constitution in order to transform its policies. The book also describes a third revolution: the departure from Labour of the Social Democrats, who formed their own party, and made an alliance with the Liberals which turned British politics into a genuine three-horse race for the first time since the twenties.

A perceptive reader will find here material from which to attempt to judge whether these are permanent revolutions, leading on to the possibility of hung parliaments, coalition governments, and possibly further party realignments; or whether they will be reversed.

The book had its origins in my weekly columns in the *Listener*, and I am grateful to the editor, Russell Twisk, for permission to use material from these. I also wish to thank Donald Trelford, editor of the *Observer*, for agreeing that I might draw on articles written while I was his deputy.

Finally, I offer my thanks also to Madge, my wife, who not only tolerated and sustained a preoccupied companion through recent holidays and weekends, but brought a mind unscarred by political obsession to bear on my typescript, and contributed a necessary list of dates as a guide through the three-party maze.

Claygate, Surrey.
Spring 1987.

CHAPTER 1

WANTED:
A PHILOSOPHER'S STONE

The eighties is the decade when Britain's post-war consensus flew apart. Its fissiparous tendencies had long been evident, but what caused the eventual breach was the emergence, on both flanks of politics, of powerful personalities who decided the times were ripe for radical change. This pattern of revolution was confused, however, by other equally powerful personalities in the Centre, who wanted to break the mould and create a new political consensus.

The decisive event in this political revolution took place before the decade began. This was the seizure, first of the leadership, and then of control, of the Conservative Party by Margaret Thatcher, at the head of a faction in the grip of an economic doctrine they originally called monetarism but quickly transformed into a political creed called Thatcherism. From the election of Britain's first woman Prime Minister in 1979 flowed a remarkable series of events, in her own party and in the Opposition. She recited a prayer of reconciliation attributed to St Francis of Assisi when she arrived at 10 Downing Street, but she mothered a Conservative revolution that was the decisive, and divisive, happening of the decade, both for the nation and for her own party.

Margaret Thatcher produces stronger reaction than any other political leader in modern times. People either love her or hate her. In part this is because she is the first woman to achieve such prominence, and therefore attracts more favourable or unfavourable prejudices than more familiar political figures with grey heads and grey suits. But it is also because she is a woman with a dominant, even obsessive personality, an acute sense of public relations, and a propensity to deliver her opinions, on anything from economics to morality, in a tone that defies dissent.

Mrs Thatcher's advisers have encouraged these traits, with the intention of winning for her the enviable role of Mother of the Nation that gave other pioneer women politicians, like Indira Gandhi and Golda Meir, unique pre-eminence in their countries. As I write the Prime Minister, during a television interview on her wardrobe, has been advising the nation on the folly of ironing its hem-lines, thus making it more difficult to lengthen garments later. But perhaps, like a Bishop or a Pope, her views when not speaking '*ex cathedra*, on a matter of faith or morals' – or, in this case, politics – need not be taken with tragic seriousness by those disposed to heavy ironing.

Whatever her opinion on fashions in hem-lines, the Prime Minister is not susceptible to changes in political fashion. Friends and opponents agree that her outstanding characteristic is constancy, a reluctance to change her mind. When matters were going badly for her during the Westland crisis, a minister used in private conversation a phrase I had last heard from my grandmother: 'We're all as God made us,' he said, and added darkly, 'and he didn't make Margaret Thatcher to say "I'm wrong".'

Her victory in 1979 convulsed the Labour Party also. The following year Labour elected its first Left-wing leader since it began seriously to aspire to power in the inter-war years. The choice of Michael Foot in preference to Denis Healey was a last despairing effort by its MPs to avert the internal revolution that threatened to overwhelm and split the traditional Labour Party and deprive it of future hope of office. But a section of the Labour Party was also in the grip of a compulsion to revolutionise its structure and policies. Tony Benn, one of the most eloquent Labour politicians in the Wilson–Callaghan era, had become disillusioned with what he saw as a betrayal of socialism by their governments, in which he had served. This reflected a mood on the Left which looked back to Clement Attlee's immediate post-war governments as a Golden Age of radical socialism – though that was not at all how the Left saw them at the time. In 1979 the recrimination after defeat turned into a campaign for internal constitutional changes and an acrimonious battle to put Tony Benn in Denis Healey's place as deputy leader.

Michael Foot's final attempt to paper over these widening cracks was blighted in 1981, when an influential group of Labour MPs broke away to form the Social Democratic Party, the first new major political party in Britain since the first year of the century, when the Labour Representation Committee turned itself into the Labour Party and began the long march to power. The Social Democrats and their Liberal allies, who had an astonishing success in by-elections and opinion polls in their first year, now aspired to replace Labour, as Labour had replaced the Liberals sixty years earlier.

For a time this seemed likely to be the most significant revolution of the eighties, for Mrs Thatcher's government was divided and in the doldrums. Then in 1982 came the Argentine invasion of the Falkland Islands, inflicting what at first looked like a mortal political blow to the Government. But when the British Task Force won back the Falklands, disaster turned into triumph for the Prime Minister. As Victor of Port Stanley she was able to staunch the Alliance tide and overwhelm Labour's incipient recovery. The decade of revolutions was to continue its unpredictable course.

These remarkable political events did not occur in a vacuum. The eighties may prove to be the decade when British politicians inadvertently detach themselves from an uncomfortable hook. For a generation and more, governments of both complexions have suffered from the public's belief that there must be a comparatively simple solution to the nation's economic malaise if their politicians, like the No. 2 company in the car hire business, would just 'try harder'. One result of this decade may be a final shattering of that illusion.

Not that the origins of this mood are hard to fathom. Because of the trauma of depression in the thirties it is understandable that every government since 1945 has gained power by promising greater prosperity than its predecessor. For the first two post-war decades, natural recovery from wartime austerity, accelerated by scientific and technological achievement, lent credibility to such claims. Harold Macmillan's tenure of office between 1957 and 1963 was the last flowering of that economic recovery, which had allowed R. A. Butler to foresee that British standards of living would double within twenty-five years, and had caused Harold Wilson to taunt the Conservatives for engineering a four-year economic cycle to win elections. But since Sir Alec Douglas-Home's time, the belief in inevitable economic progress has come to seem less plausible. Harold Wilson's White-Hot Technological Revolution failed to materialise; Edward Heath's 'no lame ducks' policy, subsequently amended, culminated in a three-day week and a further issue of crutches to ducks; the Wilson–Callaghan Social Contract provided, in its later years, a welcome respite from the hyper-inflation that some thought inevitable in the mid-seventies, but it eventually crumbled because any kind of national consensus on distribution of wealth and incomes still eluded them.

This left Margaret Thatcher, dedicated to creating an Enterprise Culture in Britain, relying on incentives to produce the competitive and productive performances that would enable us to survive in the world of Americans, Germans and Japanese and the emerging world of super-competitors like Taiwan, Hong Kong and Korea. Hers was the most *laissez-faire* government for at least half a century. It would test the theory that 'setting the people free' (Churchill's slogan in 1951) would transform the nation's economic prospects. By the second half of the decade this economic miracle had still to appear, and sceptical observers of post-war politics recalled the less famous second part of Alexander Pope's couplet:

> Hope springs eternal in the human breast;
> Man never is, but always *to be* blessed.

Or, as Bacon put it, hope makes a good breakfast but a bad supper. Yet economic millenarianism – a belief that politicians can lead us to a land flowing with milk, honey, stable prices, full employment, lower taxes, better public services, and higher living standards for all, and all at once – runs deep in the modern British character. It has taken many forms, and wandered across party boundaries, as in the 'cold bath in Europe' theory, with British industry transformed by an exhilarating climate of competition in a larger market. This theory excited politicians of various complexions before Britain's entry into the Community, but membership produced a less significant change than either protagonists or opponents believed. Europe proved to be no more of an economic elixir than earlier ones.

What made Margaret Thatcher's first government stand out was the conviction displayed, for example, in Sir Geoffrey Howe's first Budget. Edward Heath had, after all, tested the effect of lower taxes in producing incentives, without exciting results. Yet Howe, with the enthusiastic backing of the Prime Minister, gambled in switching sharply from direct to indirect taxes, with most benefit going to the better off, and the harder-up penalised by price increases. Political and economic experiments can rarely be conducted in test-tubes. The revolution of the New Conservatism had to be attempted during the nastiest world post-war recession. Even so, if this revolution also failed to produce the revival the British craved, the belief in miracle cures generally – not just Mrs Thatcher's particular brand – might begin to fade, and millenarianism go just a little out of fashion. George Eliot coined an enlightening concept in marital politics: that to 'begin life again at a lower level of expectation' than in the immediate post-honeymoon period represented an access of wisdom.

Yet in the early eighties, even as Mrs Thatcher's experiment hit the first destructive waves, it seemed improbable that, three or four years on, the electorate would jump straight from the frying-pan of monetarism-plus into a fire of massive new public ownership and protectionism, which was what at least the National Executive Committee of the Labour Party – though by no means all its parliamentary leaders – was advocating. In 1983 the Conservatives were returned with a larger and overwhelming majority, but the victory owed much to the Falklands and to a divided and demoralised Opposition.

Both groups in that Opposition were in ferment after their defeat. The iconoclastic mood that had earlier set Labour off on its self-destructive period of constitutional chaos was matched by a new iconoclasm within the Alliance. Roy Jenkins, the Social Democrats' first leader, had been a gentle reformer who, in partnership with David Steel, a Liberal leader who was complementary in age, experience and attitudes, had ridden the first wave of Alliance optimism. By contrast, David Owen, his successor in 1983, was a man of the same political steeliness that had made Margaret Thatcher the dominant figure in the politics of the eighties. From a weaker base than hers he displayed the same freedom from self-doubt and a parallel capacity for hard work to tackle the political Everest that towered above the third party.

Long before the SDP was founded, it was clear that an influential and vocal group in society, and especially in the media, favoured a realignment of parties, induced by or followed by a change in the British electoral system to proportional representation, and with the expectation of more or less permanent government of the Centre. In some business circles in the seventies, before a last fling with the new brand of Conservatism became an option, an earlier variant of Centrist politics had been mooted – a Businessmen's Government stretching politically no further than from Lords Robens and Marsh, former (and disillusioned) Labour ministers, to Cecil King, proprietor of the *Daily Mirror*, and John Davies, then of the CBI. The intention was to avoid violent swings in economic policy, which the advocates of the scheme blamed for British industry's indifferent performance.

But both before and after the creation of the Alliance there were sharp differences of opinion about the effect of political changes on economic performance, as well as on the merits of proportional representation. Its supporters believed PR was both fair and beneficial, but others were hesitant about jettisoning an electoral system which, though it differed from those in continental Europe, had elected Disraeli, Gladstone, Salisbury, Asquith, Lloyd George, Baldwin, Attlee and Churchill, brought Britain successfully through two world wars, and maintained it as the most stable democracy in the world. It was not simple conservatism that made many people resent this electoral system being called 'a crooked roulette wheel in a bent casino'.

The Alliance had put PR back on the agenda. But that party's progress against Labour became more difficult when, following Michael Foot's resignation immediately after the 1983 electoral disaster, David Steel and David Owen found themselves taking on Neil Kinnock, Labour's improbable counter-revolutionary. Kinnock, though a man of the Left by origin, instinct and conviction, set the demoralised Labour Party's sights on the one legitimate aim of any party in a democracy: to gain power in order to achieve as many of its policies as possible. He demanded that his followers should never forget what happened to them in June 1983, and that they should subordinate their internal quarrels to the objective of regaining power. In the process he earned the implacable opposition of less flexible Left-wingers: by 1986 Dennis Skinner regarded Kinnock as further to the Right than Harold Wilson, and a Right-winger responded to this belief by saying that Kinnock was also to the Right of Roy Hattersley, who had been his Centre–Right opponent in the leadership election. Yet Kinnock also had his sticking-point: unilateral nuclear disarmament, the cause of the Left in his generation, as pacifism had been in the thirties and opposition to German rearmament in the fifties. That conviction complicated the political geography of the eighties even more.

The objective of all the political turmoil in this decade has been a cure for Britain's economic weakness. Some sceptics thought the causes of this weakness lay deeper than party politics. Ingredients suggested included an inability to adjust to the inevitable consequences of an end to empire and to changed world trading patterns; a tendency in Britain to give higher prestige and priority, in education as in rewards later, to the humanities, which have made this a civilised place to live, rather than to technical and managerial skills, which have made others richer; and the failure of a remarkably unyielding class system to adjust to the erosion of deference.

Even in a decade of political revolution the economic debate followed familiar tracks: over the best mix in the mixed economy; how much intervention in industry; whether inflation was best controlled with or without policies – statutory, voluntary, or fiscal – for wages and prices. Argument continued also about the balance between public and private spending, and about whether direct or indirect taxation, in varying mixes, would help or harm incentives and social justice. The Welfare State remained at once beloved and controversial.

In such debates politicians had a leading role in creating the climate in which other economic decisions are taken. But British public opinion over many decades had asked more of them than that. They were expected to find the philosopher's stone, to make the critical breakthrough. But during the eighties people reluctantly faced the fiercesome possibility that politicians were neither all-knowing nor omnipotent; that by exhortation, by improving education and training, manipulating the tax and social welfare systems, by jawboning about wages, Whitehall and Westminster could help or hinder, but that there was no purely political solution to the British sickness, and that much of the real action was taking place – or failing to take place – well away from the centres of political power in London.

Politics are vital in a democracy, as a safeguard as well as a stimulus. They can sustain or poison a nation's life. But they are best understood, especially in a period when the rhetoric is heightened by the deep divisions between the political parties, if we occasionally remind ourselves about the limitations of a government's power.

CHAPTER 2

THE HEADMISTRESS TAKES OVER

It is notoriously difficult to decide which came first, the chicken or the egg. Has the Conservative Party changed so fundamentally in this decade of revolution because it is led by the most unyielding Prime Minister since Neville Chamberlain? Or is Margaret Thatcher the kind of leader she has become because of the attitude taken by ministers, indeed the whole political Establishment, to a woman at the top?

The Prime Minister is a product of natural selection. Any politician who reaches the top of what Disraeli called the greasy pole has special qualities. The first woman to get there was bound to have extra rations of toughness and self-assurance, and a willingness to walk alone. Mrs Thatcher has all of these. She was born tough. Some colleagues suspect she became self-assured in the cradle. She is something of a loner.

As early as the 1979 election she stood out from her colleagues. Probably because she was the first woman party leader, her press conferences at Central Office drew huge attendances. The overcrowding and heat from television lights were almost unbearable, and experienced campaigners like Willie Whitelaw, Geoffrey Howe, Keith Joseph and Jim Prior wilted visibly. Their leader's demeanour recalled the story of a Hollywood make-up man in a Rita Hayworth film being directed by her then husband, Orson Welles. He suddenly shouted: 'Cut! Miss Hayworth is sweating.' Welles grasped him by the lapels: 'Buddy,' he said. 'Horses sweat. You and me, we perspire. Miss Hayworth glows.'

During that election Margaret Thatcher glowed, and not just physiologically, for she was on a nervous high, enjoying herself, feeling like a future Prime Minister. Her style in that campaign revealed what her style in office would be: risk-taking, combative, unyielding. Colleagues detected the first signs of a headmistressy streak, although that may have been in the eyes of the beholders, who had no experience of being led by a woman.

It is easy now to forget how junior Margaret Thatcher was when she succeeded Edward Heath. Just before she became Prime Minister, a close colleague commented to me on her attitude to this: 'Do you remember how Harold Wilson always talked about his experience as President of the Board of Trade? And Ted Heath used to talk about having been at Industry and the Foreign Office. Well, what do you think Margaret talks about? Not about having been Minister of Education, but about her briefs in Opposition – the Treasury, taxation and so on.' He implied that she was embarrassed at never having held a more heavyweight ministerial post.

Her election as leader was one of the great surprises of British political history. It was caused by a combination of circumstances: the unpopularity of Heath, which Tory canvassers discovered on the doorsteps during the two elections of 1974; the loyal refusal of Willie Whitelaw to stand until Heath had withdrawn; the self-effacement of Keith Joseph. The astonishment in her party about her election may be hard to recapture at this distance in time, but what is stamped indelibly on my memory is the attitude to her leadership of many shadow ministers she inherited from the Heath years. They had suffered a trauma: not only had they known her as a junior, and not notably assertive, member of the Heath Cabinet and been astonished at how events had leapfrogged her to the top; more important, Tories had never expected to be the first party with a woman leader. Any who had given this subject any thought would have placed a modest bet on Labour, or later the Alliance, as the natural home of feminism. So when it was the Conservatives who took this revolutionary step in the politics of the sexes, the shock was all the greater.

Yet when all the excuses have been made Mrs Thatcher had cause for irritation, for her colleagues cannot wholly have concealed in Shadow Cabinet the condescending attitude many of them expressed to journalists. It may be summed up in a phrase: 'We'll have to look after this inexperienced woman, and keep her on the right path.' So if the first woman Prime Minister is a product of natural selection, her conditioning in office, as an unconventional but dynamic feminist, was certain to accentuate the same qualities and faults: determination, aggression in debate, occasional resort to feminine charm, stubbornness.

Jim Prior notes: 'In the early days I think Margaret was worried that we would not accept her authority'; and he honestly adds: 'I dare say she was right, since most of the powerful voices were ranged against her.' Over the months and years of her first Administration, she imposed her authority, gradually winnowing out recalcitrant opponents, bringing in those who backed her policies, or at least owed to her their preferment.

It is wrong to think these were years of unrelieved hostility between two wings of the Cabinet. Even the most implacable political opponents had their happier moments. Jim Prior once drew her attention to a journalist's comment that in a broadcast she had 'sounded sexy'. Her reply, as ever, was quick and assertive: 'And when ever did you think I didn't sound sexy, Jim?' But although it is tempting to attribute the revolutionary colour of the Thatcher government to its leader's sex and personality, we must also note the circumstances in which it took office. The removal of Heath was not just personal. It was that, but it also represented an intellectual reaction against the economic posture of governments since the war, Conservative as well as Labour.

This Government came to power in the grip of a theory. It is true that various ministers adhered to that theory with differential fervour. Tories normally think of themselves as the Party of Good Government, rather than as missionaries of any one of the fifty-seven varieties of good government that political philosophy offers. Nevertheless, most Conservatives were united in believing that Britain was suffering from loss of incentive and enterprise. They believed that, because public expenditure had been allowed to swallow up too large a share of the nation's wealth, and because the revenue to match – or, rather, not quite match – that expenditure had been raised disproportionately through direct, instead of indirect taxes (income tax rather than VAT), the will to invest, to take risks and to work hard for extra wages or salary had been eroded.

Some ministers worried more than others about the failure to match revenue and expenditure. For some, the Public Sector Borrowing Requirement was a hated totem of profligate years under Wilson and Callaghan, and even of the Heath–Barber boom of the seventies. For others, the large contingent of Heath survivors, this did not matter so much. In the more pragmatic breasts around Mrs Thatcher's Cabinet table the old devil of Keynesianism still nestled, but on the main incentives argument everyone agreed.

Mrs Thatcher was lucky to have as her deputy a man with a strong sense of his duty to the leader. Willie Whitelaw, who might so easily have become leader himself, was by conviction a Tory of the old school, unimpressed by new economic theories, with a strong sense of obligation to the under-privileged and unemployed and a strong aversion to some people he found himself serving with. But he believed his over-riding duty was to maintain the unity of his Party and the Government. Under his soldierly code, if he was not prepared to put that duty first, he ought not to have accepted the deputy leadership. As internal debate grew fierce, some natural allies on the 'wet' wing of the Cabinet became exasperated by his loyalty to the Prime Minister. They complained that he did not stand up to her as his seniority would, uniquely, have allowed him to do.

Whitelaw believed that, if he reserved his criticism for their private encounters, he could have more influence as a brake on the Prime Minister's instincts. By this method throughout her two terms he has kept a hand in appointments to the Government, and ensured that men and women he considers to be able are given their chance, even if their opinions do not fit neatly into the new orthodoxy. Above all, he has provided the cement that has held the Cabinet together.

The Prime Minister also established special relationships with the two senior members of her first Administration who served in the Lords. The Lord Chancellor, Lord Hailsham, has been politically maverick – a reform Tory during and after the war, candidate for the leadership in 1963, unpredictable of opinion in the Thatcher years. Sometimes he seemed likely to become a leader of dissent against the new economics. But he admired Mrs Thatcher personally, and she reciprocated by keeping him in his job into ripe old age – partly, colleagues thought, because she sympathised with his loneliness after his wife was killed in a riding accident.

The Foreign Secretary, Lord Carrington, was another Tory grandee of whom the Prime Minister at first seemed in some awe. She gave him free rein in foreign affairs, for her experience in 1979 was limited. Against her own instincts she took his advice on the form of independence for Rhodesia/Zimbabwe. In return for this free hand abroad, Carrington often refrained from intervening against her in domestic matters, as *his* instincts dictated. In 1981 he succeeded in prolonging for a few months the Cabinet career of his deputy, Ian Gilmour, the most articulate critic of the new economics. But Gilmour was eventually sacked, and Carrington's influence on domestic policy was limited.

In her Chancellor, Mrs Thatcher had a man who shared her economic enthusiasms, though his attitudes on social issues were different from hers. Geoffrey Howe had been a founder of the Bow Group, which in its early years had been on the Left of the Conservative Party in welfare state matters, but he had also been principal architect of Edward Heath's trade union legislation. When this was overturned, and as successive incomes policies ran into trouble, he became convinced that the British economy needed to be taken by the scruff of the neck and shaken – though the emollient Sir Geoffrey would not have used such aggressive language. He had worked his way gradually to belief in the New Conservatism. That theory demanded a retreat from the government intervention in the economy that had been the policy of every administration since Winston Churchill's wartime coalition. It aimed to reverse what its adherents saw as a drift towards corporatism, and to reinstate market mechanisms as the principal determinants of the economy.

Its great evangelist, both in Opposition and in Government, was Keith Joseph, the man whose combinaton of economic zeal and political diffidence had left the road to the leadership open for Margaret Thatcher. It was his speeches in the months after the Heath government fell that set the agenda for the New Conservatism. Sir Keith was better as a political thinker than as an operative. As Industry Secretary in Mrs Thatcher's Cabinet he found himself forced by circumstances – that word of Burke's so beloved by traditional Tories! – to act against his instincts. Colleagues on the Left of the Cabinet felt the government did not get credit for the subsidies they voted to save the steel and motor industries because Sir Keith looked so uncomfortable when announcing them. But the Prime Minister would hear no criticism of him, and indeed this kindly man had few enemies even among those who thought him wrong.

Margaret Thatcher's ill-luck was that her attempt to launch an economic revolution, to restore private enterprise as the engine of the economy, and to revive investment, coincided with the worst world recession since the thirties and a doubling of energy prices. No one had predicted the severity and persistence of this recession, and even when the tremors of this second oil shock subsided they left their damaging mark on the world and British economies. So the theory on which the new Government was based ran into trouble for an unexpected reason, as economic theories usually do. J. K. Galbraith – who is not the American guru the Prime Minister most fervently admires – once wrote: 'Economics is not durable truth; it requires continuous revision and accommodation. Nearly all its errors are made by those who cannot change.'

From Mrs Thatcher's point of view, the difficulty about that prescription was that she remembered with horror the deviation by Heath and Anthony Barber from the Selsdon Programme that the Conservatives had welded from similar economic ideas before the 1970 election. Indeed, one of the dominant influences on the Prime Minister and her closest colleagues has been U-turn Psychosis, also known as Barber's Syndrome. She has been obsessed by the belief that what Tennyson called 'honest doubt' is the enemy of revolutionary political action. And it was on economic and political revolution, leading to a revival of Britain and the final defeat of socialism, that Margaret Thatcher had set her heart.

In her early years the problems of recession were aggravated by anxieties about inflation. Under Labour, the retail prices index had risen to 25%, fallen into single figures during various incomes policies, but had begun to rise again when these crumpled during 1979's Winter of Discontent. Prices were rising annually at 10.1% when Labour lost office. Within a year this figure had risen to 21.9.

One reason for this startling rise was a promise the Conservatives had given during the election to honour the findings of the Clegg Commission, set up by Labour to adjudicate on public sector pay. This added 25% to the public wage bill. Another reason was Sir Geoffrey's first Budget, in June 1979. Even during the election the Conservatives' tax promises had been controversial. Denis Healey and Shirley Williams said they would have to double VAT to pay for their promises of lower income tax. Joel Barnett, Labour's No. 2 at the Treasury (whose book *Inside the Treasury* was subsequently to make him Mrs Thatcher's favourite Labour author) said anyone earning less than £192 a week would be worse off under the Tories, and that their intention was to switch money from the poor to the rich. Margaret Thatcher and Geoffrey Howe said such calculations were ridiculous, and Central Office accused Labour of ignoring the relief Conservatives intended to give lower down the pay scale by raising tax thresholds.

Before the Budget, the CBI and TUC heard of the possibility that there would indeed be a 15% VAT. They protested to Prior – who had become Employment Secretary, and was closer to the two organisations than other ministers – that this would inflate wage claims. Prior had a sympathetic chat with the Prime Minister, and hoped the increase would not be as sharp as that. This proved to be optimistic.

The Government was determined to cut sharply the top rates of income tax. The rate for earned income then stood at 83%, and Howe, with the Prime Minister's backing, wanted to bring it down to 60%, for the Conservatives had come to power believing that this was a disincentive to economic growth. But they wanted simultaneously to make a sharp reduction in the standard rate, to convince average earners that the political climate had changed for them also. The smallest cut that might make such an impact was 3p, from 33 to 30p in the pound.

That was a much more expensive business because of the large number of taxpayers involved. It has been said that God must have loved the poor, he made so many of them; the same applies to average earners. The Treasury found that to finance such widespread cuts, which would cost more than £4 billion, the VAT rates would have to be increased from 8 and 12½% to 15%, and petrol tax would have to go up sharply. The retail price index rose four points because of this, and cuts in subsidies to nationalised industries added a further two points. Overall, expenditure cuts of £3 billion were made, leading to higher prescription charges and other unpopular moves.

The Prime Minister was disappointed by hostile reaction in the opinion polls and the press. But the Budget taught her a salutary lesson: the British public still believed that good fairies should be able to deliver golden apples without blemish. It had yet to learn the lesson that there could be no income tax cuts without rises in VAT or other indirect taxes, or a reduction in public services, or both. Fewer subsidies might mean fewer jobs. Short-term pain might be a price worth paying for long-term pleasure, but the Government was not offering free lunches.

Reports of Margaret Thatcher's anxiety about the slump in her Government's popularity in those early months after the Budgets raised the question of whether she was a true gambler who would stake all on the economic theory she believed in. Would she keep her chips on the black if the wheel kept stopping at red? In the event, her faith remained stronger than any other minister's, and she was her Government's most fervent keeper of the Friedmanite flame. She was not, however, oblivious of the political consequences of economic dogma. Highly pragmatic decisions on gas prices and mortgages showed she would not always let the market rule if the result offended her natural constituency. She might lack Willie Whitelaw's or Michael Heseltine's concern about the North–South divide, but she had at least as sensitive a feel for Britain's Finchleys as Richard Nixon had for his famous Middle American touchstone, Peoria, Illinois.

Each government insists on learning the hard way. Labour advocates of currency devaluation in the sixties saw only the benefits for British industry, and rarely foresaw the pressure on prices – and therefore wages.

Conservatives, dazzled by their belief in the automatic, almost magical benefits of an Enterprise Culture, did not foresee what the switch to indirect taxes would do to wages. In fact, politicians as a class contrive to remain comparatively oblivious of the almost iron laws of the labour market.

This is, alas, the rough end of the economist's trade, and not taken seriously enough. When Nigel Lawson was City Editor of the *Sunday Telegraph* and I was Labour Correspondent of the *Guardian*, the National Economic Development Council, over which he now presides, was in its infancy. He and Samuel Brittan, economic columnist of the *Financial Times*, often showed considerable boredom at the obsession about wages among those of us assigned to reporting the labour market. They themselves were interested in the then fashionable French indicative planning: even future Chancellors and economic gurus are entitled to their youthful flings. Judging by his speeches, the Chancellor is now more interested in wages.

But throughout this Government's life there has been no question of seeking an incomes policy, voluntary or statutory. The Prime Minister has painted even her more doubting colleagues into a corner. Her economic strategy had to work in the way she intended, for there was nowhere else to go, no escape road. The Government's rhetoric from the beginning has been so opposed to any kind of policy on incomes that retreat in that direction was politically impossible, even when inflation increased alarmingly. So ministers watched the retail price index rise to 22%, a rise accelerated by a minimum lending rate of 17% in November 1979. Unemployment began its relentless spiral that was to take the total to three million and more. It has remained Mrs Thatcher's most grievous problem throughout her two terms.

Quite early on, when there was a swing of 13% to Labour in the Southend by-election, Francis Pym warned colleagues that 'too much haste in change would damage the very social fabric that it has always been the first principle of the Conservative Party to preserve'. But against this was the belief of the Prime Minister, Keith Joseph and others that what a radical government had to fear was its own lack of determination when the going got rough. They believed that if they altered course, as Heath and Barber had done in 1972, there could be only one result: what the Conservative Right called 'the ratchet effect of socialism' would move Britain steadily towards a more collective and interventionist state.

In many ways this Conservative revolution was a mirror image of what was taking place on the Labour Left. Just as Tony Benn and those who supported him felt that Labour governments always sold out on Labour policies that had been drawn up in Opposition, so Mrs Thatcher's wing of the Conservatives felt that the Macmillan and Heath governments had done much the same.

It was Margaret Thatcher's battle over unemployment, public spending and taxes with the group of ministers she had dubbed 'wets' that moulded her style as Prime Minister. Her determination to win this battle, and eventually to remove from key positions those ministers who represented a threat to the economic thrust of her Government, was preconceived. Before the 1979 election she gave an interview to Kenneth Harris of the *Observer*. His method was to provide his subjects with a long draft of their interviews, which they could then review. I was at that time the *Observer*'s Deputy Editor and Harris showed me the draft. I came on two sentences which I urged him to try to retain at all costs: 'It must be a conviction government. As Prime Minister, I could not waste time having any internal arguments.' He agreed they were important, and Mrs Thatcher did not edit them out. They must be the most widely quoted sentences of Margaret Thatcher on her way to the Premiership.

Despite her resolve, Mrs Thatcher did find herself having 'internal arguments', and although she often seemed to enjoy these, she never quite forgave those who challenged her. The pattern of her dismissals of ministers demonstrates what a cautious, but ruthless political leader she had become. Those chosen for the sack have not been the men who caused her most irritation in Cabinet but those unable to cause her too much trouble on the back benches. Thus Peter Walker has stayed, and Jim Prior and Michael Heseltine were left to go of their own volition.

The pattern was set in the reshuffle of January 1981. Norman St John-Stevas had been her first Leader of the House, combining this post with that of Arts Minister. It was an imaginative appointment. Stevas, editor of Bagehot, was fascinated by constitutional reform and threw himself enthusiastically into encouraging the growth of select committees of the House of Commons, which would scrutinise the work of government departments and give ordinary MPs more say. But so far as the Prime Minister was concerned he had two faults. One was that he was an unreconstructed 'wet', and did not hesitate to join his friend, Ian Gilmour, in arguing the pragmatic Tory case on economic policy. The second was that his uncontrollable sense of humour and mordant wit produced a steady flow of anecdotes that did not always treat his political mistress with the reverence all Prime Ministers come to take as their due. His descriptions of his leader stretched from 'the Blessed Margaret', an affectionate but not wholly devout adaptation of the terminology of his (Catholic) Church, to 'The Leaderene', which sounded less respectful. The tone suggested a scolding housewife: if John Mortimer's 'Rumpole of the Bailey' had been on television at the time, the wit-kissed Norman might readily have adopted his description of his wife, She Who Must Be Obeyed. Alas, it could not last.

The Prime Minister offered St John-Stevas, for whom she retained great affection, the chance to leave the Cabinet but to remain as Arts Minister, an offer he declined. In *The Times* report of the same, quite small reshuffle, an obscure paragraph recorded another change: 'The other new Minister of State for Industry is Mr Norman Tebbit, a Right-winger, who was formerly Under-Secretary for Trade.' The reformation of the Thatcher Government had begun: as opportunity occurred, or was created, the Prime Minister promoted her own supporters into key economic posts and gradually weeded out the 'wets'.

Sir Ian Gilmour, who was dismissed in September 1981, was the most articulate of these. He is the philosopher of modern Toryism, a former owner and editor of the *Spectator*. Mrs Thatcher seemed at first to admire him but they were chalk-and-cheese so far as policy was concerned, and as he elaborated his discontent, both in Cabinet and in only slightly coded public speeches, her irritation with him grew. Prior and Walker were equally critical of economic policy, both in private and semi-public, but each of them had a strong base in the parliamentary party and beyond. To sack either would be to risk creating a rallying-point for rebellion against her leadership. Gilmour, though a popular figure in the Commons, did his best work at his desk rather than on a public platform or in a smoke-filled room. He wrote better than he spoke. So he was expendable, at no great political risk.

His press statement showed how deep the rift was: 'Every Prime Minister has to reshuffle from time to time. It does no harm to throw the occasional man overboard, but it does not do much good if you are steering full speed ahead for the rocks. And that is what the Government is now doing. . . . It will soon become clearer than it is now that there must be changes in economic policy, if only because the social consequences of what is being done are not acceptable.' When Sir Ian was sacked, there were 2.4 million unemployed.

Two others on the Left of the party were dropped in the September reshuffle. Lord Soames was of the Conservative blood royal, son-in-law of Churchill, former Ambassador to Paris, former Vice-President of the European Commission, now Leader of the Lords. As last British Governor-General in Salisbury, he had helped in the uneasy slither from Mrs Thatcher's instinctive support for the white minority to what quickly turned into black single-party rule. Mark Carlisle was a likeable QC, who as Education Secretary resisted spending cuts and paid the price.

At the time of St John-Stevas's sacking in January 1981 a consequent change indicated the shape of things to come. Francis Pym had been Shadow Foreign Secretary in Opposition, but in 1979 was appointed Defence Secretary to allow Carrington to have the Foreign Office. When St John-Stevas went Pym succeeded him as Leader of the Commons. Mrs Thatcher has always taken care to select emollient men for this job: Stevas, Pym, John Biffen. Its principal function is to get the Government's legislative programme through, and this requires an ability to create a rapport not only with Conservative backbenchers but with the Opposition, which can otherwise make life miserable for the Government whips and, at one remove, for its backbenchers, who suffer endless all-night sittings.

There is a certain charm, of course, in watching the sun come up from the terrace of the House of Commons, only yards away from the inspiration of Wordsworth's sonnet on Westminster Bridge:

> Dull would he be of soul who could pass by
> A sight so touching in its majesty.

But as June turns into July the appetite for seeing the sunrise can become sated, so a government business manager who knows his job tries to protect his followers from too many all-nighters.

Francis Pym had been a first-class Chief Whip under Ted Heath, and he was an effective Leader of the House, principally because MPs on all sides liked his old-world courtesy. The man who was an indirect descendant of the seventeenth-century John Pym, of Long Parliament fame, understood Westminster's traditionalist ways. The relationship between the two sides, although adversarial, is not a simple matter of 'them' and 'us'. One successful member of the present Cabinet learned a painful lesson in his second speech in the House. He was young, brash, and determined to do well, so he demolished, with forensic skill, the speech of an elderly miner from the Labour benches who had spoken just before him. He left the chamber rather pleased with himself, only to be confronted by a red-faced Knight of the Shires: 'You, sir, are an absolute shit. Don't you know that man is one of the nicest people in this House?'

Pym had not been moved from Defence to the Leader's job just because of his parliamentary skills. The Prime Minister detected in him a man who was likely to make trouble for her if he remained in charge of the Services. This was a period when Defence budgets were coming under strain because of preparations for a new generation of nuclear weapons, and especially for the costly Trident system. Pym fought some doughty battles to preserve conventional forces and even threatened to resign. Mrs Thatcher's acute nose for danger twitched and she replaced him with John Nott, who was more of her own economic mind. Ironically, later in 1981 Nott was to join John Biffen, another independent soul, but up till then thought of as a True Light believer in monetarism, in a rebellion on public spending.

Another formidable critic of Mrs Thatcher was also moved in the September reshuffle, and Jim Prior's career took the first step towards an inevitable, though much later, end. After he had allowed her to over-rule his open unwillingness to be exiled to Northern Ireland, he gradually became more alienated. Both he and she must have known – or perhaps *should* have known – that no major political progress was likely there in the foreseeable future. He extracted a promise that he could stay in the mainstream of Government policy-making by remaining a member of the

Cabinet's key economic committees. But Jim Prior soon found that Ulster's preoccupations make a wider role in government difficult to sustain. This is the experience of many who have had responsibility for Northern Ireland, stretching back to Jim Callaghan who as Home Secretary took the first shock of the crisis and found himself semi-detached from the work of the Wilson government in its final months before the 1970 election.

To ordinary Conservative supporters, the seismic shifts that were taking place within Margaret Thatcher's government did not seem as significant as they did to the participants, or to commentators. To some supporters, a dripping Keynesian 'wet' and a dry-as-dust Friedmanite monetarist looked much alike – neither was a socialist. I was once lunching with Jim Prior, and listening to his explanation of his version of Tory philosophy, when a middle-aged waitress gave him hers: 'My old Dad, who was a retired policeman, always said to me: "Vote for the Tories, dear; they've got money, so they know how to look after your money."' Prior beamed his appreciation of this homely wisdom, but it must have been a salutary reminder of how herculean a task a politician faces in conveying his view of the world to his ordinary, not-very-political supporters.

For to a large proportion of voters politics is less a matter of judging whether the Conservatives have swung too far to the Right, or Labour too far to the Left, or whether the Alliance is offering policies sufficiently different from those of the failed consensus. Rather it is a *mélange* of inherited loyalties, personal prejudices, transient impressions and a feel for the way the tide is running.

One thing is sure: the fierce debate going on within the Cabinet half-way through Mrs Thatcher's first term would have been more dangerous to her if Conservative supporters had not been comfortably aware of concurrent chaos in the defeated and divided Labour Opposition.

CHAPTER 3

KEEPING THE SHOW ON THE ROAD

Labour's defeat in 1979 provoked an internal revolution that shook the party to its foundations and came near to destroying it as an effective political machine. This was the first election since 1935 in which two million votes separated the two major parties. An inquest was inevitable. The Centre and Right were worried that fundamenal changes in British society since the war, for which Labour claimed credit, might have eroded its own constituency: that there were now so many more 'haves' than 'have nots' that the election of Labour governments would become ever more difficult. The Left was convinced that the duplicity of successive Labour leaders and governments, a retreat from socialism, had undermined their support. The scene was set for a titanic battle over constitution and ideology.

Since Labour's beginnings in 1900, it has always been a turbulent coalition. The division between socialism and trade unionism (or Labourism, as some call it) has always existed, but the thread grows ever more tangled. This division has given Labour its federal structure, its unsatisfactory block-voting system, its oddly constituted National Executive Committee, and the most byzantine internal politics known to man. These problems all came home to roost after the 1979 election defeat.

The dominant political philosophy of the Wilson and Callaghan governments had been the revisionism of Anthony Crosland. In the fifties and sixties Labour had effectively – though not formally – abandoned public ownership as an end in itself, and elevated 'equality' as its principal objective. But equality without undue pain depended on continued economic growth, and successive governments, Conservative and Labour, had found it impossible to sustain growth without inflation.

This put Labour's trade union allies in the frame, for their behaviour was crucial both to the resolution of the party's internal crisis and to finding a plausible remedy for the national economic failure that had undermined the Callaghan government. After the Winter of Discontent unions were more unpopular than ever before. Although Len Murray was an intelligent general secretary, his General Council was in disarray. The unions, which had created the Labour Party eighty years earlier, looked in poor shape to rescue it from its internal troubles.

What worried Labour's leaders was an apparent change in group loyalties in British life. Adapting the classic antithesis about their movement, they found it short nowadays of the compassion of Methodism, but full of the economics – or at least the rhetoric – of Marxism. The unity of Labour's historic constituency was crumbling, as Jim Callaghan painfully learned during that Winter of Discontent and the election.

A new mood of unenlightened self-interest seemed to prevail, even among Labour activists. As long ago as the 1970 Parliament, an MP had reacted sharply when told that to carry conviction Labour might have to argue more explicitly its Galbraithian case on 'private affluence and public squalor'. His reply was brusque (expletives having been deleted): 'If you think that I'm going on the knocker in my constituency arguing for higher income tax to pay for social benefits for large families, most of them West Indian or Irish, you're mad.' In more civilised form, that subsequently became the implicit assumption of many Labour ministers. Without growth they found it hard to convince traditional Labour voters that the social wage – health, education, the Welfare State, public services generally – was as important as the pound in their wage-packets.

Jim Callaghan has a favourite quotation from James Maxton, the Clyde-side Labour veteran: 'If you can't ride two horses, you ought not to be in the bloody circus.' By the time Callaghan became Labour leader and Prime Minister in 1976, he needed to be able to ride more horses than that – unions which had lost their way, a Left wing which blamed a Labour Government for 'again betraying socialism', an NEC majority that dallied with the same view, and an emergent social democratic wing which was alienated over Europe and the general direction Labour was taking. Add to that the Government's need to accommodate demands for greater devolution in Scotland and Wales, and the fiery opposition to this of such rising figures as Neil Kinnock, and you had a party that was beyond the management skill of even the most consummate political manager of his generation. Once the Callaghan government lost its majority in the Commons, and so required support from the Liberals, the circus had become one that not even Barnum could have controlled.

The missing element in the inquest on Labour's defeat was any examination of the unions' unpopularity. Millions of trade unionists had voted for the Conservatives in 1979. Predictably, this made Margaret Thatcher sceptical about how representative their leaders were. The Thatcher years have been a bleak period for a generation of TUC leaders who would like to be treated – as Bevin, Deakin, Citrine, Cousins, Woodcock, Feather, Jones and Scanlon were – as almost an estate of the realm.

The union leaders could not claim they had not been warned. George Woodcock, the TUC's greatest general secretary (1960–9), used to lament the different time-scales on which he and politicians had to operate. His efforts to persuade the unions to reform themselves seemed to proceed *sub specie aeternitatis*, while governments were mostly interested in changes that would come within a single Parliament lasting four or five years.

The politicians contemplated the TUC with the same exasperation that Andrew Marvell expressed *To his Coy Mistress*:

> Had we but world enough, and time,
> This coyness, lady, were no crime . . .
>   . . . I would
> Love you ten years before the Flood:
> And you should, if you please, refuse
> Till the conversion of the Jews . . .
> But at my back I always hear
> Time's wingèd chariot hurrying near.

Or, as the politicians would phrase it, the rattle of ballot-boxes in the next general election. The politicians' patience was limited. As long ago as 1966 Woodcock had warned the unions that they would be blamed if governments failed:

'If the unions were not prepared to work with governments to make it possible, or not impossible, for them to fulfil their economic and social obligations, either governments would renege on their obligations, and no longer accept the duty to maintain full employment, or they would make moves to restrict the activities of the unions by trying to restrain free collective bargaining and perhaps even by trying to limit the right to strike.'

Twenty years later, the number out of work is about 3.25 million, and legislation introduced by Mrs Thatcher's Government has sharply reduced the unions' power and influence. The supply of either beer and sandwiches or coffee and biscuits at Number Ten has notoriously dried up.

But as Labour picked up after the election, all this was in the future. A hazard of modern government is that it exhausts its practitioners. By the time Jim Callaghan lost office he was sixty-seven and felt weary. His Government had lived through perpetual crisis, from the IMF in 1976, through the Lib-Lab Pact, the rows over devolution, and the Winter of Discontent. The pressures of decision-taking, as the Queen once consolingly remarked to him, are relentless.

Yet a couple of months after the election Callaghan felt fully restored. He intended to get Labour into better shape before handing it over to Denis Healey, who looked the best man to tackle Margaret Thatcher. But first Callaghan wanted to launch a solid attack on a Government he believed might become vulnerable quite quickly. For he himself felt a deep revulsion against what he believed to be the thrust of the Thatcher government. He thought she would divide the nation – North against South, the able and intelligent against the poor and unfortunate. The prospects of such widening gaps angered him. This is what Callaghan's politics are all about: he is non-ideological but concerned with the welfare of those from the same underprivileged background as his own. (He once answered a young socialist who was taunting him about lack of interest in one-parent families by saying he had become a member of one himself at the age of eight, when his father died.)

All such plans for conventional Labour v. Conservative politics were overwhelmed, however, by an internal revolution in the Labour Party whose scale and virulence neither Callaghan nor anyone else foresaw. The Left, led by Tony Benn and orchestrated by the Labour Co-ordinating Committee, began to campaign for constitutional changes which Callaghan believed would be disastrous. Specifically, it wanted control of the Manifesto to be taken away from the parliamentary leadership; Labour MPs to face reselection once in each Parliament; and future Labour leaders to be chosen by a wider constituency than just the Parliamentary Party.

Behind these demands was a profound disillusionment with successive party leaders, and indeed with most Labour MPs. While Labour was in Opposition in the early seventies, Tony Benn and his allies on the NEC had made the running on policy. But Benn complained that 'people understandably distrust political parties which say one thing in opposition and do something different when they are elected'.

Benn was raising what other Labour leaders, on the Centre and Right, saw as a genuine dilemma. They did not believe that Labour's traditional voters would support in an election some of the policies that Labour activists in the unions and constituency parties voted through at annual conferences. Yet because they knew union block votes were stacked against them – just as they had been stacked against the Left in the forties and fifties – they had got into the habit of letting such policies go through, sometimes almost on the nod, and ignoring them in government. So Labour's policy documents had come to seem weasel-tongued, and that sin was now finding the leadership out. A convulsion seemed inevitable.

Labour's history has left it with a constitution and structure designed for a party of opposition at a time when government seemed a remote dream. In theory the annual conference is the source of all power, and the NEC, elected at the conference, wields that power during the rest of the year. But since Labour began to take its turn in government, a rival centre of power has grown up: the Parliamentary Labour Party, which has a direct mandate from the voters. That rival power is vested in the Cabinet or Shadow Cabinet and, even more, in the leader.

Labour's constitutional row revolved around an issue that is difficult for any party aspiring to internal democracy: the tension between its political activists and the people who vote for it. The Conservatives solve this problem by making no pretension to internal democracy: their conference is merely advisory to the leader, in whose hands power and patronage reside. This is an open acknowledgement of the Tories' Shakespearian reverence for 'degree', or hierarchy. But Labour's internal democracy was flawed. Both conference decisions and the make-up of the NEC were dominated by trade union block votes, which represented a largely sleeping membership but were wielded by small delegations from each union. Some unions actually paid more subscriptions – and therefore had more votes – than they had members. Millions of trade unionists had a purely financial relationship with Labour. They did not object to paying a political levy – as Mrs Thatcher ruefully discovered when she introduced compulsory ballots on the subject – but they took no active interest in union or party politics. More than twenty years before the constitutional crisis of the 1980s, I wrote an article analysing the bizarre nature of the union block vote. The then editor of *Tribune*, now Neil Kinnock's chef de cabinet, Richard Clements, gently informed me that his paper had mounted a similar critique several years earlier, because the Right-wing union steamroller of that period was demolishing the policies for which *Tribune* stood.

Some complained that Constituency Labour Party delegates were not much more representative. Many CLPs did not have mass memberships of anything like the numbers on their voting cards. The antics of the Militant Tendency were also keeping many older Labour people away from their local party meetings.

Many Labour MPs, bruised by the abuse they had endured since the election defeat, saw a party conference constituted in this way as being remote from the eleven million people who had voted Labour. They feared they would be forced in their local parties to kowtow to unrepresentative cliques of the extreme Left, whose devotion even to parliamentary democracy was not certain.

There was also unspoken resentment of union leaders' power in the party – unspoken because no one at an annual conference cares to refer back the Tablets of Stone. But many saw humbug in an examination of every aspect of Labour's internal democracy which, nevertheless, left undefiled the holy of holies: the system of election for the NEC. Eighteen members out of twenty-nine were elected wholly or mainly by an un-representative union block vote; and even the seven constituency representatives were elected by delegates whose views seemed remote from those of Labour voters. Arguably, the NEC contained some of the worst rotten boroughs since the 1832 Reform Act. So the Labour Party, one of the great parties of the state, and a formidable engine of reform in Britain, needed to reform itself. But its anachronistic machinery never seemed up to the task. To outsiders, slaughter of some ancient and sacred cows might seem a prerequisite to reform, but that was never likely to happen because among insiders there was confusion between what might seem right in the abstract and what might produce the right results – from their own point of view.

The 1979 conference in Brighton narrowly defeated a call for a new system of electing the leader; accepted the reselection of MPs; and asked the NEC to produce a plan to take over sole control of the Manifesto from the parliamentary leadership (a decision subsequently reversed). The battle was certain to continue. Two Chinese journalists, exuding oriental amiability, approached an angry Denis Healey on the Brighton seafront and asked, with apparent innocence, whether he was pleased with the decisions. Healey exuded Yorkshire amiability. Not much, he confessed (without undergoing the Chinese water torture). But the decisions would be changed next year, he added confidently. What's more, if they weren't he'd be over to Peking to find out how to run a Cultural Revolution.

Whatever the *People's Daily* may have made of this piece of occidental inscrutability, Healey's witticism captured the gallows humour common on the Centre-Right at this time. The leaders of any party that has lost an election face a formidable task. They must simultaneously make news and make sense. Deprived of the support provided by Whitehall – civil service briefs, red boxes, black limousines – they must try to turn shadow ministers into substance in the minds of voters in a still distant general election. It is a task demanding hard work, detailed study of policy, wit, political *nous*, the killer instinct, an eye fixed constantly on the Government's weaknesses, and good luck. Labour's internal troubles deprived Callaghan of at least the last two. He became even more certain that he wanted to hand over the party, in as good shape as possible, to Healey.

The two men were different in character and style. Callaghan, in the fullness of his years, was measured, careful, puritanical; Healey rumbustious, colourful, with a touch of Renaissance Man and a turn of language that Jim would never have used, even in his Navy days. Callaghan believed Healey deserved his turn. That feeling has often been decisive in determining who will be Labour leader. It is what, after all their passing rivalries and antagonisms, Harold Wilson had felt about Callaghan.

Healey's status as heir was vulnerable, however, to the erosion of time. The risk was that, in alliance with Callaghan, he would be cast in the role of full-time apologist for the last Labour government, a latter-day Ted Heath. A fierce debate was developing over Labour's choice between a mixed economy, which Callaghan, Healey and most former ministers favoured, and the Left's Alternative Strategy – more public ownership and industrial intervention, import controls, and withdrawal from Europe.

To add to the Labour leadership's anxiety, the Militant Tendency was making more difficult the reform that would really help: the revival of mass membership, on the principle that it is difficult to run a people's party without large numbers of people. Militant's 'entryism' was damaging Labour, not just in public relations terms but by driving many ordinary members away through boredom or distaste. The Tendency had also captured control of the Young Socialists. Its attitude to Labour's traditional members was shown by a document which leaked. This uncharitably dismissed many local Labour parties as 'shells dominated by politically dead men and women' and 'ossified little cliques'. The Right-wingers were

'Neanderthal fossils' and the Tribune Group 'pathetic'. Militant had grandiose ideas, expecting within the next decade to build 'a world party of socialist revolution' and become 'the decisive force on the planet'.

Meanwhile it was strongest in London, Liverpool and other large inner cities, and in a more down-to-earth section of its political thinking recognised, with prophetic insight, that Labour might turn against it: 'We have to be scrupulously sure that we do not in any way give these gentlemen an excuse to take action against us.' It was to be some time before 'these gentlemen' moved against Militant but another paragraph in the same document showed how far out of line with their own traditions this Trotskyist organisation was:

> 'We must never forget to train our cadres to the theoretical possibility of the unions as organisations being thrust aside, in a period of revolution, or prior to an insurrection, and that workers' committees or Soviets should take their place. But that is a theoretical possibility only. As Trotsky says, we do not make a fetish of any organisation.'

Militant might claim not to be obsessed with organisation but Labour's older factions, of Right, Centre, Left and Far Left, certainly were. For unrepresentative though the trade union structure might be, it still represented both the power within the Labour Movement and its claim to have political 'bottom'. Ernest Bevin had taken on George Lansbury when his pacifism threatened to take over the Labour Party in the thirties; Arthur Deakin, Will Lawther and Tom Williamson had elevated Hugh Gaitskell to the leadership in the fifties, in preference to Aneurin Bevan and Herbert Morrison; and Frank Cousins, Jack Jones and Moss Evans had broken the long hegemony of Labour's Right in the sixties and seventies. The fight for control of this formidable machine would be conducted implacably.

In a bleak period, it seemed all that held Labour together was an instinct for survival. With a new iconoclastic generation, some of it deeply infected by exotic ideology, this rebellion was harder to handle than earlier ones. Labour's danger was that it would wander in circles of bitterness and fatuity for a decade or more. But the paradox was that the assistance of the unions, so often the pillars of negativism, was needed to save it.

As Labour MPs embarked on this long night of the soul, they probably understood better a passage in which Harold Wilson answered a charge often levelled at him, of 'deviousness' or 'papering over the cracks':

> 'To bridge a deep political chasm without splitting a party or provoking dramatic ministerial resignations is sometimes regarded as something approaching political chicanery. This is to subordinate the realities of 200 years of democratic politics to the demands of sensationalism . . . In my view, a constant effort to keep his party together, without sacrificing either principle or the essentials of basic strategy, is the very stuff of political leadership. Macmillan was canonised for it.'

But in this decade of political revolution such thinking had gone out of fashion. To the Thatcherite wing of the Conservative Party Macmillan was part of the problem. To many Labour people, just five years after Wilson's resignation, both 'principle' and 'basic strategy' seemed to be at risk; and no one could expect 'canonisation', for few Labour people were interested in their saints any more. Only sinners.

The 1980 conference in Blackpool confirmed Callaghan's view that he should resign at once. He had appealed to delegates: 'For God's sake, stop arguing; the public is crying out for unity.' But recrimination continued. Mandatory reselection and a wider electoral college to choose the leader were confirmed and, even though NEC control of the Manifesto was rejected, it was another bad year for the leadership.

Tony Benn was the darling of that conference. As chairman of the Home Policy Committee, he made wide-ranging commitments from the platform about how the next Labour Government would behave: its first Industry Bill must be law within days, and a Bill renouncing Britain's membership of the EEC within weeks. For good measure, he announced that, when these Bills failed to get through the House of Lords, 1000 new peers must be created, and the peerage must be abolished when a Bill to abolish the Lords had been passed.

On nuclear defence the conference took a unilateralist stand, called for the closure of American bases, but opposed withdrawal from NATO by a margin of 7 to 1. Earlier that year Neil Kinnock, who had joined the Front Bench, received a gentle rebuke from Callaghan when he voted against the party line on defence. Kinnock felt Callaghan treated him reasonably, saying: 'Listen, I'm just trying to keep the show on the road.' Others, on both wings of the Labour Party, felt keeping the show on the road was not enough.

An opinion poll on the day before Callaghan retired showed him to be the most popular politician in Britain. He had the virtue of his faults. What he lacked in longer-term vision, in any natural disposition to innovate, he made up for in common sense, and in instinctive rapport with ordinary people. The end of his career at the top unhappily coincided with the collapse of the Labour machine which he – like most politicians of the Labour Right and Centre, including those who were to found the SDP – accepted uncritically so long as they could make it work for what they regarded as 'sensible' policies.

Jim Callaghan was not one of nature's radicals. He simply used the instrument he found to hand to pursue the purposes he believed in – greater social justice and a saner handling of the economy. He took a canny view of the extent to which politicians can change the world, or even their own party. His private mood in the 1979 election had been almost elegiac. He knew he was likely to lose, yet felt he had come within an ace of winning. The unions had robbed him of that possible victory by wrecking his solution to a problem he had wrestled with for nearly a quarter of a century at or near the top of his party: how to win union co-operation in the fight against inflation and for uninterrupted economic growth. For a couple of years he seemed to be succeeding, and saw inflation fall from 26 to 8%. Perhaps it was because Callaghan saw this as the tough crux of modern politics, on which all hopes of rising living standards and social reform must ultimately depend, and because ordinary people sensed this was right, that he ended his career more revered in the country than in either Fleet Street or his own party.

The leadership election was conducted under the old system, with only MPs voting. At first it seemed Denis Healey's principal rival would be Peter Shore, but the Left urged Michael Foot to stand. Tony Benn stood aside, saying the contest should be deferred until the new electoral college had been created.

Foot was only a year younger than Callaghan, so if Callaghan would be too old at the next election, why would Foot do? To many MPs he looked like the candidate of a peaceful future. Because the old system of voting was being used there was a danger that the Labour Party in the country would end up with a different leader from the parliamentary leader elected by MPs. It was the 'two Popes' problem, and with the spectre of reselection to face, MPs feared support for Healey might damage them in their constituency parties, for his long Chancellorship had dented his popularity with both rank and file and union leaders.

In opposition Healey was proving as formidable a performer as he had been in government. There are only a handful of men in modern politics – the late Reginald Maudling, Harold Wilson, Edward Heath and Denis Healey being the most obvious – who, deprived of a departmental brief, can make a speech that thrills the House of Commons. As Labour MPs observed such prodigies of intellect and oratory, the friendlier among them might echo Goldsmith:

And still they gazed, and still the wonder grew
That one small head [in Healey's case, read 'large'] could carry all he knew.

But the less charitable echoed Melbourne's sardonic comment: 'I wish I was as cocksure of anything as Tom Macaulay is of everything.' Healey was the captain of Labour's Right. His seniority, the offices he had held and his intellectual clout made him its natural leader: Crosland was dead, Roy Jenkins in Brussels. It is a sad irony that since Hugh Gaitskell's death Labour's Right has produced these three men of leadership quality who have not so much complemented as neutralised each other. Jenkins and Crosland were old friends who drifted apart over policy (and not just Europe). Denis Healey had always been a political loner. Shakespeare thought ambition was the sin by which the angels fell; but surely it was pride.

This time, however, unlike 1976, a group of like-minded shadow ministers supported Healey – Roy Hattersley, David Owen, Eric Varley and Bill Rodgers among them. There were strains: these were younger men, not without their own ambitions; Owen and Rodgers already had grave doubts about where Labour was heading. The principal doubt about Healey, current among political workaholics, was whether he would work twenty-five hours a day to beat the Left. 'The next year [said one such doubter] will decide whether that man turns into a country squire [Healey had a house in Sussex] or becomes Prime Minister of the United Kingdom.' They wanted him to organise himself more ferociously, make aggressive speeches, and start talking about 'the kind of Labour Party I want', the traditional way of bidding for leadership.

In Opposition Healey had begun to do some original thinking on the revival of manufacturing through the use of North Sea oil revenues. But he suffered, like the rest of Labour's Centre-Right and the 'wet' wing of the Conservatives, from being identified with policies which, in the sixties and seventies, had not brought Britain the success it craved. This revolutionary decade in politics was not to his advantage. He was at odds with the party conference mood on defence, Europe and incomes policy. His unpopularity with the unions derived from his courage in fathering the kind of deal on wages which the Callaghan government had needed to survive. He had since mended some of his fences with the union leaders, but they would not readily forgive the abrasiveness they remembered from when he was Chancellor.

So Healey was fighting from behind. Some of Labour's political opponents thought the party was mad not to jump at the chance of having him as leader. One Conservative minister said to me at the time: 'Denis Healey was a beachmaster in the Italian campaign. You didn't get that job unless you were a special kind of man. He's the sort I'd be glad to go into battle with.' He was not talking about battle so much as the politics of a hung Parliament. Healey was the kind of man that football commentators describe as 'showing a lot of character', a euphemism for being tough, individualistic, out of joint with the times, his own man – what Celts call 'thrawn'. Shirley Williams once said that his outstanding characteristic was incurable optimism, a deep inner exuberance. When he tripped over a brick and bloodied his nose, he just got up and carried on. It was a political quality that Churchill had supremely, because even in darkest times he kept detecting light at the end of the tunnel.

In the next few years, Healey had abundant opportunity for exercising the capacity to pick himself up from the ground. In the first ballot for the leadership he was ahead of Foot, with 112 votes to 83. But John Silkin had 38, Peter Shore 32, and it was inevitable that in the second ballot most of these would go to Foot. He won by 139 votes to 129. The job of uniting the quarrelling Labour Party had been given to its first Left-wing leader since the thirties.

There is a tough-minded view of Labour which sees its historic division as being between doers and dreamers, between those who concentrate on winning power to achieve attainable reforms, and those who preserve their ideals inviolate from compromise and let power come if it will. In that categorisation Michael Foot had once seemed to be a dreamer. He had declined office in the 1966–70 Government, partly because Harold Wilson did not oppose President Lyndon Johnson over Vietnam. In any case, Foot had seemed more at home on a *Tribune* platform or in his study writing about Swift or Byron than as a Beatrice Webb drudge, 'trailing his filing system' into Whitehall.

Yet after he joined Wilson's later Government in 1974, and particularly after he became Callaghan's deputy in 1976, Foot had taken a different path. He was too well liked for even the most Jacobin of his supporters to suggest he had been corrupted by power but by 1976 he had clearly decided that, having accepted the job, his duty was to keep Labour in office, through all his doubts over policy and all the compromises of the Lib-Lab Pact. This was uncannily like the decision Willie Whitelaw was taking on the other side of the political fence.

Both the victories over constitutional changes and now the election of the first Left-wing leader since Lansbury presented the Left with a triumphalist temptation. The Right, in its time, had not been a shining example of tolerance, and the Left had long resented its assumption of a divine right to run the Labour Party. This attitude existed both among Labour politicians of the Right and among commentators, who believed that Labour could only be elected if it was led from the Right or Centre, and that it was the only alternative to semi-permanent Conservative government. But now some Left-wingers were saying darkly that the Right must reconcile itself to being in a minority, as the Left had had to do for so many years. They believed that the public could be won over for more socialist policies if the Labour Party pursued its mission to 'agitate and educate'.

Apart from what voters might think, however, this failed to take account of people inside the party who were becoming restive about its new direction. What would Shirley Williams, Bill Rodgers and David Owen do now that Denis Healey had failed to win the leadership? He was their last hope of resistance to what they saw as policies and organisation that would make Labour unelectable. The cruel fact for the Left in Labour politics is that it has nowhere else to go, whereas the Right has always had the option of realigning itself in the Centre. The mood of disillusionment on the Right reached climax when a special conference at Wembley in January 1981 sealed Labour's constitutional revolution. It was a mood Michael Foot had no chance of changing.

The issue that was to dog Foot's leadership, as it had dogged other leaders of the Left from Aneurin Bevan onwards, was nuclear weapons. His personal convictions were those of CND: he had been an Aldermaston marcher from the start. During the leadership election he had said he would send American Cruise missiles home if he found them in Britain on becoming Prime Minister.

Before the war Lansbury's views on pacifism and disarmament had caused Ernest Bevin to denounce him at a Labour conference for 'hawking his conscience from body to body'. Nuclear disarmament was also the anguished final test of Aneurin Bevan's political life, sensitively but sorrowfully described in Foot's biography. It was ironic that Foot himself now faced the same issue, the toughest hurdle on the course to which his leadership was committed: Labour unity.

Foot's account of the 1957 conference at Brighton recalls how Bevan – who was his hero as well as the youthful Neil Kinnock's – not only accused the Left of 'an emotional spasm' but begged the delegates not to send a Labour Foreign Secretary (himself) 'naked into the conference chamber'. That famous phrase, Foot says, referred not to the nakedness of having no nuclear arms but to the consequences of abandoning them unilaterally, 'making a shambles of all our treaties, commitments, obligations', as Bevan put it. Foot defends Bevan against charges of having made a cynical contract with Hugh Gaitskell:

> 'Of course it was true that party considerations influenced his conduct, and why not? . . . He saw the chasm opening at his feet, he saw the renewal of old battles, he saw the destruction of any hope for a new Labour Government, he saw the accusation of his opponents – and perhaps of history – that he could have forestalled the catastrophe, but that he preferred the ease of his own conscience and the comfort of his friends.'

There are dangers in reading too much into an enthusiastic biography, as Roy Jenkins once admonished me when I sought to judge his own views on Ireland from his biography of Asquith. Yet any thoughtful unilateralist reading these passages could not be sure what course Foot would take now. His own instincts, as we have seen, were unilateralist, but he had been elected to restore party unity. Yet he was tempted by his belief that public opinion might be moving on this subject, and that youth especially might make the non-nuclear cause its own. It was an issue that was to be Labour's nightmare in the 1983 election, as well as a primary cause of the breakaway that created the SDP.

The Right now feared it was entering a losing battle. The real leader of the new Left was not Foot but Tony Benn. He had withdrawn from the front bench after 1979, stood aside from the leadership election, but was now shaping up for a campaign to revolutionise the Labour Party. It was a campaign which would make or break him. He is a man who is easy to misjudge. A common view of him, popularised in hundreds of cartoons, is of a demon king, Catherine-wheeling half-crazed ideas, but driven by a quite uncrazed lust for power. Benn's weaknesses are of a different kind. He is a man of often original mind, willing – though only up to a point – to seek radical solutions. His flaws are those of a romantic temperament.

Leaving personality and political ambition aside, Benn's dominant themes at this time had support even outside his own party. He argued that British democracy could not be made to work well for much longer unless people and Parliament were given the information that would allow them to influence decisions before they were taken. He wrote and spoke about problems of consent: the mutual vetoes of *laissez faire* economics, a hunger for industrial democracy. He argued that such problems could only be solved by new experiments in what he called democracy and his critics called populism. On such subjects as open government, parliamentary committees with greater power, and industrial democracy, many of his critics, even in the Alliance parties as well as Labour's Right, agreed with him. But their complaint was that, although he was avid for the slaughter of other people's sacred cows, he was tender with those he loved. Specifically, he either had not thought out or was unwilling to contemplate the changes needed in trade unionism if his vision of society was to succeed.

A time when the whole future of the trade unions was under discussion was not the moment simply to laud the quality of their leadership. The charge from Benn's critics was that, whether for reasons of personal ambition or self-deception, he hopelessly idealised working people and their institutions, and was willing to turn an often brilliant intellectual spotlight on everything except the Labour Movement itself. Yet Benn had laid an unerring finger on the problems facing Labour's Right (not to mention the Conservative Left). He pointed to lost economic growth, which had undermined the Galbraith–Crosland thesis of high welfare spending as the principal method of social reform, and argued that to administer what he called 'decaying capitalism' compassionately did not make it work. That option, he maintained, had been destroyed, not by Labour's conference in 1979, but by the International Monetary Fund during the equally traumatic conference of 1976, when Healey had to return from Heathrow and hurry to Blackpool to steady the delegates' nerves.

Benn was engaged on a campaign that was to culminate in his challenge to Healey's deputy leadership in 1981. This was the event that many Labour people believe put paid to their chances of winning the general election of 1983, for it split the party down the middle. Coinciding with the SDP defection, it was disastrous. Neil Kinnock maintained it provided the Social Democrats with 'an oxygen tent', and added that Labour needed the contest 'like it needed bubonic plague'.

CHAPTER 4

BREAKING THE MOULD

Just before Parliament broke up for the summer recess of 1980, my wife and I went to a party at Shirley Williams' house in Hertfordshire. It was attended by many leading Labour moderates and by journalists. As she said good-night, she smilingly told us: 'You've just witnessed the wake of Labour's old Establishment.'

A few days later she, David Owen and Bill Rodgers published their first manifesto of discontent, and nine months after that they had broken with Labour and formed the Social Democratic Party. The eighties had pro-duced a third revolution in British politics.

What was it that drove Shirley Williams, once Labour's happy warrior, out of the party in which she had grown up? For months she had been racked with doubt. Whether to stay or to leave? Whether to return to Parliament after her defeat at Hitchin in 1979 or to revert to a role as thinker and writer? As Labour drifted to the Left, she became isolated on its National Executive Com-mittee. It was all a sad change from a few years earlier when she had seemed likely to become the first woman Prime Minister.

Strangely, her election defeat in 1979 seemed more shattering for her admirers than for herself. When the news came through to BBC Television's election studio, a young woman on the production staff burst into tears, while in front of the cameras Norman St John-Stevas displayed an apolitical sense of shock. By contrast, she came to enjoy the personal and academic freedom that release from Westminster brought. In part this reflected an ambiguity in her character: how ambitious was she? But it also mirrored her feelings of relief at escaping from day-to-day contact with a Labour Party that was in sour and frightened mood.

The most devastating analysis of Labour's condition, however, came not from Shirley Williams but from Roy Jenkins, former Chancellor and Home Secretary, but by then nearing the end of his Presidency of the European Community. In November 1979 he gave the Dimbleby Lecture. Con-templating British politics, he quoted Yeats:

> The best lack all conviction, while the worst
> Are full of passionate intensity.

He called for the revival – some would say the creation – of a Radical Centre in British politics. His timing was good. Margaret Thatcher's new govern-ment was hitting its first waves, with a 15% mortgage rate on the day he spoke.

But it was Jenkins' savage account of his old party that caught public attention. He took a bleak view of Labour's impending constitutional changes: MPs supported by 20,000 or 30,000 Labour voters would be in danger because a 'People's Court' of twenty or thirty activists didn't like them. Labour would have its leader selected and its manifesto written by people whose views were abhorrent to most Labour MPs.

The Jenkins analysis was sobering, but others who shared his political outlook thought a Labour débâcle was not inevitable. They believed Labour's Centre-Right was not beaten yet and thought that old friends of Jenkins, like Shirley Williams, Roy Hattersley, David Owen and Bill Rodgers, were entitled to more cheer from him for the grim battle in which they had engaged under the leadership of Jim Callaghan and Denis Healey. There was no love lost between Jenkins and Callaghan or Healey, who were old rivals.

Roy Jenkins extended his critique beyond Labour's post-election quarrel. He blamed Britain's economic failure since 1956, the year of Suez, on political ossification; and he called for redrawn party lines, isolating the Marxist Left and creating his new Radical Centre as an alternative to Margaret Thatcher's more dogmatic Conservatism. Some who later joined him in the SDP saw a fault in the analysis. Clearly a Conservative Party led by Mrs Thatcher, who was further to the Right than any of her modern predecessors, and a Labour Party led by Michael Foot, who was further to the Left than any of his, left a gap. But critics pointed out that in post-war Tory and Labour governments centrist voices had been dominant. Under Churchill, Attlee, Eden, Macmillan, Douglas-Home, Wilson, Heath and Callaghan, the economic and social attitudes Jenkins was espousing had not lacked advocates. Indeed, Thatcherite Conservatism and the Left's victories in the Labour Party were largely revolts against those ideas.

Less than two years earlier, Margaret Thatcher had won endorsement from the electorate for policies outside the centrist segment. She had achieved power when Callaghan's attempt to pursue consensual politics, notably on incomes and employment, had run foul of his own supporters in the unions. So the new leaderships in both big parties could be seen as aberrations from the pattern of forty years. The prevailing climate of British politics in a period of economic decline had been moderate and centrist.

The Jenkinsite answer was that what Britain needed was consistency in economic strategy, instead of frequent political upheavals. Specifically it demanded more positive support for the mixed economy, without constant Conservative sniping at the public sector or repeated Labour threats to private enterprise. Ever since the 1973 miners' strike brought down the Heath government, there had been observers who feared Britain was becoming 'ungovernable' and thought what was needed was a coalition, 'a Businessmen's Government'. This talk had fizzled out in the later seventies but the mood persisted in some quarters. It recalled a *Punch* cartoon in which a bearded old man had replaced his sandwich board reading 'The End of the World is Nigh' with the terser 'End of the World – Official'. By 1980, with the Thatcher government engulfed in a world economic recession, disaster theorists gave their prophecies another trot around the block, confident that if they were fulfilled they would be remembered, but if they proved wrong people would forget.

Roy Jenkins' anxieties raised the debate to an altogether more serious political level. Clearly his return from Brussels in January 1981 was an event of importance. If a politician of such weight raised his standard at Dover – or more probably Heathrow – a revolution in political alliances might follow. What the revolt against the existing party structure needed was a fresh burst of energy, and Jenkins had been long enough away from British politics to be able to claim a new perspective.

Critics jeered that his name was not synonymous with energy, that he was too laid back to father a political revolution. This was an unfair – and, as it turned out, inaccurate – deduction from his life-style and political attitudes: not just the boring old claret joke, which he derides, but a certain fastidious rationality that shies away from newspaper contents' bills that read 'Jenkins Acts', with the verb employed in the histrionic, rather than the practical sense.

When he was Chancellor Jenkins worked hard, but the contrast with some other ministers was that he liked to finish in time for what he called 'a proper dinner'. One of the hidden strains in his relationship with Harold Wilson (of which the Prime Minister was probably unaware) was that Wilson enjoyed long, discursive evening chats over drinks and sandwiches at Number Ten, while Jenkins preferred an agenda followed by a meal.

The Dimbleby Lecture was catalytic. It provoked others who were worried about Labour's drift to think afresh. From the moment Jenkins delivered his thunderbolt, it seemed possible that politics would undergo revolution on a scale unknown since the Asquith–Lloyd George schism during and after the first world war. 1981 was going to be far more dangerous for Labour than any of the previous defections by Dick Taverne, Ray Gunter, George Brown, Reg Prentice and Woodrow Wyatt. Each of these had either personal grievances against Labour or suffered a loss of political faith.

Shirley Williams, Bill Rodgers and David Owen still regarded themselves as democratic socialists, committed to reform of British society along more egalitarian lines, inheritors of the tradition of Tawney, Attlee and Gaitskell. But with each successive disaster for Labour's leadership their breakaway came nearer. This process can be traced through the reactions of Shirley Williams, one of the most attractive politicians of her generation, as public attitudes to her showed, and a key figure of the Labour Right. She had been born into the Labour Movement half a century before. Her father, Sir George Catlin, she recalls, 'used to wheel me to Labour meetings in a pram', and her mother, Vera Brittain, author of *Testament of Youth*, instilled in her a tradition of plain living and high thinking which marked her politics. Both parents were active in Left-wing causes, notably the Peace Pledge Union and the Jarrow March against unemployment. T. S. Eliot and Pandit Nehru were visitors to their house in Cheyne Walk.

Shirley Williams' own career seemed preordained (although Lady Astor warned her she would never get on in politics with 'that hair'). After a spell running the Fabian Society, she was elected a Labour MP in 1964 and was given office by Wilson in 1966. But it was in opposition in the early seventies that her star really began to rise, and the storm clouds to gather. Less than a decade after entering Parliament she topped the Shadow Cabinet poll; but Labour's long quarrel over Europe had begun and Shirley Williams was embarked on the pro-European course that would make this a breaking-point for her.

When Wilson returned to office in 1974, she climbed through the ranks of his and Callaghan's Cabinets, first as Prices Secretary, then at Education. Callaghan preferred her to more senior ministers as chairman of Cabinet Committees. This was when talk of her as a future Prime Minister began. But she seemed less single-minded than Margaret Thatcher: no one could quite imagine her going for the jugular as Mrs Thatcher did when Heath was in trouble. Some observers doubted whether she had ever seen herself as a Number One – an important qualification in politics, where self-doubt is no asset. They recalled Fabian teas at Labour conferences where she introduced gurus like Tony Crosland in reverential tones that presented herself as a natural lieutenant. Yet by 1980 she was taking a lead among the Gang of Three, declaring to a fringe meeting: 'We are going to fight to save this party, and by God we think we can.' At that time, although deeply worried, she said she was not interested in a centre party with 'no roots, no principles, no philosophy and no values'.

However, when Foot defeated Healey for the Labour leadership, she announced in November of that year that she would not be a Labour candidate and hinted at the need for a new party. David Owen had already declined to stand for the Shadow Cabinet, and Bill Rodgers, though elected in ninth place, refused to take any portfolio other than defence.

At the Liberal Assembly in September, David Steel had pointed the direction in which Labour doubters should look:

> 'Without Liberal leadership, a Liberal agenda, and Liberal commitment, their efforts are doomed. The trail of British politics is littered with the skeletons of well-intentioned breakaway groups who tried to go it alone. With us they could make a formidable contribution. Without us they will perish.'

Privately Steel had advised Roy Jenkins that it would be better to have a new party rather than simply to join the Liberals. He was already looking forward to 'a great government of national reform'.

Shirley Williams, meanwhile, was looking back at the destruction of the Labour Party as she had known it. What broke her will to continue with Labour was her belief – sad rather than bitter – that new recruits on the Trotskyist or near-Trotskyist Left had not only imported dangerously false doctrines but were rapidly exporting all fraternity. Her intellectual contribution in that period was to identify the essentials of democratic socialism which she then felt distinguished her both from the far Left and from the centrist ideas of Jenkins. The test she offered for Labour Party membership – 'If it were a choice between democracy and socialism, would you choose democracy?' – was one many new recruits could not have passed.

So the Social Democrats' argument with the legitimate (i.e. pro-parliamentary government) Left was about pace and economic methods. Their argument with the Trotskyist Left was irreconcilable. The strongest case for a breakaway was their belief that Labour was in terminal decline and that British politics was undergoing a fundamental shift, comparable to the eclipse of the Liberal Party in the twenties. What made the decision difficult was uncertainty about the national attitude.

It was true that the Labour vote, as well as the combined votes of the two major parties, had been in almost continuous decline since the fifties. But did this mean voters were ready to strike out in a new direction? It was argued that disillusionment with the old politics and the volatility of the voters marked a real political fracture, but when public opinion polls asked questions about policy, the voters' trumpet gave forth an uncertain sound. In the summer of 1980 MORI had asked 1911 people which of a list of policies they liked. Those with a positive score were a bewildering mixture, both in their variety and order:

More money for the NHS and for retraining the unemployed; allow families to invest £1000 tax free in British companies; keep the grammar schools; introduce import controls; sell more council houses; take Britain out of Europe; invest more in micro-electronics; reduce company taxation; consult with unions more in running the economy; introduce a wealth tax, an incomes policy and proportional representation.

How was a politician to produce a manifesto out of that lot? The man in the street seemed to be thrashing around for something different – almost *anything* different – to arrest the economic decline Britain had suffered under successive governments. The problem for any new party was to discover what tranche of policies would be consistent enough to attract heavyweight politicians, yet inspiring enough to launch a political crusade that would attract the public.

The daunting scenario facing the agonised politicians contemplating a break with Labour was this: unless they were able to produce a new political and economic wonder-cure that would sweep aside Conservatives and Labour in a single election, they risked making matters worse. A new party would be formed consisting of a disparate group of MPs and ex-MPs, at varying distance from their radical roots, some activated by public duty, some mere refugees from reselection conferences. Some might be elected in a three-cornered fight, but more of them would just split the anti-Government vote. New boundaries were going to make it harder for the Tories to lose the next election anyhow.

Even if Labour was defeated again, a party that was eighty years old and with strong roots in the trade unions and the working class was unlikely to fade as quickly as the Liberals had done after the Asquith–Lloyd George split. Yet unless it did fade, or unless the new party failed, the Left in Britain would be divided and out of office for a generation. Too often commentators discuss such issues only in terms of politicians' careers; any politician who believes in what he is doing is right to consider seriously his own future prospect of office. But those considering the anguish of cutting their links with Labour were guided by another criterion: could they hope to create, outside that party, the base for another government of social reform? Roy Jenkins, as biographer of Asquith, was probably more acutely aware than the others of the dangers. He had been meeting discreetly with David Steel and he hoped a swift, surgical operation, grafting the Right of the Labour Party to the Liberals, would create a strong new instrument of reform, suited to the mood of the country.

On 25 January 1981, the day after Labour's special conference at Wembley, Roy Jenkins, Shirley Williams, Bill Rodgers and David Owen met at Owen's house in Limehouse and announced the formation of the Council for Social Democracy, the embryo of a new party. Michael Foot begged them to remain with Labour. Some Liberals, notably Cyril Smith, were doubtful about the whole enterprise. But on 9 February Shirley Williams wrote, in her resignation from the Labour NEC, that 'the party I loved and worked for no longer exists'. The following month Owen, Rodgers and ten other Labour MPs resigned their party's whip and joined with the Liberals to co-ordinate parliamentary tactics.

One Conservative, Christopher Brocklebank-Fowler, crossed the House later that month to join them. A leading Conservative was to speculate later what would have happened if, say, Peter Walker and Ian Gilmour had led a dozen other Tories into the new party. He thought it would have swept the country and formed a majority government after the election. But there is no evidence that other Conservatives did seriously consider defecting, though some 'wets' hoped the creation of the SDP would help them to drag the Conservative Party back towards the Centre.

On 26 March the SDP was officially launched in an unprecedented atmosphere of media hype, and the process of 'breaking the mould' of what the Gang of Four came to call the old, class-based politics had begun. A death notice had appeared in *The Times* at the end of January: 'Labour Party, on January 24, 1981. After a long illness, at Wembley. Funeral Westminster. No flowers.' Was the notice a little premature? Or was a new age in British politics about to dawn, marking the most fundamental shift for two generations?

The mood among Labour Right-wingers who decided to stay in their party was sombre. They knew that large numbers of former Labour supporters had written their party off. Peter Shore said that 'the Roman spectacle of a great party tearing itself to pieces' could not continue without mortal damage. Many believed the next general election was already lost. By contrast, among Social Democrats there was euphoria. Encouraged by a poll that showed a new Centre grouping more popular than either Conservative or Labour, one of them forecast that they would form the government after the next election. The immediate public support was impressive: on one day Owen received more than 1000 letters, and the week after Limehouse Shirley Williams had sat among piles of mail she did not have time to open. Telegrams, cheques and offers of help poured in. The leaders had had to abandon their original plan not to launch the party until after the May council elections, although it was decided that the SDP was too new to contest these.

Not everyone was swept away, however. One realist said: 'It's going to be a bloody, rough, tough, destructive, cruel battle, and in the end we may well lose.' David Owen, who was anxious that old friends should not tear each other apart, warned both Social Democrats and the moderates who had stayed in the Labour Party that they ought not to abuse each other, since they might have to work together in future. This was a warning that was forgotten as the two groups drifted apart. Yet it acknowledged what both knew to be the truth: both the Gang of Four and Labour men such as Denis Healey, Roy Hattersley and Peter Shore shared reformist, egalitarian and liberal values. They differed principally in their judgement of whether or not Labour's steady drift to the Left could be arrested.

The argument that influenced those who stayed in the Labour Party was that Britain was almost unique in the West in producing alternative governments based on a moderate party of the Left capable of handling economic and social matters sensibly. This had contributed to an enviable social peace, was why Britain had a derisorily small Communist Party, and why until recently the ultra-Left, Trotskyists and the like, had been irrelevant. Those who fought on within the Labour Party thought this was a tradition not to be lightly abandoned. The weakness of the Labour Right's argument was that the only way they could frustrate the far Left was to mobilise trade union block votes. Yet what they saw wrong in the new constitutional system for electing the leader was the dominance of those same, unrepresentative block votes. Some day Labour would need more fundamental reform, but at this time of travail, with the Party fighting for its life, nobody was even contemplating that.

The Social Democrats' inner strength was that they had shrugged off such problems by forming a new party. Their leading figures had been growing more and more frustrated down the years over the political direction of their old party; and also by its thrombotic institutions, most notably that union block vote, which seemed to make sensible reform impossible. Jenkins, Owen, Rodgers and Mrs Williams seemed to receive a new injection of vigour as they embarked on their new politics. But life is never free from problems. The Social Democrats knew they would have to do a deal with the Liberals, who already occupied the centre ground that Roy Jenkins, at least, coveted and the others were to learn was their inevitable citadel in the stormy years ahead. The Liberals, despite the trauma of the Thorpe Affair, had gained steadily during the seventies. By 1979 they had doubled the national vote of two million they gained in 1970. The Lib-Lab Pact had also given them a taste of power.

The relationship was never likely to be easy. People who have spent years in the political wilderness are not easy to live with. Liberals felt they had borne the heat and burden of third-party politics, their pleas for proportional representation unheeded by those who were then in power but now needed their friendship. A cry of 'Johnny come lately' was inevitable as the Liberals beheld the razzmatazz with which the new party was launched. They were also scornful about the Social Democrats' electoral skills, contrasting them with the ill-financed but ingenious machine they themselves had built up on many a hard-fought by-election and local council field. One Liberal said of his prospective allies: 'None of them has any idea how to organise a parish council, let alone a general election.'

Mutual suspicion also appeared near the top: David Steel and David Owen had an edgy appearance together on Robin Day's Question-Time. At the dinner beforehand it became clear to Peter Walker, the Tory member of the panel, that they scarcely knew each other personally. He also came to the comforting conclusion that Owen, Rodgers and Mrs Williams would be more difficult for Steel to deal with than Roy Jenkins; that would be a help to his own party. On the air, Owen made it brutally clear that he wanted only an electoral pact with the Liberals, and that otherwise the relationship should be an arm's-length one. He and Shirley Williams still used the word 'socialist', so a closer deal with the Liberals would be difficult. But Steel was against what he called 'a cynical exercise to preserve MPs' seats'. He was looking for 'an alliance of hearts and minds'. He thought Owen and he would agree on most policies.

So even as the realignment took place, a truism of British – perhaps of all – politics appeared: coalitions of one kind or another are necessary, whether within parties or between them, and where the lines fall is a matter for painful debate and choice, particularly on the Left.

In David Steel the Liberals had, at this crossroads in their history, a leader who was arguably the shrewdest politician in the country. Apart from a period of personal exhaustion after the 1983 election disappointment, he has played with great skill and resource a hand that has not always been strong. The Liberals cherish variety in their leaders: Jo Grimond was the first of modern charismatics, with a rhetorical propensity to march his troops towards the sound of gunfire; Jeremy Thorpe made better jokes, had a sharp organisational talent, and could do marvellous impersonations, either of West Countrymen or fellow politicians. But Steel is more solid than either. The Alliance owes much to his cool head, capacity for self-effacement, and sheer guts. While the Liberals' collective virtue is their open-mindedness, Steel's is his single-mindedness. He once said that he did not want the Liberal Party to be the political equivalent of going jogging. Although in private he will admit uncertainty on many issues, he has the capacity, enviable in a political leader, to make up his mind. As a son of the Presbyterian manse, he possesses what Tennyson called 'the faith that lives in honest doubt'. This makes him a formidable coalition politician, firm about the general direction in which he wants to go, flexible about even quite important detail. Despite Liberal carping, his performance during the Lib-Lab Pact had been a virtuoso one.

Steel displayed his shrewdness and an ability to use his allies in the Alliance's first, heady year. He knew the acquisition of three men and a woman with experience of Cabinet office was an advantage to be exploited; and he had the support of Jo Grimond, an old friend of Roy Jenkins, in persuading the Liberal Assembly in Llandudno in the autumn of 1981 to endorse the Alliance with the Social Democrats. That week began with one of the most emotional political meetings in modern times. As Grimond, Steel, Jenkins and Shirley Williams spoke, the atmosphere was of evangelical religious revival rather than politics. The Assembly itself overwhelmingly supported the Alliance with the SDP.

David Steel quoted his first speech as Liberal leader in 1976: he did not want to lead a 'nice debating society' or 'an academic think tank', or to be 'an occasional safety valve in the political system'. He wanted power, even if Liberals had to share it with others. That was five years earlier. Now 'some others' had arrived, and Steel was already talking about an Alliance Government: 'I have the good fortune to be the first Liberal leader for over half a century who is able to say to you at the end of our annual Assembly: go back to your constituencies and prepare for government.'

Huge problems remained. The two parties' electoral pact had to be consummated by allocating parliamentary seats equally. This demanded from Liberal candidates who had already been selected a painful renunciation. The process went on through 1981 and 1982, and after a sticky start it was completed with less blood on the sand than many expected. But the Alliance had its first unfavourable publicity during this process, which contributed to a drop in its ratings.

At some levels there seemed little love lost initially between the two parties. One *Liberal News* correspondent in 1982 openly used the unkind description of the SDP that was becoming common among Liberals – 'the Soggies'. A Liberal trade unionist wrote a detailed denunciation of the SDP paper on the unions; another Liberal warned that the relationship would probably go sour. But the leaders, like most successful politicians, had a more determined streak. Liberals and Social Democrats faced the choice that Benjamin Franklin put to his fellow-signatories of the Declaration of Independence: 'We must indeed all hang together or, most assuredly, we shall all hang separately.' The allies knew their political lives were at stake.

Some Liberals, oppressed by the impact on their slightly zany political habits of these new technocrats, would have liked to write their own Declaration of Independence. Steel, however, less innocent than his cherubic appearance suggested, reminded such doubters of an uncomfortable truth: since the war, whether under Clement Davies, Grimond, Thorpe or himself, the Liberal Party had been fighting principally to avoid its own extinction. The Alliance was their best chance in modern times of achieving power. Behind the posturing, the real debate was between those who hoped within their lifetimes to see Liberals in government again, and those who in their hearts preferred the cool, pure air of the wilderness.

The Social Democrats meanwhile badly needed an early success with real voters. Two of the Gang of Four, Roy Jenkins and Shirley Williams, were outside the Commons; although the SDP had nearly thirty MPs, the party would only be given legitimacy if new MPs were elected on its ticket, for Labour members at Westminster were giving a hard time to former colleagues they now regarded as renegades. Some Social Democrats had wanted to resign their seats and fight by-elections, as the Ulster Unionists were to do five years later in protest against the Anglo-Irish agreement, but this was rejected as too risky.

Three months after the party was founded, Roy Jenkins, standing with Liberal support in a by-election at Warrington, almost created a political sensation when he cut a huge hole in the Labour majority. Labour's vote slumped from 62 to 48% in a northern stronghold of the most traditional kind, with an apparently impregnable majority of rock-hard, working-class Labour voters. Jenkins' paradoxical claim that his first defeat in the twelve elections he had fought was his greatest victory seemed a just one: from looking like a politician of the past, he had suddenly become overnight a man with a future, who could work near-miracles in the most unpropitious circumstances.

Originally it had been suggested that Shirley Williams should fight Warrington. Roy Jenkins, with the stigma of his unpopular Europeanism, and open to the taunt that he was a pensioner of European bureaucracy who had done well out of his job and abandoned his Labour roots in the process, looked a less suitable candidate. But although he might have the air of an

Edwardian grandee, when engaged in a by-election Jenkins retained those instincts of a fairground bare-knuckle fighter that any successful democratic politician needs. His combative spirit, political experience and sheer talent put the Social Democrats' show on the road from Warrington onwards.

However, the result contained also a warning for the SDP. Their erosion of the Labour vote was impressive, but the foundation of their success had been the collapse of Conservative support. This evoked disturbing memories of the experience of successive Liberal leaders: Grimond, Thorpe and Steel all aspired to replace Labour with a radical party of the Left-Centre, but each did best when Tory voters became disillusioned with that party. Each had seen his hope turn to disappointment as Conservative fortunes revived and the Labour vote steadied. There was really no future for the SDP as another Orpington-style alternative to Toryism-in-trouble. Another worry was that, according to a poll, one-third of Warrington voters thought the SDP would withdraw from Europe and another one-third did not know what their stance was. The new Alliance had a major task ahead in getting its policies across to the public.

Electorally, euphoria served the Alliance well in those early months. Three months after Warrington, in October 1981, the Liberals, standing with SDP support, took Croydon North-West from the Conservatives. In November Shirley Williams returned to the Commons with a sensational victory in the Tory seat of Crosby in Lancashire. In retrospect this was the Alliance's high-water mark in that Parliament, for soon after it the tide began slowly to ebb. But not before Roy Jenkins returned to Westminster in March 1982 by winning Glasgow Hillhead. The Alliance was on its way.

By early 1982, however, there were signs that the party had moved smoothly from infancy to menopausal difficulties with no adolescence intervening. The SDP had an unpredictable system of electing a leader, and MPs trained in Labour battles did not easily forget the habits of a lifetime. So even though the candidates, Roy Jenkins and David Owen, were determined to fight their fifteen rounds without bruising each other, they were persuaded that to reach their largely unknown electorate within the new party – a 'credit card party', as their opponents delighted to jeer – they had better go on television. Democratic politics, after all, had to be about choice, and there were significant differences between Jenkins and Owen. The former President of the European Commission had found his re-entry to Westminster politics from Brussels an irksome experience; perhaps having set his stall out against ping-pong politics, he found some illogicality in indulging in the combativeness that the House of Commons loves. David Owen, aggressive by nature and stung by Labour taunts flying round him as he spoke, had no such inhibitions; he took to jousting as to the manner born. Like a character of George Eliot's, Owen has 'a hyperbolical tongue – it catches fire as it goes'; Jenkins has a slower fuse.

Yet there were disadvantages for the party in the leadership election, and to a lesser extent in the subsequent one for the presidency between Shirley Williams and Bill Rodgers. The SDP's early popularity owed much to the intimacy of the Gang of Four. The public liked the idea of a small group of friends who had dedicated themselves, at considerable personal sacrifice, to set the world to rights. The elections for party posts put a slight bruise on that cheerful countenance. The four were still friends, but the harsh world of political reality had intruded into the idyll. The original political family had to turn itself into a party for all seasons.

During the leadership contest, Jenkins argued that the Alliance must not attempt simply to replace the Labour Party, as Owen's call at that time for radical Left-of-Centre policies seemed to imply. In an interview with me on the Nine O'Clock News, Jenkins recalled the twenties and thirties when, with the Left of British politics split, the Conservatives ruled with only brief interruptions. It was a problem that oppressed them all: only by winning Conservative as well as Labour votes, he said, could the Alliance avoid responsibility for a reprise of those years, and he asserted his determination both to elbow Labour out of the way and to defeat the Conservative Government. Roy Jenkins' childhood during the Depression was spent in the Labour stronghold and industrial desert of South Wales. His formative years were when his father was a miners' union official and later a Labour MP. The divisions between Liberals and Labour, and the apparent permanence of Conservative rule, must have left a strong mark on him. He had identified in those inter-war years and during his work on Asquith's life the key problem of realignment: that it tends, by splitting one side of politics, to give the other flank supremacy for the generation during which the changes take place. The Alliance had to show that it could break this mould also.

So Jenkins' own temperament and his political judgement both drove him in the same direction. He did not wish simply to return British politics to a Gilbert and Sullivan world where

> Every little boy and girl that's born into the world alive
> Is either a little Liberal or else a little Conservative.

The party structure which had existed before the Great War, even with an SDP additive to the Liberals, did not attract him. Instead his dream was that he could create a new political Centre, drawing support from both Tories and Labour.

Roy Jenkins, as had been expected, was elected leader.

CHAPTER 5

TORIES AT TRAITORS' GATE

The divisions over economic policy persisted throughout Margaret Thatcher's first term, but reached their climax in 1981. Jim Prior believes this must have been the most divided Conservative Cabinet in history. He once found himself sitting on the Treasury Bench while a Right-wing backbencher delivered a speech that Prior regarded as absolute nonsense. He was therefore surprised to hear both the Prime Minister and Keith Joseph punctuate the speech with 'hear, hears', and Mrs Thatcher say at the end that she regarded the MP as 'one of the most promising of our young men'.

So the disagreements ran deep. But as Prime Minister, Margaret Thatcher was a more formidable figure to her colleagues than she had been as Leader of the Opposition. The contrast with Ted Heath's style was also notable. It had sometimes been difficult to know where he stood in a Cabinet debate until he summed up, or even until the minutes were circulated later. Mrs Thatcher set out to guide the discussion from the start, leaving others to challenge her.

Mrs Thatcher is a forceful and effective debater, but prime ministers do not find enough hours in the day to master every subject. She seemed to judge a minister's case by his pertinacity. (In this respect, her style was similar to Heath's.) One minister said it was her habit to challenge a minister in Cabinet 'in a quite savage way'. If he crumbled under the assault, began to apologise, and said he would bring in another paper from his department, she assumed she was right. But if he stood up to her – as my informant implied that he did – the Prime Minister assumed he was right and dropped her objections.

What fortified the Prime Minister in her internal struggles was a belief that she had caught a public mood in 1979. In part this was a reaction against the Winter of Discontent, against rotting refuse and unburied bodies; but in part it was more fundamental, a feeling that the entire post-war consensus had broken down, that successive Labour and Conservative governments had failed, that something new must be tried. Margaret Thatcher offered a new faith and a new face. The fact that she was the first woman Prime Minister, and a person of manifest courage, had appealed to an electorate in desperate search of fresh leadership. So she came in on a tidal wave for change, even if her supporters were by no means clear what changes to expect. Like the alderman and art, they didn't know much about politics but they knew what they liked – and especially what they didn't like. Specifically, they didn't like their lives disrupted by strikes, and they did like the promise of lower taxes.

The Prime Minister had surrounded herself with economic ministers who shared her philosophy: Geoffrey Howe and John Biffen (then a believer) at the Treasury, Keith Joseph at Industry, John Nott at Trade, David Howell at Energy, and Angus Maude as Paymaster-General. Only Jim Prior, at Employment, was a dissenter. Some Tory critics awarded an almost Mephistophelean role to the Financial Secretary to the Treasury, Nigel Lawson. One said that even outside the Cabinet he had influence 'where it mattered' – in Downing Street – and that he was 'a hard man' who, like many economic journalists, did not understand 'the real world'. The future Chancellor's reputation was made before he even entered the Cabinet.

What the more cautious members of the Cabinet gradually realised was that the Prime Minister was convinced she had a better understanding of what the public wanted from her than they did. This was to take the British economy by the scruff of the neck and shake it, until it was changed utterly. They had underestimated her determination that she was right. At this time one spoke to me with awe of her empathy with housewives, but it went much wider than that. The Prime Minister and her closest colleagues were reacting not just against price rises that worried housewives, and the policies of the Labour government they blamed for these. They were opposed to the whole interventionist philosophy that Conservative governments also had followed, inherited from a wartime system designed to achieve the greatest national cohesion in face of a common enemy.

Even ministers bitterly critical of some policies recognised in Margaret Thatcher qualities that pleased them. Francis Pym believed she was a most effective champion of the private enterprise system in which he also believed. Ian Gilmour admired the way she tackled the unions. So the Cabinet was not polarised in any simple way and ministers moved from side to side on different issues. But the group Mrs Thatcher categorised as 'wets' had been shattered by the aftermath of the 1979 Budget, and by the squeeze that followed the tax cuts of that first summer. They had reduced the cuts in public expenditure by more than £1 billion, but only two months after the Government was formed a minister was shocked to hear that an old people's home in his constituency was having to be mothballed. As unemployment moved upward, and they contemplated a Treasury forecast that it would rise to 1,650,000 in 1980, some Tories began to worry about the next election. By February 1981, even before the most controversial Budget of the Parliament, Jim Prior was contemplating gloomily a total which would rise to over three million. He believed the Government needed to get this down to two million, though even that would only be possible because of the changes in counting methods that were being planned.

By the end of 1980 unemployment was just short of two million, but it rose inexorably from then on, standing just below three million at the 1983 election, and moving on upward in the new Parliament. In 1980 also, under the influence of high oil prices and interest rates, the pound had risen to a dollar parity of 2.40, which accelerated the decline in employment in manufacturing. Faced with all this adversity, the Prime Minister showed no sign of doubt. One critic at the time complained that she was sailing into the eye of the storm, bound to the mast, her ears waxed against the siren songs of ministers complaining that they were running towards the rocks. But even more turbulent political days were ahead of her.

The most traumatic day in the economic life of the Thatcher government was 10 March 1981, when Geoffrey Howe presented his third Budget, first to the Cabinet and then to the Commons. Because in the previous autumn ministers had not agreed to control public spending as sharply as Howe wished, money supply and borrowing were now to be tightly controlled, taxes on drink, tobacco, petrol and North Sea oil were to rise, and the income tax allowances would not be raised to keep pace with inflation – a decision critics said would widen the poverty trap. One minister said after the Cabinet that the whole affair had been handled with incredible political naiveté. Two senior ministers, the Foreign Secretary, Lord Carrington, and the Leader of the Commons, Francis Pym, had not been warned that they faced a savagely deflationary package. He added that the Cabinet had been split down the middle and that, in his judgement, all the men of weight and experience – by which he meant those who agreed with him – were on the same, unhappy side.

The President of the CBI, which had wanted modest reflation, called it 'at best a brush-off, at worst a kick in the teeth'. It was not the last time that business and the Prime Minister were to be at odds. At a City luncheon she also implicitly rebuked colleagues for being unwilling to meet the bill for their own spending. What really shocked the 'wets' was that they had assumed decisions to subsidise British Steel and rescue the BL motor company represented a softening of the Government's posture, a return to flexibility in face of a worldwide economic blizzard. But the Budget undermined that theory, and the July Cabinet on public expenditure saw the sharpest difference of view so far. Jim Prior records in his book, *A Balance of Power*, that both he and the Social Services Secretary, Patrick Jenkin, went to that meeting armed with the personal election addresses of Geoffrey Howe and Keith Joseph, to show that they had promised to protect pensioners against inflation.

This July Cabinet was notable for a re-drawing of the political battle-lines. Both John Nott, now Defence Secretary, and John Biffen, who had replaced him at Trade, joined the doubting camp when the Treasury presented its public-spending plans. Nott's intervention was said to be devastating and began an estrangement from the Prime Minister that was never fully healed. He had been a more ruthless cutter of defence spending than Pym, but now he wanted to spend more himself. In Cabinet he was scathing about the Treasury paper: he purported to believe that, since the Chancellor had been away, he could have had no part in the preparation of the worst such paper Nott had ever seen. From the man who Denis Healey had predicted would be Chancellor within eighteen months of the Government's formation, these were harsh words. Perhaps he saw that post eluding him for ever.

It was the most serious reverse the Prime Minister had suffered from her own colleagues. She adjourned the discussion on public spending, but in the autumn reshuffle she struck back to regain the ground she had lost, exiling her most formidable critic, Jim Prior, to Northern Ireland, giving him what proved to be merely a face-saver in continued membership of the Cabinet's economic committees. The three sacked 'wets', Ian Gilmour, Mark Carlisle and Lord Soames, were replaced by three Thatcherite supporters, Norman Tebbit, Nigel Lawson and Leon Brittan. Lord Thorneycroft was dropped from the party chairmanship and replaced by Cecil Parkinson, who had a seat in the Cabinet as Paymaster-General. The whole balance of Mrs Thatcher's Government was changed, in her own favour.

What made the quarrel so bitter? The critics saw a basic illogicality that offended them. They could not detect the economic sense in paying unemployment benefit to large numbers of people, and they feared that the fruits of North Sea oil were being allowed to drip away during the recession rather than being used for industrial regeneration. Unemployment also had social dangers. The most obvious danger was to race relations. The impossibility of getting work might drive young blacks into a lifetime of what the American ghetto calls 'hustling'; it might aggravate the spasmodic riots in the inner cities. But the less obvious peril was that a whole generation of working-class young people would lose the habit of work. This result was not unthinkable, if a young man or woman moved from a not very inspiring education to a dole queue, with a brief intermission in a work experience programme that did not produce a job.

If families did drift into an unemployment culture, it would be hard to rescue them. Anyone who doubted this had only to look at Londonderry and Strabane in Northern Ireland, where endemic unemployment was a prelude to the troubles. Of course, the technological revolution between now and the end of the century would change the patterns of work and leisure for many people, but to be wholly without a job, and for a long period, was something different and more dangerous.

What made the rift in the Government's ranks so deep was that, while the central economic group round the Prime Minister and her Chancellor believed that any weakness now on public spending would undermine the whole basis of Government policy, a growing number of ministers felt the

Treasury was prescribing blood-letting for an already anaemic patient. That year's party conference in Blackpool was the most turbulent the Tories had witnessed since 1963, when Harold Macmillan's illness provoked a leadership battle in the same town. This time it was the party that was sick. Dissident ministers delivered a series of broadsides at fringe meetings. Most of these took place at a restaurant called the Lobster Pot. I mentioned this watering-hole in conversation with a grand Conservative lady of the Loyalist Tendency. She rewarded me with a sparkling if menacing smile: 'The Lobster Pot? Oh, we call that Traitors' Gate.'

It had been that kind of week. The division was neatly encapsulated in a *reductio ad absurdum* exchange between a Thatcherite Young Conservative who jeered at Ian Gilmour's Economic Charter for 'wets'. 'If Sir Ian wants to reflate by £5 billion, and thinks it will help, why be so cautious? Why not £10 billion? Or' – with the infinite irony of precocious youth – 'why not £15 billion?' Sir Ian unwound his lanky figure from an inadequate chair, and answered with matching irony: 'If three million unemployed, why not six million? Or nine million?'

Coded criticisms from three serving ministers, Francis Pym, Peter Walker and Michael Heseltine, culminated in a direct attack from Jim Prior on the whole basis of the policy. He argued that there was a strong case for higher public spending, and criticised the Government's rhetoric as myopic. In private, criticisms were equally fierce. One minister who was normally a Thatcher ally offered this enigmatic advice: 'I believe that events will bend Margaret, but she is very unpredictable – except that she's basically a Fundamentalist.' And he slipped off into the Blackpool night, promising further exegesis on a later occasion.

Not all the hard words came from the Prime Minister's critics. Edward Heath had a rough reception, and one young man was cheered when he contrasted Mrs Thatcher's vision of making Britain great again with Heath's of making himself great again. This offended old friends like Willie Whitelaw, and in *l'esprit d'escalier* which such nastiness produces among loyal people Heath's old deputy later wished he had left the platform in protest. Tory conferences do not often provoke such feelings. But when Mrs Thatcher came to wind up the week she made clear that she would not change direction 'just to curry favour'.

It remained a bleak year for Conservatives, because although the Official Opposition was obsessed with its internal difficulties, the new Alliance of Liberals and Social Democrats looked like a serious threat to the Government and to the whole political status quo. But if 1981–2 was the winter of Margaret Thatcher's discontent and the nadir of her Government's fortunes, spring came suddenly and in the most improbable way: through a humiliation, followed by a triumph, in the South Atlantic.

Neither the world nor the domestic economy offered much cheer between the Cabinet troubles of 1981 and the landslide Tory victory in 1983.

In blacker moments Mrs Thatcher must sometimes have felt, like Keynes, that the dollar was behaving 'like the Gold Standard on the booze'. Nothing was stable. In the event none of this mattered, for her Falklands triumph and a divided and demoralised Opposition lifted the nation's eyes from its economic anxieties. At the time, nervous Conservatives could not be sure that they were electorally safe, yet once it appeared probable that British servicemen were going to be in action in the Falklands, the public's instinct to back the government of the day suspended normal politics. The Conservatives did well in the council elections and had a triumph in the Beaconsfield by-election – a sharp contrast with Roy Jenkins' victory in Glasgow only a couple of months previously.

As the Government entered what turned out to be the final session of the Parliament in November 1982, even as the Falklands Factor might have been expected to fade and even with high unemployment, Mrs Thatcher had a commanding lead in the polls. She had acquired during the anguished months of the Falklands crisis an enviable role. Her image was now that of the Pilot Who Weathered the Storm. This has always had a potent appeal in British politics. Dickens records a story of Government backbenchers who were quite capable of remaining soundly asleep throughout a colleague's speech until he came to the passage about 'Mr Pitt, the Pilot Who Weathered the Storm', when they could join in enthusiastic cheering without ever reaching full wakefulness.

The euphoria of the Falklands victory evaporated the Prime Minister's political problems at home. There were still worries on the Tory side. In November 1982, polls suggested that three voters out of four regarded unemployment as the most important issue; this compared with only two out of five in May when, at the height of the Falklands crisis, Mrs Thatcher's irresistible persona persuaded a small majority that the economy might improve in the following year. By November most people took a gloomier view. The debate on the Queen's Speech showed what issues the Opposition parties would have liked to dominate the coming election. The Prime Minister emphasised the Government's reduction of inflation to 7.5%, the fall in interest rates, and the growing raft of measures being introduced to take the sharpest edge off unemployment, which ministers did not believe could be cured quickly. But for Michael Foot and David Steel the issues were a far worse unemployment record than any other Western Government's and, surprisingly, the tax issue.

A few weeks previously a Treasury answer to a well-judged question by Michael Meacher, Labour Member for Oldham West, had showed that a family on average earnings was paying 14.5% more tax than before 1979, even allowing for inflation, and that only those on five times average income were paying less tax. But because pay settlements had been higher than inflation, most people still *felt* better off. The Prime Minister, by now the unchallengeable war leader, did not deign to argue with the other two party

leaders on taxation. They might call her 'the greatest tax-cutting dema-
gogue of all time' (Foot), and accuse her of presiding over 'one of the
sharpest rises in taxation on ordinary families that has ever been experienced' (Steel), but she replied with an aggressive tour d'horizon, ranging
from the Falklands through protectionism to electricity prices. She was
clearly confident that voters would be content with her stewardship.

Not all Tories were so confident. Some wondered how permanent the
cure for inflation would prove. Steel argued that what Mrs Thatcher called
realism in pay bargaining was caused by fear of unemployment and would
not last. He said the price of so many lost jobs was not worth paying for 'that
relatively modest decline in inflation' – from the 10.3% she inherited to 7.5.
The Opposition began to complain about the cost of unemployment to the
nation. They put this at about £17 billion per year in benefits and lost tax
revenue. Yet Tory 'wets' were surprised, and some a little disappointed, at
Labour's handling of the unemployment issue. A rebellious minister with
whom I had lunch that month seemed irritated as he sampled the Beaujo-
lais Nouveau. Why on earth were the public not more interested? And why
did Labour not know how to use the issue? After all the internal arguments
over the economy in 1981, which the 'wets' had begun to think they would
eventually win, they were understandably annoyed that the only two issues
now appeared to be the Falklands and Mrs Thatcher. It was not just the
Opposition's fox that General Galtieri had shot.

The truth about unemployment seemed to be that those in work were not
as concerned about those without jobs as the politicians expected them to
be. Was the country suffering from what Dean Inge once called 'fatty
degeneration of the conscience'? The paradox was that, by the time politicians realised unemployment was not affecting voters' attitudes so much,
this ceased to be true, for during Mrs Thatcher's second administration
more and more people had had personal experience of unemployment,
either affecting them or their children. MPs began to think it was a more
potent issue again. That is the fascination of politics: history often repeats
itself, but never precisely.

But this is hindsight. As the election came nearer Tories with marginal
seats became more twitchy about unemployment, and their nervousness
infected colleagues sitting on the more lusciously upholstered shire
counties. Some looked at the graphs issued with the unemployment figures
and wondered if the Government's luck would last for ever. The graph
issued just before the election, which went back to 1965, toddled along in
the foothills for its first fourteen years and then turned itself into a veritable
Everest after 1979; the world recession might bear most of the blame, but
Tory dissidents did not hesitate to join the Opposition in worrying about a
connection with inner-city riots. Unemployment among young blacks was
growing four times as quickly as among whites.

However, as the election approached the ranks closed. The Manifesto had to be prepared. Manifestoes are important in two ways. They may not be read much by ordinary voters, but they are combed by those who influence the election debate at one remove: leader-writers use them to judge how a party is facing the prospect of governing; commentators in print and broadcasting search them for evidence of policy shifts. Perhaps most assiduously of all, opponents pore through them to seek pieces of unexploded ammunition. But they are also important for their use in internal debate if the party does achieve power. When Douglas Hurd was Ted Heath's political secretary at Downing Street, he kept a Manifesto pinned to the wall, and stroked out each commitment as it was carried out. In any government, any policy included in the sacred document, however much regretted in the light of circumstances, may be forced into a Queen's speech if its protagonists can counter all rational argument with the words 'but we had it in our Manifesto'.

The machinery by which manifestoes are drawn up is often controversial itself. Labour has formal arrangements, the Tories more informal. On this occasion Mrs Thatcher had commissioned Geoffrey Howe and Cecil Parkinson to oversee the preliminary work; they in turn had established subject working parties, where Conservative worthies from the National Union, selected backbenchers and assorted academics threw in their ideas. Simultaneously, the Prime Minister had some ideas factories of her own at work. In one branch eight Cabinet ministers, half their political advisers, most of the Think Tank, Old Uncle Ferdy Mount and All were contemplating the somewhat amorphous subject of The Family and the State. This vagueness must have sent the adrenalin pumping through the arteries of sociology dons, braying (to adapt Evelyn Waugh) for broken grants.

The most elaborate network of consultation inevitably produces some wounded feelings, even in a party where upper lips are traditionally stiff. There were officers of backbench committees who thought they had more to contribute than the arbitrarily chosen MPs, the academics, or the Party's version of the Great and the Good. So they were given other opportunities to influence the only mind that mattered: that of the Prime Minister. At one such chat in Downing Street the subject of unemployment was discussed. The officers of the Finance Committee are, by and large, as 'dry' as the Australian bush in economic thought. But they included Chris Patten, now at last moving up the ministerial ladder as his abilities demand, but at that time serving out a sentence on the back benches, in the chill of his leader's displeasure about his articulate dissent on economic policy. Patten, both intellectually and in political courage, was perhaps the most formidable of the 1979 intake of Conservatives. At the Finance Committee's soirée the Prime Minister gave an attentive hearing to his arguments in favour of a June election. When economics came up, one of his colleagues assured her that 'scarcely anyone' in the party nowadays believed in reflation. Patten, never one to duck a challenge, confessed that Scarcely Anyone was among his aliases. He was rewarded with a brisk lecture from the Prime Minister on where he was wrong.

Mrs Thatcher and her Chancellor were less concerned with arguments about public spending, which they believed they had settled in Cabinet, than they were about what tax cuts they should make in advance of an election. Sir Geoffrey's first Budget in 1979 had set out to help the well-to-do, in the hope of generating economic activity; this time he concentrated on the lower end of the tax scales and on social security benefits. About 1,750,000 low-income earners were taken out of tax, thus diminishing what used to be called the Poverty Trap, but by then had turned into the Why Work Syndrome. (In such coinages is our economic debate conducted.)

But a far more fundamental debate had been going on in Government since the previous year. This concerned the future of the welfare state and its implications for public spending. For a time it seemed that the key event in the election campaign would be a leaked document from the Think Tank on the rising tide of public spending. The welfare state was now consuming 40% of national wealth, and ministers did not see how they could ever redeem their promises to bring taxes down unless they found ways to save money. If such ideas were put in the election manifesto they would represent a U-turn, though of a quite different kind from that demanded in the past by Tory 'wets'. It would be the first attempt since the war to cast doubt on the existing form of the welfare state. The Think Tank report was an attempt to take arms against the sea of troubles Margaret Thatcher saw engulfing Britain and her own Government – more specifically against a tide of public spending that was rising in relation to falling industrial production.

To privatise the National Health Service and university and other education, to put a lower ceiling on pensions, unemployment and other social benefits, would have been seen as the most distinct change in direction this revolutionary government had taken. Ministers were to maintain later that the radical proposals which leaked in this period were merely 'options', but a change in direction was at least conceivable to one wing of the Cabinet as being within the new tradition established since May 1979; while to others it seemed like a break with the traditions of post-war Toryism.

What the debate underlined was the absence of an agreed philosophy. Every Conservative praises Disraeli, but his One Nation theory is open to varied interpretation in modern times. Dizzy, after all, presented Toryism as a national party because it allowed aristocrats to represent the peasantry, who were the majority. The natural enemy of both was Whig oligarchy. In the 1983 election it was not the peasantry whose votes mattered but the Midlands car workers and the whole post-Industrial Revolution caste they represented. Marxists called them the proletariat and wanted them to unite; Robert Worcester of MORI called them the C2 socio-economic group, and wanted them to answer his questions about how they would vote and why; Mrs Thatcher simply wanted them to support her despite high unemployment, as they had done in large numbers in 1979.

These were traditionally the most politically mobile people in post-war Britain. What the Conservatives were trying to discover was how best to retain their support. Was it by protecting their dole money, their Health Service and their children's free college places? Or by cutting their income tax further and 'letting the money fructify in the pockets of the people', as Churchill had advocated when Attlee was creating the welfare state in the forties? Another smart-alec remark of Galbraith's summed up the dilemma: 'Politics is not the art of the possible. It consists of choosing between the disastrous and the unpalatable.'

The argument rumbled on in the Think Tank, in Mrs Thatcher's Family and State group, and elsewhere in the Conservative Party. Opinion polls showed that the public remained dedicated to the Beveridge principles that the State should undertake the main responsibility for insulating people from ill health and poverty. If anything, people had become more of that mind since 1979, yet the increasing number of old people and the new, but expensive, possibilities of medical treatment made radical ministers look longingly towards more private provision: throwing more responsibility on to families and generally reducing the role of the state.

However, when Labour started to campaign on what it called 'the secret manifesto', and to warn voters about the 'dismantling of the welfare state', the Prime Minister saw the red light. The section of her Manifesto on the subject turned out to be much less exciting than advance leaks had suggested, or than some Tories might have liked: 'The Conservative Party believes in encouraging people to take responsibility for their own decisions. We shall continue to return more choice to individuals and their families. This is the way to increase personal freedom. It is also the way to improve standards in the state service.' But it went on to deny any intention to dismantle the welfare state, and to proclaim a determination that the public services should provide good value for beneficiaries and taxpayers. The Government welcomed the growth in private health insurance, the Manifesto said, but Mrs Thatcher was to assure voters again that the National Health Service was safe in her hands. As the campaign proceeded she committed herself in successive pledges to keep various benefits in line with the cost of living. When, in the new Parliament, Norman Fowler was set the task of creating 'a new Beveridge', he kept stumbling over commitments dating from the election campaign.

Another issue which reverberated through the campaign and into the new Parliament was local government and its finances. Mention of rates was beginning to embarrass ministers. Mrs Thatcher had long favoured their abolition but neither Michael Heseltine, Environment Secretary in her first four years in government, nor anyone else had found a satisfactory rating reform. In the months before the election a Cabinet committee under Willie Whitelaw was still wrestling with this appallingly complex subject. What would satisfy the CBI, which was worried about business rates, might alienate householders – and voters. So instead of promising to abolish the rates, the Manifesto eventually offered legislation for rate-capping and to abolish the Greater London Council and the Metropolitan Councils. This was legislation that was to consume much parliamentary time after 1983, cause immense political damage to the Conservatives, and eventually drive from office Mrs Thatcher's latest Environment Secretary, Patrick Jenkin.

In January 1983, when Heseltine was moved to Defence to fill the vacancy left by John Nott's return to the City, his friends feared his high standing with the Party would suffer because of his failure to solve the rates problem. A colleague said privately that this would be monstrously unjust: it was the Prime Minister herself who had allowed the party to become so heavily committed to rating reform. But he sighed, and offered the opinion that 'Michael might be the victim of her retrospective guilt transference'. Truly there are more things in politics than were dreamed of even in Freud's philosophy.

Although Mrs Thatcher and Michael Heseltine were never close, she was impressed by the efficiency he had introduced in his sprawling empire at Environment. His reputation as a self-made businessman, his addiction to management objectives and efficiency targets, accorded with her own beliefs. She probably realised he had found time to discover more about such subjects than she had herself. Yet Heseltine had never seemed to get the posts his standing with the Party in the country might have indicated. His appointment to Defence was the Prime Minister's attempt to solve problems: the campaign of CND, now aimed at a new generation of voters, had to be countered; and the burgeoning cost of service spending had to be contained. When he was appointed the Prime Minister warned him that he must expect to stay there for a long time, so that he would have to live with his mistakes. He was still there when they clashed over the Westland affair in 1986.

It had been notable that Heseltine, like Peter Walker, had been passed over when the party chairmanship fell vacant with Lord Thorneycroft's departure in 1981. For Mrs Thatcher that would have meant appointing a man of a very different political colour to a position close to her throne. Instead she turned to the second rank of her Government and appointed Cecil Parkinson, who was politically and personally more congenial to her.

Perhaps the least congenial minister, as far as she was concerned, was Peter Walker. He had been Ted Heath's campaign manager when she fought him for the leadership, and she had left Walker out of her Opposition front bench. Throughout her first administration he languished at

Agriculture – a backwater for a man who had been Geoffrey Howe's boss at the Industry Department a decade earlier. But even in the most arid surroundings Walker is never a man to hide his political light under a bushel. His departmental officials revealed that Britain's balance of payments had benefitted by about £1.7 billion from agricultural success. Even this did not make him the apple of his leader's eye. When it came to Thatcherite economics, Walker did not so much wear his heart on his sleeve as wave a banner above his head. His rumbustious fringe speech at the 1982 party conference sparked a new set of rumours that he would be sacked in January, and Walker murmured to friends: 'Why wait till January?'

He has a proper political conceit, and would undoubtedly have been a more dangerous presence on the back benches than anyone Mrs Thatcher has sent back there. When agricultural spending cuts were mentioned to him he once told the Prime Minister and Chancellor that, if they wanted that kind of policy, they had better find another man; and one Treasury letter pleading that Agriculture should match Industry in its spending sacrifices produced from Walker a tart one-liner: had they thought of bringing industry up to agriculture's level of contribution to the national economy?

Other ministers fought their corner against the current orthodoxy, and Mrs Thatcher quietly let them do so. George Younger, then Scottish Secretary, led a doughty national rearguard action against the closing of Ravenscraig steel plant. The Prime Minister seems to admire Younger, who tells her quite sharply what's what. The state of Scottish Conservatism was a warning that she needed to take a lot of notice of her lieutenant there.

The election was ever more present in the minds of ministers. Like most prime ministers, Margaret Thatcher was cautious about rushing prematurely to the country for a fresh mandate. The polls looked favourable in the spring of 1983, but Downing Street is a cocoon that its occupants find difficult to leave, even in propitious circumstances. While Mrs Thatcher ruminated in public speeches on her need for two more terms to achieve an economic revolution, her more practical advisers were urging her to cash in on her good fortune after the Falklands and face the voters in the summer of 1983.

Margaret Thatcher has been a singularly lucky politician as well as a skilful one. The circumstances in which she wrested Heath's leadership from him were evidence of her good fortune. A few years as Education Secretary were not the ideal launching pad for such a venture, but venture she did and she won. Luck is one commodity politicians need to survive and prosper. When the Harding administration was formed in Washington, with Calvin Coolidge as Vice-President, a friend of his remarked: 'Something will happen to Harding. I have known Coolidge ever since we were students together at Amherst. He has never won the first place, but something always happened after the event to put him on top. Something will happen now to put him in the White House.' Harding died in mid-term and Coolidge became the first New England President since the Civil War.

The obvious likenesses between Calvin Coolidge and Margaret Thatcher do not extend much beyond common respect for puritan values. He was negative; she is positive. He lacked ambition; she patently never did. He was painfully taciturn; that is not one of the Prime Minister's weaknesses. But both, like successful military commanders, have had more than their necessary ration of luck. The issue for Mrs Thatcher in the early months of 1983 was how to ride the luck that her achievements in the Falklands crisis had brought her.

Margot Asquith once said of Curzon: 'He has an expression of enamelled self-assurance.' Some might apply the words to Margaret Thatcher, but that may be an oversimplification of what has never seemed an especially complex character. Her public pronouncements are self-assured; so is her conversation. When swift decisions are needed, she can take them. But there are moments of jitteriness. Soon after I moved to the BBC, I did a television interview with her and was nervous. But it became clear that she was more so, and she made no bones about it. She does not like to make mistakes. The election decision was a vital one. Beneath the self-assurance Margaret Thatcher has the natural caution of a woman. It showed that spring.

CHAPTER 6

A PEOPLE'S PARTY WITH TOO FEW PEOPLE

If Margaret Thatcher was uncertain, Michael Foot had more fundamental cause to be so, for his party seemed to be falling apart. The crusade for constitutional change, which Tony Benn had made his own, had reached its climax at Labour's special conference at Wembley in January 1981. The previous few months had been disastrous for the Centre–Right: not only had they lost the leadership to Michael Foot, but the final split had begun. In November 1980 Shirley Williams had said she would not be a Labour candidate in the next election; David Owen had declined nomination for the Shadow Cabinet; and although Bill Rodgers had been elected to serve in it, he refused to take any portfolio other than defence, which he was not offered. The Social Democrats were near to breaking point.

At Wembley the Left skilfully marshalled union block votes to produce the electoral college that they preferred and the Right detested. This gave 40% of votes to the unions and 30% each to Labour MPs and the Constituency Parties. The next day the Gang of Four – Roy Jenkins and the three Labour front-benchers – issued their Limehouse Declaration. The Social Democratic Party was on its way. It was a split which made Conservative victory in the next general election inevitable. Some observers thought it might eventually signal the approaching end of Labour's 80-year history.

Labour's immediate turbulence was not over. The Wembley conference was followed by Tony Benn's campaign to win the deputy leadership from Denis Healey. Michael Foot was furious at the damage he believed this campaign would do to his already stricken party. At one stage he challenged Benn to fight him for the leadership instead. Like all good political dramas, this one was played out at a number of Brechtian levels. On the headline level of 'Foot slams Benn', it seemed the party leader had scored points: Benn had denigrated the policies of a government from which he failed to resign; had severely, perhaps fatally, damaged Labour's election chances; and had provoked a spirit of political intolerance and personal venom within the Party. However, at another level Benn could feel misrepresented: he was often characterised in the media as 'a cream-faced loon', a Labour equivalent of Keith Joseph or Enoch Powell; but just occasionally as a Margaret Thatcher, asking his party awkward, sometimes dangerous questions about its philosophy, its record, its political direction. To cast Benn as an Eastern European autocrat was to defile the language. His campaign against politicians' tendency to say one thing in Opposition and do something different in Government had wider appeal than was admitted by the political Establishment and by commentators, both of whom are preoccupied with politicians' practical problems.

This dilemma of equivocation in politics has no easy solution. David Owen denounced the politics of 'fudge and mudge' from his political standpoint, and Benn from his quite different position would have subscribed to the scorn. Yet British polity has often benefited from fudge and mudge. If Willie Whitelaw, as Home Secretary, had not been skilful in making law-and-order noises to the Conservative conference while refusing to countenance the penal policies Tory activists wanted – hanging and flogging – Britain would be a less civilised country. If Harold Wilson and Jim Callaghan had not 'talked Left and acted Right' for the benefit – or the mystification – of delegates they regarded as unrepresentative of Labour voters, Britain might have been less stable, or alternatively Labour might have failed to be elected at all. But these chickens were now coming home to roost, and tension between the conference and Labour MPs was worse than it had ever been. Not that such tension had been invented by Tony Benn. In 1945 Attlee and Harold Laski, then Party chairman, had a fierce exchange about this relationship, and since the fifties and early sixties, when Richard Crossman and others had conducted a Conference Must Decide campaign, a dangerous option had always been available to a Labour politician: if he could not persuade his fellow MPs, elected directly by the nation, that his policies were right, he might appeal to a wider, though less representative constituency – the Labour Movement, dominated by the block votes of the unions.

Michael Foot spoke out strongly for the rights of MPs, whether against Tory colonels in constituency associations or trade union moguls. Like Edmund Burke, he argued that real democracy must appeal to the judgement of Members of Parliament – 'not Honourable Midgets or Right Honourable Marionettes, but real men and women exercising their own independent powers of judgement on the great, complex issues of the age.' It was ironic that it fell to Foot to challenge the wisdom of Labour's annual conference, for apart from Aneurin Bevan he had been the supreme post-war artist of that conference, playing it like a Menuhin or an Oistrakh. Now he admitted its resolutions were 'not necessarily compatible' with one another, and that 'it is not a question . . . of merely transferring resolutions from the conference agenda to the House of Commons order paper'. Populism, in fact, was not enough.

This was not a lesson Tony Benn was willing to accept. Observers were divided as to whether he was a practical, often ruthless politician seeking power, or a visionary proposing a transformation of the British system towards a more sensitive democracy. Either way he did not look to Michael Foot like an ideal running mate in the next general election. Benn had moved gradually from Right to Left, passing both Foot and Neil Kinnock on the way. Harold Wilson once said of him, 'He immatures with age.' His fiercest critics feared he wanted to turn Labour from being representative of one of the great interests of the nation into a sect like the Exclusive Brethren, which would frighten off millions of Labour voters.

Benn was a talented politician, one of the two best debaters in British public life (the other being the maverick Enoch Powell). He could be warm, friendly, and with a well-developed compassion for the underdog. It was personality as well as policy which had won him a following whose admiration shaded into hero-worship. But his last spell in government had seared his soul. With every speech and broadcast now he was revealing the depth of his disapproval of the Callaghan Government's policies – from the IMF intervention on public spending in 1976, through the successive phases of incomes policy, and with what looked in retrospect like an intolerable strain of conscience over defence, Europe, Ireland and much else. Voluntary resignation is out of fashion, but it is hard to think of a case where resignation would have been more appropriate. His mood in 1981, the purging fervour of a Savanarola, derived from those unhappy years.

Denis Healey has his failings too. He combines the best intellectual equipment in British public life with the political instincts of a bar-room brawler. No one suffers fools – or those he thinks are fools – less gladly. He had made many enemies in the Labour Party and the unions, some of them unnecessarily, and he paid the price for that during the contest with Benn. Yet Healey's faults were the obverse of his virtues. When he spoke at a fringe meeting at that year's TUC, his performance may have been less polished than Benn's and less insinuating than that of the third candidate, John Silkin, but it was also that of a statesman who knew what he believed and said what he knew. There was remarkably little trimming to wheedle supporters. He went the second mile in saying things he knew would be unpopular. On defence, incomes policy and the economy, and even on Europe (where his own views have varied down the years), he chipped away at the prejudices of his followers rather than simply pandering to them.

The TUC conference was a rehearsal for the Labour conference a month later. Michael Foot made what Healey called 'the best speech Michael has ever made', but a Right-wing union leader called it 'brilliant, brave, but a year too late'. Healey's campaign managers were delighted when Foot called Benn's campaign 'trivial and infantile'. As the votes were lined up, the imperfect nature of trade union democracy was again demonstrated. From soundings taken by various unions it became clear that Healey had far more support among the rank and file than among activists and officials who controlled the block votes. The largest union, the Transport Workers, found this, to its leaders' surprise, but it still failed to vote for Healey. The Left-wing Public Employees' leadership did bow to membership pressure and supported him.

The TGWU vote became a subject of scandalised comment. Its 1¼ million block vote represented no less than 8% of the electoral college. Its shaky method of choosing whom to back had its roots in TGWU history: in writing the union constitution the founding genius, Ernest Bevin, gave power to the executive, and great power to the general secretary, himself. From the twenties to the mid-fifties, he and his longest-serving successor, Arthur Deakin, ruled the union with a rod of iron, and delivered its vote to Labour's Right. But the TGWU's sudden switch in the fifties and sixties to support for nuclear disarmament, nationalisation and other Left-wing policies was not the result of any Pauline conversion among dockers, lorry drivers, busmen and other members. It was their new leader, Frank Cousins, who espoused these causes and imposed them on the union through the power he inherited from Bevin and Deakin.

Not that other unions, on either side, were models of democracy. The engineers, whose leadership was now Right-wing, had a rulebook whose complexities made the dietary dicta in the Old Testament seem simple. The electricians, under Communist control in the fifties and that of the Right since then, gave total power to whichever group ruled.

Until Labour's Brighton conference in October, when the voting took place, Benn had seemed to be borne on a magic carpet, as though propelled by inexorable historical forces. But during the campaigning of spring and summer many Labour people saw what damage was being done to their party. Early successes for the SDP, notably Roy Jenkins' near-victory in Warrington, convinced them that the internal quarrelling must soon cease. When the destination of the union block votes had been decided, a quirk of mathematics left the decisive voice to a small, undecided group of Tribunite MPs, the most prominent of whom was Neil Kinnock. They had voted for John Silkin in the first ballot, but could not bring themselves to support either Benn or Healey in the second round and abstained. Healey won by 50.426% to 49.574. The counter-revolution in the Labour Party had begun. Tony Benn's hair's-breadth defeat, if not the beginning of the end, was at least the end of the beginning.

For narrow though the margin was, an election result can rarely have proved such a watershed in a political career as this defeat was for Tony Benn. At the same conference, the widespread anxiety about the damage being done by internal strife led to changes in the National Executive Committee. The control which Benn had exercised since the early seventies began to slip. The loss of five Left-wing seats represented the biggest revolution since the Bevanites had swept in at Morecambe in 1952 – another great turning-point in Labour history. The results did not immediately transform Labour's policies, but they did create an Executive that would support the leadership's efforts to re-establish some independence for Labour MPs. Michael Foot picked up an old phrase Harold Wilson had injudiciously used when faced with a Westminster revolt: Foot said if there were to be no 'dog licences' from Prime Ministers, there must be no intimidation from Constituency Labour Parties either. MPs (and their leader) must be allowed to exercise conscience, judgement and experience of electoral consequences when taking account of conference decisions. And he reminded the unions that MPs had a wider franchise than they had.

The conference unexpectedly gave Foot another constitutional victory by allowing the Parliamentary Party to retain its role in drafting the Manifesto. Earlier, when it had seemed likely that he would be defeated, a shadow minister said gloomily that this was 'the dying bee-sting of the old NEC'. Another year passed before Tony Benn and Eric Heffer were removed from their key chairmanships over Home Policy and Organisation, but the Centre-Right now felt it was winning.

Labour still had appalling problems. The fight for control of the NEC was bound to go on, and on past experience no cautious punter would have bet on the assiduousness of the moderates in the dusty committee-room work for which Tony Benn's supporters had such addictive enthusiasm. Many leading Labour politicians have found the nit-picking at NEC meetings hard to bear. Shirley Williams regarded her freedom from attending these meetings as one great benefit of her departure from the Labour Party. Denis Healey made no attempt at them to conceal his contempt for his more zany opponents. As soon as the agenda got under way, he would produce the largest briefcase known to man, extract the day's newspapers and – using a pen-knife attached to a bunch of keys worthy of the Governor of Dartmoor – rattle his way through a daily chore, the maintenance of his personal cuttings library. This habit did not endear Healey to Left-wingers proposing controversial motions through the rustle of paper, but it helped to preserve Healey's reputation at Westminster as the best-briefed Opposition politician.

The Centre-Right had surprised observers at Brighton by the zeal with which it fought its corner. The election for the deputy leadership had put it on its mettle. One middle-aged moderate confessed that she had come expecting Brighton to be her last Labour conference, but that she was going home spoiling for a fight. Reselection was continuing, however, and although its effects were less horrendous than MPs expected, some had been emasculated by fear; and London, Labour's chamber of horrors, still had most of its reselections to do. In the event, Ken Livingstone was to be one of the few successful challengers there; in 1981 he remained an unreconstructed leader of the outside Left, although his position changed subsequently; he was still seen as a thorn in Neil Kinnock's flesh rather than a support.

The other anxiety for the Centre-Right after the 1981 conference was that their victories had depended on union votes. The Constituency Parties remained alienated from Foot's leadership, and deeply hostile to the Centre-Right. This conference had been divided more sharply than ever down its centre aisle. The CLPs, particularly their young members, looked as if they belonged to a different party from the predominantly male, middle-aged trade union delegates. But all the reservations could not blur the conclusion from Brighton that Labour's internal tide was turning. Like the tides of our sandcastle childhoods there were many contrary eddies, and more still to come, but a change in mood suggested that the Party was beginning to think again of how to win elections.

Not, as it turned out, in time for 1983, but in 1981 Mrs Thatcher's Falklands triumph was still to come and the economic disarray in her Government made a Labour victory seem at least conceivable. The early successes of the Social Democrats also spurred Labour people to fight for the survival of their party. Above all, the monumental mess Labour had made of its constitutional changes had shamed union leaders who backed them, and they were in chastened mood.

A debate was beginning about Labour's electoral future. A surprising contribution came from the veteran Marxist historian, Eric Hobsbawm. He produced what might be thought a truism in an elective democracy, but Labour members needed reminding of it: 'The best and most Left-wing party is not enough if the masses won't support it.' He denounced 'the delusion of the early 1980s that organisation can replace politics'; argued that the SDP defection had robbed Labour of a significant section of the Left-of-Centre middle class; and that coexistence between Healeyites and Bennites was essential if Labour was to remain what he called a 'People's Party', rather than becoming a small partner in future coalitions.

To young delegates on the Militant fringes of Labour, who had been awaiting the Imminent Collapse of Capitalism for shorter lifetimes than Professor Hobsbawm's, this article (assuming they ever read it) was heresy. But to union leaders, who would have been horrified by any such capitalist collapse as an interruption of free collective bargaining, the article had a message. It supported their own belief that the Labour Party their predecessors had created eighty years before must remain a serious aspirant for power, not just a vehicle for minority protest. Many union leaders who had voted for an electoral college were dismayed by the disunity the Healey–Benn election had created throughout that disastrous summer. Some were also shocked by differences revealed between their own Left-wing attitude and the views of members. There was heavy union pressure on Tony Benn to avoid further leadership elections, with the implicit threat of a slump in his vote if he insisted on standing.

If Brighton 1981 had begun Labour's long and tentative convalescence, Port Stanley 1982 turned the world of British politics upside down again. That summer was the most astonishing of a remarkable decade. By May it was difficult to remember what the political map had looked like in March. Then Westminster was absorbing the political effects of a skilful Budget that took the sting out of the Tory wets' waspishness. But they still wondered whether a government which had presided over such an increase in unemployment could be re-elected. Were the sickly crocuses of that economic spring really the forerunners of industrial revival? Or had nothing fundamentally changed and would economic growth simply set off again the familiar spiral of wage–price inflation? The economy seemed, as ever, to be the overwhelming election issue.

By May the question was whether political fortunes had been changed utterly by the terrible beauty of war in the South Atlantic. Through the sacrifices of British servicemen had electoral prospects at home been transformed? Many politicians found this a delicate, even distasteful question, but few doubted there had been a seismic change. The council elections in May were the first test.

This should have been a bad Conservative year. Not only was the Government suffering from mid-term unpopularity, aggravated by the worst world recession in fifty years. This was also a year when council seats lost by Labour in 1978, during the Callaghan government's unpopularity, came up again. This looked likely to be a grand inquest on the Conservative performance, and not a happy one for the Prime Minister. But when the campaign had been going for a week politicians knew a Falklands factor was operating. Labour results proved spotty, better in the North than in London, where internal dissension had also taken a toll. Despite Labour's self-destructive tendency, well-placed Tories insisted privately that it remained the principal opposition: not only had the Alliance surge begun to slow down even before the Falklands, but Labour's deep roots throughout Britain made it more obviously a national party.

Labour's opinion poll figures were gloomy, however, and Michael Foot's personal ones worse. Labour had several albatrosses: the Militant dispute had still months and years of vote-losing mayhem ahead; the unions remained deeply unpopular; Foot himself was greatly loved by Labour people but his style looked anachronistic as the Conservative and Alliance machines grew slicker. One uncovenanted effect of Labour's constitutional changes became clear: it was even more difficult to change the leader. In the past, a feeling so long before the general election that a Labour leader could not win would have provoked a deputation of senior MPs suggesting he should stand down. But now that MPs no longer enjoyed the exclusive right to elect, change was impossible. No single group dominated the unions, which formed the largest constituency in the electoral college, so Foot was secure from challenge unless he decided to go of his own accord.

Private murmuring grew less inhibited. Denis Healey had not wholly abandoned his hope of leading Labour at the election, for he did not believe anyone could permanently endure the battering Foot had suffered for so long. But Healey also knew Foot was tougher than his frail appearance suggested, and he made it clear that only if the leader resigned would he seek the job. Many found it puzzling that Foot did not resign. This gentle, bookish, amusing, slightly shambolic man did not seem full of ambition. People could imagine Denis Healey putting his Sussex wellies on bare knuckles as he waded through slaughter to a throne. They could conceive of Peter Shore, though with a sigh, abandoning his scholarly preoccupations to place a sharp elbow in a rival's ribs. It would cause no surprise if Roy Hattersley laid aside his essayist's pen to wield his bat like a Hutton and clear his path to power. But power has never been Michael Foot's aphrodisiac. When it was offered originally by Harold Wilson he had said, like Sam Goldwyn, 'include me out'. Eventually Wilson persuaded him, and he went straight into the Cabinet, as his seniority dictated. Yet he did not exercise power – first at Employment, later as Callaghan's Number Two and drill sergeant of the Lib-Lab Pact – as if power were life's highest priority. That lay elsewhere, in his beloved books.

Once during the Heath administration I met Michael Foot at a party, and we were discussing a quotation the Prime Minister had used about his Industrial Relations Bill: 'There is nothing so strong as an idea whose time has come.' I mentioned that one of Heath's aides had told me this sentence had been lying around in his mental luggage for years, and that he feared it might be from Marx. A shade regretfully, I thought, Foot said no, it wasn't Marx; perhaps 'one of the Americans'. He must investigate. We arrived home shortly after 2 a.m., to be told by an astonished baby-sitter that a Mr Michael Foot had just been on the telephone. He had given her a cryptic message for me: 'Tell him it's Victor Hugo.'

What kept Foot going was what caused him to stand for the leadership in 1980: he did not believe Healey could unite the Labour Party. He was not certain that Shore, whom he had originally supported, could defeat Healey, but he believed, rightly, that he himself could beat Healey. He believed, wrongly, that he could unite Labour. As his poll ratings slumped and abuse accumulated, even from old Left-wing comrades, the reason Foot resisted the temptation to resign was that he feared further schism: at best, a bruising, three-months-long, multi-sided leadership election; at worst, a battle running right up to the general election, making Labour's defeat, and perhaps destruction, inevitable.

Foot was not the only man who thought Labour's survival was in doubt. After the damage done by the deputy leadership election, Neil Kinnock had warned his restless Constituency Party that the threat to Labour's existence was the worst in its history; if they did not counter the SDP threat they would be cast into the political wilderness for years.

The Militant Tendency ran like a malign thread through the history of these years. The issue was not easy for Foot, who had always opposed witch-hunts, but some thought he could only become a viable alternative Prime Minister, as distinct from a Leader of the Opposition facing inevitable defeat, if he was ruthless with Militant. Others had been surprised by the vigour he had displayed already. Opinions were divided as to whether

Militant was an organisational disaster or just a public relations disaster. It did most practical damage in the Young Socialists, from which its influence spread into local Labour parties. Successive Labour youth organisations have fallen under the spell of whatever is the fashionable Left deviation. It seems that political parties' youth groups either become marriage marts, as Young Conservative groups once did, or set out to scandalise their seniors, like the Conservative Students, who have swung far to the Right, and the Young Socialists, who go equally violently to the Left. Political youth, even in Britain, seeks to emulate the students in a Maupassant story who went round shouting 'l'enfer et la malédiction', *pour épater la bourgeoisie*.

As the election approached, party discipline was moved on to the back-burner. What postponed the retribution was Militant's recourse to the courts. Labour's general secretary, Jim Mortimer, who as Chairman of ACAS, the conciliation service, had probably seen more of the Law Lords than most politicians, told NEC members they must tread carefully in what was a legal minefield. With the rights of individuals now involved, they must studiously follow principles of natural justice.

The Militant drama has since dragged on for years. Not the least diverting aspect was the willingness of these British heirs of Lenin and Trotsky to use the capitalist courts. Their surrealistic concept of an organisation without members, simply newspaper readers, gave Labour many hours – and many guineas' worth – of legal bafflement. The Trotskyists were resourceful; they had an efficient press officer, who dressed as if he had just graduated from Harvard Business School, and who made sure that 'entryism' would not go down to defeat without publicity and consequent electoral damage to Labour.

But Michael Foot could not afford to do nothing, for the Militant issue had become significant for his political standing. The 1982 conference agreed to set up a register of organisations, which would effectively make Militant illegal within the Labour Party, but membership remained difficult to prove. Eventually five members of the editorial board of the Militant newspaper were expelled, and more under Neil Kinnock's leadership. Neither Left nor Right has been satisfied, but the issue has been partially defused.

Those puzzled by Michael Foot's decision to ignore criticism and remain as leader failed to notice that he now had the ambition, proper in a senior politician, to be Prime Minister, and thought he could do the job well. So did his wife, Jill Craigie, the strong-minded historian of the suffragettes. One knowing backbencher, pondering whether Foot would go, recalled that the last two Labour leaders had relied on the advice of their wives, and he added: 'One right, one wrong, and who knows?'

Mrs Foot was sure Michael should fight the election. Friends credited her with his shorter haircuts, the more conventional dress, including temporary abandonment of the beloved suede shoes, but as he battled on through the arid activities of Militant and other organisational deserts, kindly observers wondered whether leading the Labour Party as it then was represented Michael Foot's proper role in life.

A story is told about a dinner Jim Callaghan gave at Chequers as part of Prince Charles's education in what some courtier called 'statecraft' (presumably to avoid that controversial word 'politics'). The mixed group of older and younger ministers doubtless discussed statecraft over dinner, but at the more convivial stage of the evening the Prince, finding himself accompanied by only a few, asked where the others were. Denis Healey volunteered an explanation: 'X', he said, needed another drink and didn't want the rest of them to know. 'Y' needed to answer a call of nature and didn't want the rest to know. And Michael Foot? 'Oh, Michael *needs* to read a book, and doesn't want us to know in case it might hurt our feelings.' Healey's affectionate joke catches an essential truth about Foot: not that he lacks interest in politics, even disguised as statecraft, but that he is no obsessional. Like Healey himself, Roy Jenkins, and a few other senior politicians, he has major intellectual interests outside Westminster.

For Foot these political times were out of joint. His twice-weekly encounters with Margaret Thatcher during her question-times were not happy occasions for him. There was no mutual respect, little real point of contact between them. He and Harold Macmillan might have relished each other more, the bibliophile turned politician against the ultimate politician posing occasionally as a simple crofter. Television appearances were no more help. Michael Foot was editor of the London *Evening Standard* when most of our mothers were preoccupied with nappies or the laundering of short pants. He had an instinct, perhaps derived from youthful experience in Fleet Street, not to answer journalists' questions. Perhaps this obstinacy was his challenge to the media's implicit claim to set the agenda for debate, but it came across as his own imprecision. He rarely seemed to say anything new or exciting on television.

By the autumn of 1982 Foot still looked the least menacing Opposition Leader in modern times. He was saddled with policies on defence, Europe and incomes that were lacking in clarity, and four other factors made his task in the general election look impossible: redistribution of constituencies would lose Labour about thirty seats; defection of the Social Democrats not only deprived his party of a valuable transept in its broad church but risked splitting the anti-Conservative vote; Margaret Thatcher had converted the Falklands factor into a valuable Leadership factor; and then there were Foot's own image problems.

The Shadow Cabinet elections that year worked a minor miracle, preserving a continued balance between Right and soft Left, with Tony Benn excluded but not humiliated, and some younger men encouraged though not elected. The Parliamentary Labour Party has been called the most sophisticated electorate in the world (usually, it is true, by its own members). This means that MPs have elevated voting to an art form – rococo, perhaps – in which they combine the moral obliquity of characters in a C. P. Snow novel with mathematical ingenuity worthy of a Senior Wrangler. Right-wing Labour men who subsequently joined the SDP are said to have voted for Michael Foot against Denis Healey in order to hasten the end of a Party whose time, they believed, had passed. In the Shadow Cabinet voting of 1982, some MPs said they had selected a few names from each of the Right and Left lists, worked in a bit of pro- or anti-Europe bias, a little support for youth or experience, and a couple of people they simply liked. When 235 or so idiosyncratic choices are combined, almost anything might have happened. Yet astonishingly Labour finished up with the same shadow ministers at the close of a heady and disturbing year.

Michael Foot's standing in the party suffered, however, when he tried, and failed, to reshuffle his Shadow Cabinet. He wanted to move Neil Kinnock, who had the Education portfolio, to shadow Norman Tebbit at Employment, where he would have replaced Eric Varley who was offered an amorphous 'co-ordinator' role. Kinnock would have brought to this key role a touch of Welsh flamboyance and his strong dislike of Conservatives. Foot's instinct that his front bench needed a fresher look was right. Oscar Wilde once complained that while the world was a stage all right, the play was badly cast, 'with our Guildensterns playing Hamlet, and our Hamlets having to jest like Prince Hal'. The economy and unemployment were subjects that Foot believed would influence most votes away from the Government, and he thought Kinnock was the best man to handle them. But when Varley mobilised Shadow Cabinet support to resist the move, Foot left the decision to Kinnock, who feared another disastrous Labour split and dropped the matter.

Labour MPs grew even more twitchy about the leadership, and Foot, sensing danger, made a speech in December that left no doubt he intended to lead the party into the general election. But his poll rating remained low, and politicians worry about their leaders' poll ratings on what American Democrats call the Shorenstein Doctrine. Hymie Shorenstein was a political organiser in Brooklyn, a satrap of Franklin Roosevelt. He once received a visit from a dissatisfied candidate for minor local office who, having contributed handsomely to campaign funds, expected to see his name more prominently imprinted on public hoardings and voters' minds. Shorenstein explained to his candidate the importance of promoting the leader of the Democratic Party's ticket, Franklin Roosevelt. Leading the local man to the East River, he pointed out how, when a tugboat pulled in to the quay, the day's detritus of an urban harbour – cigarette packets, chewing-gum wrappers, assorted junk – was drawn in with it. 'Think of Franklin D. Roosevelt as that tugboat,' Shorenstein advised him kindly, 'and of yourself as that garbage. If he comes in, you come in. That's how we're spending your money.'

By the end of 1982 it was clear to most Labour men that the Shorenstein Doctrine that year favoured the Tories. But although Tearoom gossip (which is Westminster's equivalent of eighteenth-century coffee-housing) was to continue, a change in leadership was now impossible. The conspiracy had always been half-baked. Serious conspirators do not chatter to journalists in advance, although they are avid contributors to Sunday newspaper or television reconstructions later if the plot succeeds. ('What did you do in the great revolt, daddy?' 'Why, son, it was I who persuaded David, or Terry, or was it Moss to get things moving.') The rumours of a change kept coming, but by the start of election year it was clear that Michael Foot would be Margaret Thatcher's opponent.

CHAPTER 7

'GETTING RID OF THE IDEOLOGICAL GARBAGE'

If the existence of the SDP and the Alliance had not raised expectations, Liberals would have regarded 1982 as a good year in the local council elections, particularly with a Falklands Factor operating against them. They gained 193 seats and lost only 38. By contrast, in area after area their SDP allies either lost the seats of councillors who had defected from Labour, or failed to gain seats they were contesting in these, their first nationwide elections. The chairman of the SDP Councillors' Association asked for an inquiry into what he called 'a débâcle'.

But the reasons for the contrast were easy to understand. The Social Democrats were bound to be much harder hit by the Falklands factor, for while the Liberals during a decade and more had built up local strength through assiduous practice of 'community politics' – no cracked paving stone being left unturned – the SDP had not yet had time, even assuming they had the inclination, to mobilise such support. Their strength, as Roy Jenkins explained it to me in a television interview, consisted in ability to argue their political case, actually to win people over, in the course of an election campaign. It was a sharp contrast of methods with their Liberal allies. His own by-election at Glasgow Hillhead, just before the Falklands were invaded, was an example of this. When I visited Hillhead two weeks before polling, Jenkins was staring defeat in the face. Being the honest man he is, he could not bring himself to hide that belief from me in private, although he was determined to fight to the last.

Gradually the large meetings which he and other SDP leaders addressed night after night, the canvassing and recanvassing by teams brought in from other parts of Scotland and from the South, wore down his less charismatic opponents. Such tactics could never have been repeated precisely in council elections, even if there had been no Falklands factor. But what the Social Democrats hoped was that tours by their leaders, preaching the New Politics all over the country for the first time, would receive the same kind of public attention that Shirley Williams, Roy Jenkins and others had done in the past. In the event, as the Royal Navy sailed south with the Task Force and the Falklands crisis grew graver week by week, media interest in the New Politics faded. Jenkins found himself addressing the smallest audiences he had encountered since his barnstorming re-entry into British politics at the beginning of 1981. The Alliance was suffering from something that had not happened since Suez a quarter of a century earlier: an overseas issue dominating domestic politics.

Nevertheless the Alliance parties had taken about a quarter of the votes. Before mould-breaking was on their agenda the Liberals would have thought that an excellent result for a third party, and a solid launching-pad for a general election most people thought was still some way off. It was only when the results were set against the Alliance leaders' aspiration to revolutionise the whole political scene that they detected the chillest wind since the SDP was launched just over a year earlier.

Even before the Falklands crisis, the SDP's honeymoon was ending. The task of building up a party with detailed policies and an easily identifiable position in the political spectrum had to begin. The inspiration of newness and freshness was not enough, for the Alliance was now in full competition with the established parties. The worry for the SDP was that its political progress might depend less on its own merits and efforts than on the fortunes of quite similar politicians left behind in the Labour Party. The difference in political position between men like Denis Healey, Roy Hattersley and Peter Shore on the one hand, and the SDP's Gang of Four on the other, did not seem at the time of the breach to be wider than exists within most parties. Where they differed was in their beliefs about the possibility of saving the Labour Party from destruction. The rift had begun a long time before, however, and it may be charted in the attitudes of a man who had been closer to Roy Jenkins than Healey and the others.

In the week before Labour's disastrous Wembley conference which provoked the Limehouse Declaration, a memorial volume for Anthony Crosland had been published. Since Crosland's tragically early death in 1977 there had been some danger of a hagiology developing, with his disciples purporting to face each contemporary decision in the way they believed this most fertile mind in post-war politics would have done. Yet his life and attitudes were relevant to the Social Democrats' search for their political souls outside the Labour Party.

Had Crosland lived, he might by that stage have been leader or deputy leader of the Labour Party, trying to bridge the gulf that divided Left and Right. He remained a firm supporter of Labour unity until the end of his life. Although he had many reservations about Harold Wilson, he always defended him as a man who held Labour together over Europe. Susan Crosland records him as saying that all successful political leaders have accepted three rules of conduct: keep their party together; hold the middle ground against ultras of Left or Right; shift and adapt to changing circumstances, whatever the cries of betrayal. He once said to me that it was a misreading of history to think that party leaders were outstandingly consistent. From Abraham Lincoln, through Roosevelt, Lloyd George and others, a pattern of inconsistency ran. (Susan Crosland adds Cavour to that list.)

The antics of Labour's NEC had worried Crosland when he was Foreign Secretary in the Callaghan government, but what divided him from the Jenkinsites in the Wilson period was not just Europe, about which he was lukewarm compared with them, but his belief that they were recklessly putting the future of the Labour Party at risk. In personal terms Jenkins and Crosland healed their quarrel in the final year of Crosland's life; yet it was in the differences in policy and attitude which caused his original rift with them that the roots of 1981's strained relations between the Social Democrats and the Right-wingers who remained inside the Labour Party were to be found.

Crosland had set the agenda for democratic socialist politics in his seminal work, *The Future of Socialism*, published in 1956. Indeed, his former Parliamentary Private Secretary, Dick Leonard, wrote in 1981: 'To a shaming extent, the Labour Party (or at least its moderate wing) has been living off the intellectual capital of the *Future of Socialism* ever since.' Crosland certainly felt that. He complained to me more than once that none of the younger men in his party, who did not have his own burden of senior office, were doing the fundamental thinking that a new age in politics demanded. He said they were always urging him to write a knew reformist philosophy: 'I'm too bloody busy running a department; let them do the new thinking.'

Tony Crosland believed that a party of reform could not be based on a negative. Yet the temptation for the Social Democrats now was simply to rely on a Keynesian reaction eventually setting in against Margaret Thatcher's monetarism, and to ride a wave of public unease about Michael Foot's compromises with socialist fundamentalism. Crosland had foreseen this problem long before his death, long before any Labour split was contemplated. He feared the traditional Labour Right 'lacks a truly radical appeal, and often seems insular, class-orientated, conservative and middle-aged'. His political assistant, David Lipsey, who knew his thinking in the years immediately before his death better than anyone except his wife, wrote bluntly: 'He grew increasingly out of sorts both with what he saw as the conservative pragmatism of post-Gaitskell Labour leadership and the fluffy liberalism of other colleagues, who saw rights of homosexuals and membership of the EEC as a sufficient dose of radicalism to last a decade or two.'

Now Jenkins knew he and his colleagues had to produce much new thinking about where they wanted Britain to go. Shirley Williams, in the years since she lost her seat, had begun to do this at the Policy Studies Institute. Critics of the SDP, as of the Labour Right, would have adopted Lipsey's suggestion that, while Mrs Thatcher believed in incentives and the Labour Left believed in state action, the Labour Right had 'a philosophy of "hanging on", in the hope either of a revival in the world economy or of some domestic spiritual miracle, whereby political exhortation to try harder will be transubstantiated into a political renaissance'.

It was Crosland, under Gaitskell's leadership, who had elevated 'equality', rather than public ownership, to the apex of Labour's revisionist vision, and Wilson and Callaghan had conducted their party and governments within that philosophy. Crosland defined what he meant by equality:

> More than a meritocratic society of equal opportunities, in which the greatest rewards would go to those with the most fortunate genetic endowment and family background ... more than a simple (not that it has proved simple in practice) redistribution of income. We wanted a wider social equality, embracing also the distribution of property, the educational system, social class relationships, power and privilege in industry – indeed, all that was enshrined in the age-old socialist dream of a more classless society.

It was true that Crosland's advocacy of public expenditure as a principal egalitarian instrument had been modified by painful experience in government – of self-perpetuating bureaucracies, oversubsidised middle-class commuters, the dangers of taxing workers too heavily. Yet he challenged an academic thesis of the mid-seventies that public spending was absorbing too high a proportion of Britain's resources. He believed this was not greatly out of line with comparable countries.

Roy Jenkins, by contrast, had been critical of the level of public spending at that time, and in the next generation of Labour politics, the generation of the split in the party, Roy Hattersley, notably in his book, *Choose Freedom*, took the Crosland position and Bill Rodgers shared that of Jenkins. Of course Jenkins also believed in equality, if only because he thought the natural forces creating inequality were so strong that any government of the Left-Centre must lean against the wind to help the underdog. But this was not, for him, the crusade it was for Crosland.

The fly in Crosland's ointment was one which also troubled politicians with very different philosophies and hopes than his: Britain's chronic inability to sustain economic growth. It was a constant preoccupation of his. Once, during Wilson's premiership, I asked whether a prime minister with such a distinguished academic record as an economist ought not to be providing some more fundamental solution to Britain's difficulties. Crosland came gaily to the defence of his leader, using his most effective weapon, irony: 'Ah well, if you've got a structural solution to the problems of the British economy, for goodness' sake tell us about it in this Sunday's *Observer*.' Yet it was his frustration about the failure to solve this problem which made him angry that he had never been given one of the economic posts in government that would have allowed him to face trade union leaders with the realities about wages and production that his kind of politics rested upon. My personal conversations with him revolved around the fact that we were both interested in studying incomes policies. He never tired of asking questions about what I, as an old Labour Correspondent, thought feasible. What Crosland understood better than most politicians was that social resentment disrupted relations in industry, made sensible wage policies more difficult, and generally crippled Britain's economic performance. For him wages and the distribution of wealth were the core of the country's economic and social malaise.

Among my journalistic souvenirs is a galley proof of an unpublished editorial I wrote for the *Guardian* in advance of the 1970 election results, when the opinion polls made Labour runaway winners. This urged that Crosland should become either Chancellor or Employment Secretary to tackle that problem. Four years later, when Labour did win, he was appointed to the Environment Department, and when Callaghan became Prime Minister he succeeded him at the Foreign Office. Crosland's failure to get an economic post represents one of the might-have-beens of Labour history.

This deviation beyond the period of this book is necessary because since Crosland's death there had been one major entry in Labour's Situations Vacant column. As his memory faded in the new decade, Left-of-Centre politics needed another philosopher–politician to don his mantle, a leader of thought with the patience to hammer out original ideas on the anvil of practical politics. But by then the men with the ability to tackle this task were more preoccupied with fighting organisational battles to save Labour from more immediate trouble.

The Social Democrats had the same need for new thinking for their new party, but they also were preoccupied with organisation and constitution-making. Their danger was that they might become the residuary legatees of the political process, as the Liberals had often been. Among the people who said to pollsters that they would vote Liberal were some who adored 'good ol' Enoch' and who would have been horrified if they had understood Liberal policy on immigration or on Europe. But to be a party of protest was not sufficient to match the new mood in the Alliance. They were genuinely seeking power to change Britain, and that required new thinking.

So the SDP began to spawn policy documents with a prolific zeal worthy of the Liberals, who have never been given to verbal reticence in their policy-making. The new party needed both to identify its position on the political spectrum, and to decide where it hoped to get its voters from. That, as we have seen, was a controversial issue even among the original Gang of Four. The charge against early SDP policy-making was that it was too bland, too inclined to elevate motherhood and apple-pie and cure-alls and not to face the hard choices of politics. On the other hand, Roy Jenkins warned his party against 'manifestoitis' and 'great catalogues of promises'. It proved difficult to find a happy middle way.

By the autumn of 1982 a chill had entered the Social Democrats' councils. The task of carving out its own natural constituency amid the squalls of post-Falklands politics was daunting. At the height of Alliance success in the winter of 1981–2, when it led the older parties in the polls and at one point achieved 50% support, it had made large inroads into that critical socio-economic group that includes skilled workers. Indeed, at one time it actually had the support of a majority of trade unionists. Yet in judging what the SDP constituency should be, it was necessary to look at its rapidly-evolving persona. If observers sought a stereotype for the modern Conservative Party, they might choose not a Knight of the Shires but a small businessman (what Julian Critchley has called a Knight of the Suburbs). Fleet Street had already deprived Labour of its horny-handed-son-of-toil image, and saddled it with the polytechnic lecturer.

But what stereotype would more or less fit the SDP? The party was originally a child of discontent among the Labour Party. Its founders came thence, and apart from Christopher Brocklebank-Fowler so did its MPs. The SDP might, therefore, have been expected to have a penumbra of Gaitskellism, especially since Roy Jenkins had been one of Gaitskell's closest friends. Yet after its first conference in 1981, when it had become clear how many active Social Democrats were new to politics, if an observer had been forced to identify SDP Man he might have settled on a management consultant of strong views. For example, the SDP had reacted sharply against the trade unions. This was partly because ex-Labour MPs, who had suffered from the block vote through the quarter-century since it had turned against the Right, felt liberated; but more importantly, while many of the SDP's unknown soldiers in that first year were new to politics, they had experience in industry, commerce or the professions. Some had a natural boss's suspicion of organisations which represented a different interest; others simply reflected a widespread public disillusionment with unions, which began with the Winter of Discontent. At Westminster divided views among SDP MPs produced their first embarrassing split, when some voted for, some abstained, and some opposed parts of Norman Tebbit's Bill. The Party's leaders did not want to be regarded as anti-union, but some union leaders said this was what they were.

A fierce though courteous debate took place about what kind of party the SDP ought to be. Roy Jenkins warned them against becoming 'a Labour Party Mark II', but David Owen retorted that they must not be 'a Liberal Party Mark II either'. He and the other two members of the Gang of Four, Shirley Williams and Bill Rodgers, were still strongly conscious of their Labour origins, but what the leaders gradually perceived was that they were not fully masters of their fates. The political equivalent of the Calvinist doctrine of Predestination engulfed both the Social Democrats and the Labour moderates. These two groups of talented politicians, each brave after its own fashion, could not determine which would be the Elect and which the Damned.

For the Gang of Four were now fighting for their political lives just as surely as Denis Healey, Roy Hattersley and Peter Shore. The battle between the two groups was destined to have all the bitterness of civil war. The inevitable cynicism of practical politics began to affect the new party. One speaker at its first conference had a passing flick at its ex-Labour MPs: 'Whatever some of us have said in the past, let's get rid of this ideological garbage and respond to what people want.' That sounded worryingly like what Shirley Williams had been afraid of in 1980 when she was still unwilling to join any party that might not have roots or principles.

Bill Rodgers had also had an enlightening experience at the first conference, when he opened a debate on the unions with a carefully balanced speech. Every criticism he made of union abuse was as fervently applauded as it would have been at a Conservative conference. But then he had the temerity to suggest that they should read the TUC annual report, to see the constructive activities in which unions were involved, and he accused Tories of being hostile to the very idea of trade unionism, not just to its abuses. This went down like a lead balloon. So did the statements of another senior MP and union officer, Tom Bradley, that the good in the unions far outweighed the bad, and that 'unions will not go away, and neither governments nor courts of law will abolish them'. Trade unionists present noticed this hostility. At a fringe meeting they staged a mini-revolt, accusing the party's discussion paper of 'union-bashing'. Nearly everyone at this meeting was from a white-collar union. Rodgers and other ex-Labour men were unhappily aware that, even if they recruited more manual workers, many of their members, and presumably of their potential voters, thought that what's wrong with the unions and what's wrong with Britain were nearly synonymous. The Party was learning how difficult the carving out of a new political segment of the nation was going to be.

The new Party also lacked a clear image on public spending. Although Mrs Thatcher's government was the prime advocate of limiting public spending – a task which it found extremely difficult – it was recalled that Roy Jenkins, while still on Labour's front bench, had first sounded an alarm on the proportion of the national wealth that Britain spent on public services. Bill Rodgers shared that anxiety. But the Owen–Williams wing of the SDP leadership was concerned lest Roy Jenkins turn Disraeli's Taper on his head, by producing 'Whig men and Tory measures' – in other words, that the Gaitskell–Crosland form of social democracy, which elevated public spending to the honoured plinth previously occupied, for the Left, by public ownership, would be superseded and that the SDP would swing Right.

One problem was that there was no agreement about where the Alliance was likely to get its votes from at the general election. The Liberals had hoped the Social Democrats would bring a good swathe of the Labour vote into the Alliance column. But Tories feared it would split the anti-Labour vote in the South and Midlands. The SDP itself feared what actually happened: that its votes would be spread too evenly across the country, producing too many second places and too few MPs.

The Alliance had another delicate policy problem to face. With about three million people out of work, inflation was back into single figures in 1982. Understandably workers were not pushing their wage claims too far; but most people still assumed such high unemployment would not last, and they still assumed that wage inflation would then return. It remained a prime national anxiety. The current pause was like the alcoholic who told his friend he was giving up drink and had succeeded in walking past a dozen pubs that morning; now he just had to resist the temptation of one that was actually open. What would happen to wages when a more buoyant economy encouraged employers to leave the door ajar? The Alliance acknowledged an incomes policy was essential to their plans to cure unemployment, but Roy Jenkins had lost faith in the traditional social contract. Instead the Alliance proposed a complex system of taxing employers who conceded wage increases higher than a centrally negotiated or imposed norm. By the autumn of 1982 the Alliance was worried about its profile among manual workers concerned about unemployment.

Polling figures and results from elections put the new party and its Liberal ally on a psychological roller-coaster. Robert Worcester, the MORI pollster, put two astonishing years in their febrile context when he wrote: 'A massive 16-point Labour lead in October 1980, followed by a 17-point Alliance lead by November 1981, followed by a 20-point Tory lead in June 1982. Who can really say what may happen by June 1984?'

We did not have to wait that long. The switchback had reached its flattened-out final section before the general election gave an over-whelming Conservative victory. But nothing seemed at all certain to the Alliance in the autumn of 1982, eighteen months after the SDP launch. They could not believe that the Conservatives, who had been in third place so recently, could really recover so quickly just because of a national instinct to back a prime minister during a war.

Yet by-elections told the same story. Roy Jenkins' near-miss at Warrington in July 1981 had turned into Liberal victory at Croydon in October, Shirley Williams' triumph at Crosby a month later, and Jenkins' return to Westminster from Glasgow in March. It seemed that the Alliance was able to cut deep into the Conservative vote, whether Merseyside, the London suburbs or the Clyde. This was more serious for the Tories than the normal mid-term slump to which all governmental flesh is heir. It might even be the much-heralded breaking of the mould, which would leave British politics with an unpredictable three-way split that might lead anywhere. The Falklands changed all that, giving the Government a commanding lead in the opinion polls, with overwhelming by-election victories in Beaconsfield in May, and in Merton, Mitcham and Morden where they picked up a Labour-turned-SDP seat in June. The Tories, as we have seen, were also unexpectedly successful in the council elections.

The Alliance, knowing it had lost momentum, decided on a 'relaunch' in January 1983. This is a public relations concept, much revered in struggling Fleet Street newspapers and occasionally successful there. But its track record in politics had yet to be proven. Stephen Spender once described the group of anti-fascist writers to which he belonged in the thirties as 'the divided generation of Hamlets who found the world out of joint, and failed to set it right'. In their gloomier moments the SDP pioneers felt a bit like that. For a movement that was born in idealism and sacrifice, and entered into adolescence in sometimes extravagant hope, had run rather suddenly into a middle-life of doubt. Alliance with the Liberals, and particularly allocating parliamentary seats, had been painful: the seats caused many heartaches as Liberals of long standing were asked to make way for Social Democratic candidates. No matter that the local struggle was often fought most bitterly over a constituency that realistically was hopeless.

The local elections in May had confirmed Liberals' belief that they *knew* about campaigning as a third party, whereas the Social Democrats came trailing clouds of innocence from their safe Labour havens. There were to be last-minute rows over allocation, but the Liberal leadership did not want to push matters too far. They knew they had come better out of the negotiations than their allies. It had been estimated that if the Alliance won 100 seats, Liberals would get 65 of them; if it won 50, they would get 35 . . . and so on. In the 1983 election the Liberals were to win seventeen seats and the Social Democrats just six.

What worried both parties in the Alliance, after the excitement of 1981, was that the SDP, having been born with a political silver spoon in its mouth, now seemed to have turned unlucky. Nor could its troubles be blamed solely on the dousing of its spotlight because of the Falklands: that was an aggravating factor but the Alliance had lost its position, first as No. 1 in the opinion polls and then as No. 2, before fighting in the South Atlantic began. Why? The truth seemed to be that breaking the mould of British politics was far more difficult than the new party had guessed. The British are not a revolutionary people in any sense. The Alliance was now looking for its permanent constituency. The SDP might put part of the blame on the rudderless period while it settled its leadership, but whatever the reason, from the Glasgow Hillhead by-election in March Roy Jenkins knew he was rolling the stone up a very steep hill. His victory there, based on his personal appeal in an atypical, university-dominated Scottish seat, was a morale-booster – even a life-saver – for the Alliance, but it postponed decline rather than halted it. The SDP knew it was in the doldrums.

Organisers of the autumn conferences of 1982 were reduced to some bizarre events to cheer up the faithful and attract media attention. The Liberals' Assembly at Bournemouth produced what is called 'a photo opportunity', a telegenic spectacle of immense proportions. Shirley Williams, who beneath an academic's exterior has the heart of a PR man's dream, consented to take part in a mad hatter's tea party with Cyril Smith – the least SDP-minded of Liberals at that time – alone in the hotel garden apart from half a dozen camera crews and a score of press photographers. A hardened *Newsnight* cameraman blenched as Cyril dug into the chocolate cake.

The Social Democrats stuck to their even more gimmicky idea of having a conference in three towns. This time their Romany caravan rested in Cardiff, Derby and Great Yarmouth, although – courtesy of British Rail – the leading members spent an unhappy couple of hours late one night waiting for a replacement for their broken locomotive. This produced one of the more amusing exchanges of that bleak political autumn: 'They're getting a new locomotive in March [an East Anglian railway junction].' 'Good heavens, we can't wait here that long.'

One cause of tension between the two partners was whether David Steel or Roy Jenkins should be leader of the Alliance. Steel made clear there would not be such a leader, but rather a Prime Minister-designate (or 'in-waiting', for those who preferred that term). The distinction was intended to indicate the impermanence of the appointment, and to calm those Liberals who feared Steel was so impressed by his talented new allies that he was allowing their party, and even his job, to be taken over.

Whether the blame lay in Fleet Street, with the media in general or with the voters, British politics during the sixties and seventies had become, and remained, more presidential than before. Specifically, electoral success appeared to depend heavily on the popularity of party leaders. But use of the phrase 'Prime Minister-designate', while electorally useful, might cloud discussion about who would actually get the job, should that arise. It seemed essential that, at least privately, Liberals and Social Democrats should know what they were about: whether they were choosing the best man to run the country, or the man they thought best at pulling votes in the general election and at negotiating in a balance of power. In other words, did they seriously expect to win, or were they simply seeking the best way to maximise their number of MPs in the next Parliament?

Liberals had no doubt which leader better answered the second pre-scription. David Steel had a splendid record in public opinion polls, usually defeating both Margaret Thatcher and Michael Foot in the 'best at leading his/her party' question, and ahead of Foot as 'best Prime Minister'. Unsullied by office, its failures and compromises, Steel clearly represented for many respondents the greener grass on the other side of the street. Yet a new Alliance, trying to convince people it seriously contemplated the possibility of taking power – 'the confidence factor' – could scarcely afford to turn its nose up at Roy Jenkins: Chancellor of the Exchequer, Home Secretary (twice), President of the European Commission, Deputy Labour

Leader, perceptive political biographer – a statesman and thinker of the first rank.

In a poll in the autumn of 1982, however, Jenkins had had less support not only than Steel, but than a poorly placed Foot. So the question was asked, at least by sceptical Liberals whose noses were put out of joint by the parvenus, whether Jenkins was one of those (like Edward Heath) who is widely regarded as a competent, even a wise leader, but who – perhaps through the frivolity of Demos – appears to be *non papabile*. Some Liberals feared that Steel himself had decided Roy Jenkins ought to be Alliance leader, under whatever title. Before Jenkins was elected leader of the SDP, Steel had tended in conversation to emphasise his ally's great ministerial and administrative experience and his own lack of it. But once Jenkins had safely defeated David Owen, observers noted on the same evening that the result was announced that Steel was quick to say that the top Alliance job was still very much up for grabs.

Two explanations of this change of tone were on offer, the machiavellian and the super-machiavellian. The first is interesting because it sheds light on a relationship which was to become important after the 1983 election: that between David Steel and David Owen. From the launching of the Alliance onward, that relationship had been, to put it gently, uneven. In part this was a function of age. Steel has worked well with older men – Jim Callaghan in the Lib-Lab Pact, Roy Jenkins in the Alliance; but he has the normal ambitious politician's wariness of men of his own age. In part the uneasiness also reflected Owen's then more Left-of-Centre stance, which envisaged the SDP replacing Labour rather than merging in a permanent Centrist alliance. Owen remains dubious about merger of the two parties. In this machiavellian scenario, therefore, Steel only *appeared* to concede the purple to Jenkins, in order to help him defeat Owen, and had subsequently reverted to his true position as a rival to Jenkins for the top job.

But the super-machiavellians thought Steel's earlier posture represented his true feelings: he wanted Jenkins to be leader in order to facilitate permanent merger of the two parties (doubtless with himself as the *next* leader). He was simply showing a little Scots canniness in concealing his intentions from the Liberal Assembly, some of whose members were suspicious of the whole business.

CHAPTER 8

A THREE-PARTY ELECTION

In January 1983 the Prime Minister returned from a visit to the Falklands to discover that the City was jittery about rumours of an early general election. Her office dismissed such talk as just plain silly. Now I defer to no one, not even Mrs Thatcher's Press Secretary, Bernard Ingham, in acknowledging the frenetic silliness of financial markets when faced by the mysteries of politics. In Eisenhower's time of ill-health Wall Street used to tremble at every bulletin on the presidential bowel movements. Nancy Reagan sensibly decided this would not happen again.

Mrs Thatcher, it subsequently turned out, had not ruled out what most of us would call 'an early election'; unless by 'early' the City meant polling would be around Easter. The Prime Minister's preference was for going nearer to her full term; that fitted in with her newly adopted political slogan, the Resolute Approach. But it gradually emerged that she wanted to keep her options open from June onward.

Many Conservatives understood that, in facing the voters with three million people out of work, they were attempting something difficult, even unprecedented. This was victory for a government which had lost the battle to maintain full employment, the principal objective of both major parties since the second world war. So although the Falklands victory and the boost it gave to Conservative poll ratings had produced Tory euphoria, there were doubters, particularly among MPs with marginal seats. The attitude of this group was: To hell with the Resolute Approach (which would mean polling in October 1983, or even later); politics has its banana skins, so let's go while the going – and the polls – are good.

In retrospect, a Conservative victory may seem to have been inevitable. At the time, because the polls were so consistently favourable, it seemed the likeliest result: Margaret Thatcher had assumed a unique place in public favour since the fall of Port Stanley; she also faced a divided and demoralised Opposition. But one factor inserted a rumble of doubt into what would otherwise have been unalloyed Tory confidence – the existence of the third force, the Alliance, made prophets just a little hesitant. Even for those with childhood memories of the twenties or thirties three-party politics was beyond prediction, and for the rest of us it was beyond recollection. Any previous post-war election in which one party was so far ahead would have been dismissed as a one-horse race, but no journalist who had blushed in empathy with the American headline electing Thomas Dewey, while the voters were electing Harry Truman, should ever treat probability as fact.

So how were the three parties faring? The Alliance had been in the doldrums since early in 1982. Its leaders were obsessed with Margaret Thatcher. Fifteen months before, they had enjoyed the support of half the electorate, while Labour and Conservatives fought each other for a bad second place. All that had been transformed when the Prime Minister snatched victory from defeat in the Falklands. To survive, the Alliance had to chip at her pre-eminence.

An SDP man in February said the Conservative vote was firm and Labour's soft, a view to be confirmed in June. This was good news for Alliance people hoping to replace Labour as the Tories' principal adversary. But Roy Jenkins was haunted by a historian's memory of a similar process stretching over five general elections between the wars, when a divided Left produced almost uninterrupted Conservative government. Even on the most optimistic Alliance assessment – and third parties survive on optimism – Labour's vote was likely to stay up in the high twenties for many years. So if the Alliance was to 'break the mould', rather than just solidify Conservative hegemony, it had to cut into the Conservative vote.

Liberals and Social Democrats faced a labour of Sisyphus to repeat their 1981 successes now. Local council by-elections towards the end of 1982 had confirmed their problems. This had been the Liberals' worst period in four years. In private some Liberals were critical of their allies: 'They are nice people. We don't have rows. But they're not on our wavelength. This year it's not so much the SDP Rampant as the SDP Chastened. They won't do well, but then they won't fight elections in our way.'

They meant Community Politics. Some Liberal leaders, including David Steel, privately suspected that their standing in national opinion polls had more effect on council elections than local Liberal zealots conceded. But the most fervent disciples of the cracked-paving-stone, closed-nursery-centre school of politics looked back in anger to the days when Jo Grimond and Jeremy Thorpe set the media alight with their eloquence and gimmickry, but Liberals were winning 'a series of glorious second places'. They argued that Community Politics had brought them dramatic victories in the past five years. They wanted to persuade Social Democrats these were the only tactics for a third party, not reliance on fickle media and the hothouse politics of Westminster.

The difference in perspective had an electoral element. For Liberals a public opinion rating of 20 or 22% that February was, historically, good. They were on a long haul. Liberal MPs normally did better than their party's national average, so they would hold their seats and see colleagues win some extra ones. But Social Democratic MPs had almost all been elected on different political tickets. They knew that unless the Alliance's national rating rose nearer to 30%, they were in danger. The possibility of personal disaster despite a good Alliance performance nationally was apparent to them long before what actually happened in June. The conclusion of many Alliance people was that, unless the Steel–Jenkins leadership could dent Mrs Thatcher's primacy, they stood little chance of a breakthrough. The heady days of 1981 seemed far away and, as the election approached, many despaired of recapturing that first, fine *careful* rapture.

There was not much rapture in Labour's ranks either. A Labour MP, with studied irony, contemplated his party's self-inflicted wounds: 'It just shows what fair-minded people we are. We thought it ungenerous to ask poor Mrs Thatcher to face us in an election with more than three million unemployed, so we've deliberately handicapped ourselves.' Such gallows humour was common in a Parliamentary Party that ranged in mood from anxious to suicidal. The mood had reached nadir before Christmas, when Michael Foot swiftly quashed rumours he might be retiring. His sharp reaction was necessary because caballing had already begun among supporters of possible successors.

In the New Year Labour morale took a modest turn for the better. In part this was simply because the election was nearer. A struggling football team, when it comes to pull on its boots for a cup-tie against some giants, dismisses the bookmakers' gloomy estimates and reminds itself that eleven bundles of flesh and bone have much in common with any other eleven. Labour had a few intravenous injections: its poll figures were not as bad as the Alliance's, and Labour hoped the third force would damage the Tories more. A fall in the value of the pound had reminded them that all man (and woman) is flesh, and that market-based economics are, after all, more mutable than the Laws of the Mcdes and Persians.

Labour's front bench had also been doing better: the economic tide seemed to have turned for Peter Shore; Denis Healey had undergone rejuvenation and brought fresh aggression to his attack on the Government's record abroad; Roy Hattersley was chivying the Home Office effectively on immigration. Even the Prime Minister's invincibility seemed less certain at question-time. Michael Foot's questions were shorter, his style more taut, and on nuclear disarmament, unemployment and President Reagan's stance he sometimes caught Mrs Thatcher holding an unpopular brief. Labour optimists cheered themselves by thinking that in Michael Foot and the nuclear issue of 1983 fate might have matched the man and the hours. They included multilateralists. Foot might be – or might have been – a unilateralist himself, they conceded, but he was, above all, a man who believed all political progress flowed from the election of a Labour Government. Much agony and mutual tolerance between old adversaries went into the Manifesto, in an attempt to accommodate both Labour wings. Or so they hoped.

Criticism of Foot's leadership continued, even at a personal level. His early-morning walks with his dog Dizzy (after Disraeli, one of his literary mini-heroes) had received much publicity. A leading Labour figure posed to me a question which had clearly been troubling him: 'What do you think Michael thinks about when he's walking his dog on Hampstead Heath at half-past six in the morning? Byron or the Labour Party?' I ventured the opinion, natural to anyone whose mind works more comfortably in the evenings, that any man who exposed himself so untimely to the day was entitled to think about Byron if he wanted to. But politicians are made of sterner stuff: 'He should be thinking about us. He took on the job.'

At this time of dark foreboding, another school of Labour thought dismissed all hope of victory as pipe-dreaming. So it offered an alternative pipe-dream: Mrs Thatcher would win, but so narrowly that she had to rely on Alliance or even Ulster Unionist support, and survived for only, say, eighteen months. In such circumstances, the theory went, Michael Foot would retire, and Denis Healey would succeed him as the only man with the seniority and visibility to establish himself before a second election. Such musings, it was claimed, had put the spring back into Denis's step and the song – or rather the operatic aria – back on his lips.

Meanwhile, Conservatives were speculating about who would be in Mrs Thatcher's second administration. Not that euphoria was universal: as the election came nearer MPs in marginal seats grew twitchy about un-employment, and their nervousness sometimes infected colleagues sitting on the most lusciously upholstered shire seats. The international context of the election was cloudy: the future of oil prices and therefore of the Government's projected revenue and scope for tax cuts was as uncertain for Sir Geoffrey Howe in 1983 as it was to be while Nigel Lawson was contemplating his options before the succeeding general election. Other obscure factors were the speed in world recovery; the future value of the pound against the dollar and other leading currencies; the Middle East crisis and its repercussions on oil supplies and prices; and the East–West disarmament talks, with the chance that any breakthrough might transform the world economy.

Yet when all doubts had been listed, Opposition politicians feared they would be overwhelmed by the Prime Minister's standing with voters. What frustrated many was that it was Margaret Thatcher's personality almost as much as her government's policies which offended them. So far as Alliance MPs were concerned, this applied particularly to international matters.

On Capitol Hill in Washington indigenous journalists have a handy aid to memory for visiting firemen who cannot distinguish the committees that monitor international matters in the two Houses of Congress: 'Always remember that Congressmen have affairs, but Senators have relations.' So it is the House Foreign *Affairs* Committee and the Senate Foreign *Relations* Committee. Without carrying the latent sexism too far, the Prime Minister's critics felt she was prone to foreign affairs rather than foreign relations. They accused her of taking up short-term postures to the outside world, and cited her on-off quarrel with Europe over Britain's budget contributions. Yet her critics were not enamoured of what they saw as her too steady relationship with President Reagan on the key problems of economics and defence. 'President Reagan's yap-dog,' David Owen unkindly called her, echoing the title of Roy Jenkins' book, *Mr Balfour's Poodle*. The election was hotting up and the Opposition was content with any weapon against a dominant Prime Minister. As Balfour once noted, consistency in opposition is an over-rated virtue.

Anxiety about the Prime Minister's perceived attitude to the world was to be found most acutely among the internationally-minded Alliance leadership. One of them said, with unusual irritation, that Mrs Thatcher was 'cocooned in self-righteousness'; everyone who did not agree with everything she believed in was wrong – not only the Argentines and her political opponents at home, but our closest allies, the Americans or the Germans, even the money markets when they failed to react as she believed they ought. He added: 'She has a far greater incapacity to comprehend the working of other people's minds than anyone I've ever met.'

So it was to be a personalised election. But the parties were not neglecting their manifestoes either; indeed, they were not neglecting anything. Woodrow Wilson, on the night of his 1912 election victory, deflatingly told his campaign manager: 'Whether you did little or much, remember that God ordained that I should be the next President of the United States.' British politicians in 1983, unsupported by such a strong sense of pre-destination, preferred, with Baden Powell, to Be Prepared, and with Saatchi and Saatchi to be smart. By February the Battle of the Manifestoes was being planned by rival General Staffs. How much influence manifestoes have is anybody's guess, but some politicians fight over each relative clause and parenthesis with the zeal of a Great War general contesting a few yards of Passchendaele mud.

However, the run-up to the general election was dominated, and confused, by two by-elections, in Bermondsey and Darlington. Bermondsey was astonishing, Darlington almost conventional by comparison. In Bermondsey Peter Tatchell's Labour candidature had a long overture. This began when Michael Foot, stung by SDP quotation in the House of Tatchell's ambiguous views on parliamentary democracy, declared he would never be a candidate. The outgoing MP, Bob Mellish, former Labour Chief Whip, had warned Foot that if Tatchell was endorsed he would resign and provoke an embarrassing by-election. News of that threat reached David Steel, who ordered the Liberal organisation in Bermondsey to be revived. Mellish eventually did resign and the campaign took place in bitter February weather. It soon became clear that Bermondsey Labour Party was divided not just between Left and Right but by a chasm in ages, attitudes and life-styles. Peter Tatchell and John O'Grady, a Mellish supporter standing as Real Bermondsey Labour, cast each other as Trot Weirdo and Machine Politician. Both suffered.

Bermondsey seemed fated to become an industrial geriatric ward after the closing of the Surrey docks in 1971. In this historic part of London, ancient crafts like printing and tanning had fallen on hard times. Bermondsey's antiquity could be seen in its pub signs – Thomas à Beckett (where Henry Cooper, the boxer, had trained), or Simon the Tanner, called after the house in Joppa where St Peter had his vision. But neither tanning nor brewing provided the many jobs they had once done in what, before the 1832 Reform Act, had been a brewers' rotten borough. And the vision had perished also.

O'Grady, a 62-year-old ex-serviceman who had been leader of the local council for fourteen years until the New Left ejected him the previous May, accused his Left-wing usurpers of dissipating his inheritance by creating an atmosphere hostile to enterprise, and of driving rates so high that Bermondsey business was threatened. Tatchell's counterattack concentrated on the London Docks Development Corporation, for Bob Mellish had resigned his seat not just to expose Labour to the embarrassment of having a far Left candidate in a by-election. He was also due to take up the vice-chairmanship of the new Corporation, at a salary of £16,000. O'Grady, who initially opposed the Corporation, said it was to protect Bermondsey's interests that he had later accepted a place on its board, at a fee of £3000 per year.

To Tatchell, such flirtation with the Establishment was treachery. Labour was pledged to abolish the Corporation, and Tatchell said he would fight for council houses with gardens, and jobs for local people, not well-off incomers, in the old Surrey Docks area. But the dispute on policy did not explain the bitterness. O'Grady and Mellish, who masterminded his campaign, were old-fashioned Labour men, used to acting as welfare officers for their patches, expecting loyalty, even deference, in return. Tatchell, like the Liberal candidate, Simon Hughes, was deeply into Community Politics. He himself lived in a 'hard to let' block of flats. His life-style affronted O'Grady. Tatchell supported Gay Rights, while O'Grady's election literature emphasised that he was a family man, and he displayed twin grandsons on a brewer's dray during his highly traditional campaign. The graffiti of Bermondsey were not for the liberal-minded.

These attacks on Tatchell's candidature damaged Labour without saving O'Grady from humiliating defeat. The Liberal, Simon Hughes, a barrister, by then had an organisation well able to exploit Bermondsey's complaints about broken windows, new lights on estates, and social benefits. He lashed out at Conservatism in central government and Socialism, old and new, on the council. Above all, with SDP help he was able to mobilise the anti-Tatchell vote by the well-tried Alliance by-election technique of flooding a single constituency with an army of MPs and other workers. Hughes won by a landslide, gaining 57% of the votes.

So to Darlington, which was to poll in March. The Bermondsey defeat had reopened the Labour leadership issue, and it would not now go away until the Party saw how it fared in this difficult corner of its northern redoubt. The public must have been puzzled in this period at the contrast between what leading figures said 'on the record' and what journalists were writing and broadcasting. Was there a leadership issue, or was it all 'got up by the media'? In such secret areas as a party leader's future, the danger exists that journalists and broadcasters will take in each other's washing. The most extravagant extrapolations from fact to theory go into cuttings libraries in dozens of editorial offices and are solemnly regurgitated in interviews and reconstructions. So there is a risk of exaggeration. But there is an opposite danger: some of those making the most loyal noises about Michael Foot on the record were privately playing a different tune. One, making it clear he had the gravest doubts about his leader, nevertheless accused me of naivety for even asking whether any action was likely against him. This was not a subject to be discussed even between consenting adults in private, at least if one was a journalist.

To the outsider such attitudes may seem cynical and duplicitous, but it is difficult to see how else politicians can behave. Theirs is a serious trade, whose objective is to gain power for purposes that seem to them good. So the sound instinct of anyone faced by microphone, camera or notebook was to take a loyalty oath. Conspiracies, whether for good or bad causes, cannot be conducted in the broad light of day – or, indeed, of Redhead or Timpson. This is an aspect of the much-reviled lobby system that successive exposés have failed to comprehend. It is not a matter of simple-minded or lazy correspondents taking a drip-feed of information from public relations men, but of trying to find out what is happening in the real world by talking to politicians who say – who *have* to say – one thing in public and another, somewhat different thing in private. If journalists did not do this, changes could never be brought about. As for the public having any influence on such changes, they would not even know the debate was going on.

After the Bermondsey débâcle, it was occasionally possible to read underlying thoughts about Labour's leadership between the lines of public comments, although this was also an inexact science. In the dying moments of the television programme on the Bermondsey result, Robin Day slipped in a question to Gerald Kaufman that a less reticent politician might have let slip beneath his sleepy guard. What would he answer if Michael Foot said to him: 'What ought I to do, Gerald?' The reply was opaque: 'I'd say, "Michael, you're the leader of the Labour Party."' 'Oh well,' said Sir Robin in his faux-jovial voice, 'he knows *that* already.' A Labour wit suggested later that Kaufman ought to have interrupted with 'Oh no, he doesn't; that's half the trouble'. But Sir Robin repeated his question and he got no better than the same answer. Kaufman later rejected any suggestion that this exchange left his leader swinging in the wind, but it was the nearest any shadow minister had come to side-stepping a full-blooded endorsement. On the other channel that weekend Neil Kinnock, Foot's friend and protégé, defended and praised him.

As Darlington drew nearer, the message for Foot, as for Julius Caesar, was 'beware the Ides of March'. The gossip against his leadership might seem to be all talk and no action, but if the Darlington by-election confirmed the gloomy poll findings the talk might get out of hand. The location made this a crucial test: greater nervousness existed about the Alliance among Conservatives with marginal seats in the South than among Labour men with slender holds on paradise in the North. Darlington would tell the Labour MPs whether they were living in a fools' paradise. Bermondsey might be put down to the acknowledged awfulness of the London Labour Party; defeat in Darlington would be blamed on Foot's leadership.

Darlington looked like a constituency where the wise man would stay away from the bookies. If the Alliance bandwagon, after Bermondsey, was rolling again, they might win easily, for in this new by-election era success breeds success exponentially. If the SDP candidate, Tony Cook, a local television reporter, did win, the Alliance would have decisively ended its year in the doldrums. Conservatives had a strong interest in preventing Alliance revival. Their chairman, Cecil Parkinson, believed votes for the Alliance hurt his side more than Labour. This was not an uncontested view: a Welsh Labour reader of the runes assured me at this time that if the Alliance vote nationally went above 24% – in the event it was 25.4 – it was Labour which would suffer more. Such were the arcane rules that the New Psephology imposed in a three-party system. It was only a question of time before someone said Labour's real test would be when 'Birnam wood remove to Dunsinane', and Robert Worcester and his polling friends would be stirring in the newt's eye and frog's toe.

The campaign was full of private cross-currents. One Labour MP rubbed his hands at the prospect of a generous and popular Budget: this would stop the Tory vote crumbling, as it had done in Bermondsey, he said, which would avert the danger that the Social Democrat would become the repository of all anti-Labour votes in Darlington and win another sensational but far more significant victory. Another Labour man went further in his machiavellianism, recalling a canvassing encounter with an elderly lady who said: 'Oh, I would like to vote for your candidate, such a nice man! But you see, I've always been Conservative, and I don't think I could quite . . .' The Labour MP scented danger: she might move half-way and vote SDP. It was a time for decisiveness: 'No, I quite understand,' he said, with a generosity that must have stunned her. 'In the circumstances it would be wrong for you *not* to vote Tory.'

It seemed indelicate to remind such Labour warriors of the new three-party politics that, if they were too successful in helping shore up the Conservative vote so near to a general election, they were unlikely to form the next government. Perhaps they subscribed to the philosophy of a former TUC press officer who, when faced with questions pointing to hypothetical dangers ahead, would look piously heavenwards and quote devoutly from the hymnal: 'I do not ask to see the distant scene, One step enough for me.'

The modern by-election is a distinct art-form, principally because of the aggressive style of reporters and the new methods pioneered by the Liberals and adopted by the Alliance. I spent a freezing morning observing the SDP's methods from the open back of their lorry. At the front the first blast of wind was taken by the Party leader, Roy Jenkins, and his candidate, Tony Cook, while Bill Rodgers kept up a non-stop and amusing commentary on the passing scene through the loudspeaker. A young student of politics from Yale and myself, clutching notebooks to protect our political virginity, listened in awed silence as Rodgers encouraged his supporters on the lorry to wave. The SDP's gimmick is to persuade voters that elections are fun. By their determined good cheer, their inexorable leafleting and their omnipresent outcrops of posters, planted round suburban gardens like the heads on stakes in *Heart of Darkness*, they created an atmosphere that might just give them victory.

In by-elections, however, the media sometimes become the message. Although Tony Cook was a television man himself, he did not find handling the hotshots from Fleet Street and Shepherds Bush a congenial task. There were rumours that his morale sank each morning at the prospect of facing aggressive journalists, probing his knowledge of local and national statistics. Parliamentary candidates are like nervous English batsmen padding up to face the West Indian pace bowlers; perhaps they should be given protective helmets. Cook was awarded much of the blame for the failure to set the bandwagon rolling again, but the Alliance had a more fundamental problem which a by-election in this run-up period merely illuminated: they would not be able to reproduce in 650 constituencies the atmosphere and organisation that had become their forte.

Labour, knowing how important Darlington was, poured in its heavyweights as never before. Michael Foot attracted overflow audiences in support of his candidate, Ossie O'Brien, and his oratory caught fire for the first time in months. Jim Callaghan went twice. I met him on the train back to London, and he was more cheerful than he had been for a long time. Such optimism proved justified. Labour had a comfortable majority over the Conservative, Michael Fallon, with the Alliance a bad third.

It was to prove a false dawn. Darlington was one of many seats that went Tory in June. Yet at the time it underlined Conservative anxiety over unemployment. What would happen in the West Midlands, which had been the furnace of Britain's post-war boom and the cockpit of post-war elections? Would this, its first experience of real economic hardship, erode the support there which brought Mrs Thatcher victory in 1979? And if it did, would voters switch straight to Labour, select the Alliance as a half-way house, or merely stay at home?

For all the doubts about whether Mrs Thatcher would win again, few on the Opposition side believed either Labour or the Alliance would have enough seats to form a government on its own. The most intriguing question of politics in the eighties began to be aired in private conversation: would there be a successor to the Lib-Lab Pact, a more elaborate one now that the SDP existed, a Lab-All. Pact?

In Kentucky, which was a border state during the American Civil War, brothers fought on opposite sides. I met a man in Louisville in 1966 who said his family were still divided by decisions their grandfathers took a century before. In politics civil wars have also been the most bitter. In the fifties the two political ladies between whom one would least like to have found oneself on a dark night were Asquith's and Lloyd George's daughters, Lady Violet Bonham-Carter and Lady Megan Lloyd George. Similarly, the bitterest opponents in British politics today are the Social Democrats and the Right wing of the Labour Party. It requires almost as great a leap of imagination to think of Denis Healey and Roy Jenkins serving in the same Cabinet again as to envisage Margaret Thatcher and Tony Benn joining in a Ministry of All the Talents. Yet some Opposition politicians secretly contemplated what they thought the most likely post-election scenario. This, remember, was before the Conservatives' good local election showing in May, which finally convinced the Prime Minister she could no longer resist a June election. But in April, after the Tories' failure to win either Bermondsey or Darlington, no one was so sure. So the 'coalitionists' could dream their dreams.

The dream was that Mrs Thatcher might lose her overall majority, and would therefore be regarded as a defeated leader, as Edward Heath was in February 1974, thus making it inexpedient for third parties to do deals with her. This caused some Social Democrats to warn Denis Healey's wing of the Labour Party that 'we ought to be talking'. But no politician said anything interesting in public about his intentions in a hung Parliament, and no private talks are known to have taken place. Until the results were known, the public was left to assume that each of them was expecting his own party to gain an overall majority, with his current leader as the next Prime Minister.

Yet anyone taking a cool look at the politics of a hung Parliament could see that the only people likely to remain constant as the Northern Star were Margaret Thatcher, Tony Benn and their respective supporters. This was only because they would have nowhere else to go but their existing allegiances with the more Centrist wings of their present parties. The same might not be true of politicians like Denis Healey, Peter Shore and Roy Hattersley, or Roy Jenkins, David Steel and David Owen. Or even of Francis Pym, Jim Prior, Michael Heseltine and Peter Walker (not to speak of Ted Heath). None of these was going into the election with coalition on his banner, but they knew the mathematics of three-cornered politics might force a post-election deal by someone.

Labour's Manifesto showed where the strains in any deal with the Alliance would be. Defence, particularly closing American nuclear bases, took them right back to the Gaitskellite war of a quarter-century earlier, during which Social Democrats like Bill Rodgers won their spurs. But Denis Healey had taken a stand then also, and he wanted a different Labour defence policy. Europe was fundamental for Jenkins and Shirley Williams, more negotiable for the Labour Right. To add complication this was one issue where Labour's Left was more in accord with the majority in the opinion polls, who were against the Common Market. On the economy Labour's policy was less radical than the Right had feared. Public ownership proposals were limited and amorphous. But the stumbling block for the Alliance might be relations with the unions, both on pay and the law. Different attitudes to the House of Lords and to proportional representation were other potential minefields.

Those considering even the possibility of whether a Labour–Alliance deal was conceivable were, admittedly, piling hypothesis on hypothesis. Only if the mathematical lottery which this election might turn out to be were to return Labour as the largest party, but with a substantial Alliance presence, did the hypothesis become reality. If that did happen, would the bitterness left by Labour's revolution and civil war prevent serious negotiation? It is one of the great unanswered questions in the history of this decade, and it may occur again. The instinct of many Social Democrats would have been to bargain with Denis Healey and his supporters and try to transform Labour's policies from outside, since they had been unable to do so when they were inside the party. Healey and Jenkins were chalk and cheese, as men who have held the same high office at different times, alas, often are. Healey and Owen, however, shared the immodest belief that their parties had better leaders available than the incumbents – a view that was not unknown in the Conservative Party also.

CHAPTER 9

SEARCHING FOR THE GLASS JAW

Tory backbenchers returned from the Easter recess valiant for June. Darlington had calmed MPs who were nervous about an Alliance surge. A Gallup poll identified Labour as the principal enemy, but its revival in the polls was not strong enough to alarm optimists. The subtleties of tactical voting in by-elections would fade in the summer sun. Politicians were back to what the Duke of Wellington asked of his officers: hard pounding. But opinion in the Cabinet was more complicated. Margaret Thatcher's closest ally at this time, Norman Tebbit, might have the instincts of a Mississippi riverboat gambler: he was strongest for June. The party chairman, Cecil Parkinson, reported that the grass roots wanted to take the winning tide, that Tories whose experience in life had limited their faith in Dame Fortune's constancy did not want to give her time to trip them up again.

Mrs Thatcher's own instincts were cautious, even if her public pronouncements are self-assured. When swift decisions are essential she can take them; but on the election date she wanted to be sure. The views in her Cabinet were by no means unanimous: John Biffen favoured the autumn; Francis Pym offered a not too coded public exhortation for delay, invoking the spectres of Premature Elections Past – June 1970, February 1974. Willie Whitelaw's influential voice was also against June, although in his talks with the Prime Minister at this time he found his main opponent was not always June; sometimes he found himself speaking up for the merits of October 1983 rather than the spring of 1984, in which Mrs Thatcher still found merits.

Margaret Thatcher's self-image is of a person who makes up her own mind. There is a story of a meeting she held with Whitelaw, Foot and Healey to settle the terms of reference of the Franks Committee on the Argentine invasion of the Falklands. The Labour men had negotiated some changes but the Prime Minister said she must clear these with her Cabinet. Healey is reported to have replied: 'Margaret, I haven't served in your Cabinet, but from what I hear, when you've your own mind made up, that tends to prevail.' According to the tale, Mrs Thatcher blushed becomingly, snapped closed her file and said: 'Right, let's agree it now.'

So she wanted to be decisive about the election, but even more she wanted to get the date right, and she was determined that the fingerprints of every important minister would be found on that decision. She likes to have her own way, but politically she is a believer in belt and braces, so by the time ministers and other advisers were consulted at Chequers on 8 May everyone was more or less in line.

The next day, Robin Day and I had arranged to have lunch with Edward Heath. The election date, 9 June, had been announced an hour before we met. When the former Prime Minister arrived, Robin and I were talking excitedly about the prospects. Our guest, who had not heard the news, suddenly remarked that we were 'not just speculating'. 'Oh no, Ted,' said Robin Day. 'She's just come from the Palace after telling the Queen.' In my version of the story, he added impishly: '*She's* come from the Palace, and *you're* here for lunch with us.' Sir Robin claims this is a figment of an overactive imagination.

The time had now come for Margaret Thatcher to ride her famous luck. The polls showed a lead over Labour of somewhere between 11 and 21%, but warnings against complacency that she, Parkinson and others uttered during the first week of the campaign were not mere ritual protection against *hubris*. Mrs Thatcher was certainly the favourite, but she faced obstacles that could unseat her. The first doubt was over precedent. If she did win a working majority, she would be the first Prime Minister since the war to serve a full term and then secure another mandate. (Attlee's 1945 majority was so eroded in 1950 that his government was defeated in the following year; and it took three Tory leaders, Churchill, Eden and Macmillan, to keep them in power from 1951 till 1964.) Evidence over at least twenty years suggested that voters had converted the traditional swing of the pendulum into a blunt instrument for striking incumbents over the head for failing to conjure up the elusive British Economic Miracle.

The Government was vulnerable on economics because, supporters said, its record was still at the point of promise rather than fulfilment. Inflation was down to 4.6% compared with 10.3 in 1979, but the Opposition said this was only because unemployment was at its highest level since the war, at frightful cost in output, national wealth, public services, and even worsening crime statistics. They charged the Tories with breaking most of their 1979 promises, even allowing the burden of income tax to increase. The Prime Minister counterattacked by equating the reflation advocated by the Opposition with renewed inflation. She mounted a detailed dissection of Labour and Alliance plans for reducing unemployment, with a substantial admixture of Thatcherite scorn. Conservatives believed the polls showed the British had abandoned belief in a quick economic breakthrough – or 'fix', as they described it – and were content to await the result of the two or three terms the Prime Minister said were necessary to put matters right.

The Opposition could not afford to concede that Margaret Thatcher was invulnerable in 1983. Both parties dislike both her policies and personality so much that they have always felt, in boxing parlance, that she must have a glass jaw if only they could find the right punch. Labour came nearest to finding that elusive punch when it questioned the Government's intention about the future of the Welfare State. As we have seen, Mrs Thatcher's dilemma had first become public in the autumn of 1982, when internal Think Tank and other government discussion-documents, outlining radical changes, leaked to the *Economist*. The ideas floated included introduction of a minimum level of private insurance in the NHS, widespread de-indexing of benefits, education vouchers, student loans (instead of grants), and more in similar vein.

At the 1982 Conservative conference these were said to be merely discussion-documents. Ministers had rejected most of the ideas already. Mrs Thatcher, knowing how the public revere the NHS, declared: 'The National Health Service is safe with us. As I said in the House of Commons on December 1 last, "The principle that adequate health care should be provided for all regardless of ability to pay must be the function of any arrangements for financing the NHS." We stand by that.'

Labour stuck to their attack, producing new leaked documents from the Think Tank and the No. 10 policy unit. They alleged that the Conservatives had 'a secret manifesto' to reduce the scope of the Welfare State and run down the Health Service. The Alliance joined the attack. It was the one moment when the Government looked vulnerable; it was arguable that, once the Government's hope of a swift economic miracle had faded, and as unemployment added hugely to the cost of benefits, Thatcherite philosophy demanded a rigorous review of the real level of these benefits. Some Tories believe this is the only way to bring about a lower-wage economy and so create more jobs.

During an election, however, these were not popular arguments, even though the Prime Minister, assisted by her Falklands triumph and divisions in the Opposition, seemed to have an unassailable lead. A nervous Conservative leadership feared that voters would punish any party that did not defend their beloved Welfare State. So the anguished cry 'the NHS is safe with us' was heard frequently in the land. Ministers hurriedly pledged themselves to maintain a whole raft of benefits in line with inflation – not only pensions, but payments to widows, invalids, guardians, victims of industrial injury, among others. For years into the new Parliament civil servants had lists of 'pledged' and 'unpledged' benefits to which they referred inquirers as obstacles to radical change. During the election ministers retained a freer hand on supplementary, child and housing benefits. They were to return to this subject in the Fowler Review of 1985.

Labour enjoyed some lightening in its mood, dating from the sauna-bath experience of Bermondsey and Darlington when the party jumped in and out of the snow of despair and the scalding shower of hope. But it was qualified hope. Insiders acknowledged that floating voters from the *Guardian*-reading middle class were going to be hard work for Labour canvassers, because of their constitutional shenanigans, the SDP schism, and the policies on defence, Europe and the unions. Much better, one MP argued, to concentrate on working-class voters, on internal unity, leave policy where it was and dismiss the support of even liberal-minded leader-writers as a lost cause.

Men like Denis Healey, Peter Shore and Roy Hattersley, however, could not be content to leave the battle for this intellectual middle-ground unfought. It was ground they knew that one day they must win back. Throughout his political career, Shore had been a fully-paid-up-intellectual-in-benefit. Although Hattersley proudly proclaimed himself a gas-and-water socialist, and had perhaps the most profound commitment among leading Labour men to greater equality, he knew this could only be achieved by convincing a segment of the middle class that it was both just and efficient. As for Healey, a Right-wing Conservative remarked privately before the election date was fixed that he was 'quite simply the cleverest man in this place'. He urged orisons on the Tory benches for Michael Foot's preservation right up to Dissolution, and said Margaret Thatcher's over-riding task was to ensure she did not have to fight against a party led by the Right Hon. Gent. from Leeds East. A minister asked me around the same time whether I had considered the consequences if a Number Eleven bus struck down both the Prime Minister and Leader of the Opposition. I offered him the consoling thought that the two did not wander hand-in-hand on busy London bus routes. Sweeping aside such leaden-footed practicality, he made clear that he was contemplating the awful prospect of a Conservative Party, deprived of Mrs Thatcher's by-now elevated public standing, confronted by a Labour Party led by Healey.

Denis Healey is one of the few multi-dimensional characters left in contemporary politics. I once had dinner with him and Conor Cruise O'Brien, and witnessed a display of intellectual pyrotechnics that left the rest of us feeling like Wimbledon spectators, eyes swivelling from left to right and back. In 1983 his political appetites sharpened. Just before Parliament was dissolved, he so infuriated the Prime Minister with his persistent *basso* cry of 'cut and run' that she lapsed into her long-lost Lincolnshire dialect to accuse him of being 'frit' (frightened) of an election. Healey's political weakness is that he does not know when he *ought* to be 'frit', and is always spoiling for a fight.

This was the strangest period in Healey's life. His supporters still cherished the faintest hope that if the election were delayed until October some change might make him Labour leader. One called him 'landlord of the Last Chance Saloon'. Tolstoy once complained to Bernard Shaw that he seemed to treat life as a joke, to which Shaw replied that if it was a joke, he wanted to make it a good one. Healey's mood in 1983 often seemed the same: he laughed because he was too old to cry, but he knew Labour's chances were not good. A final blow for Michael Foot came on the day the election was announced: a poll indicated that if Healey were leader, Labour would be neck-and-neck with the Conservatives instead of trailing far behind. But the leadership issue had really been long dead. Healey knew after Labour's victory at Darlington that his last chance was gone.

A sad consequence of Michael Foot's elevation to the leadership, and of the dire circumstances in which he inherited it, was that the fun seemed to go out of his politics. One of the wittiest men in politics stopped making people laugh. Power changed Harold Wilson but he never went as far as that. Yet when the election trumpet sounded, the old political warrior in Foot received a shot of adrenalin: he spoke and wrote eloquently about social conscience, the egalitarian fire in his belly was ignited, and he pulled out the literary organ stops – always a sign that Michael Foot is enjoying himself. The Footian heroes – Shakespeare, Milton, Hazlitt and Paine – were mobilised. The desperate thought occurred to some of his less fervent admirers in the Labour Party that, although he might not be the most efficient departmental minister, or the best manipulator of Labour's internal politics, perhaps his forte was fighting elections.

Foot reserved his real fire for great public meetings in Glasgow, Liverpool and the provincial cities where his political heroes like Nye Bevan and his adversaries like Hugh Gaitskell had enjoyed election triumphs. He was wary of the new style of electioneering, unhappy on television, suspicious of the daily press conferences. For other party leaders these press conferences were the occasion to grab the political initiative; Foot treated them as mere pipe-openers to his day, leaving Healey, Shore and other shadow ministers to hurl thunderbolts at the enemy from the scarlet splendour of the Transport House platform.

Michael Foot's disdainful attitude to media coverage was a problem to his campaign managers. There could not have been a sharper contrast with the Prime Minister's approach to her television interviews. Not for him the request that Mrs Thatcher's aides made, that she should be shown both the wide shot and the tight shot before questions could begin. Foot would have regarded that as intolerable narcissism. He must be the only student of life and letters who reveres Cromwell, Milton and Swift, and yet remains a full-blooded romantic. His campaign relied not on a list of Labour's political priorities, carefully chosen after study of private polls, but on the inspiration of the moment. Throughout his life he has enjoyed argument; to him an interview with Robin Day or Brian Walden did not seem a different art-form from an up-and-downer at the Tribune Group or in the Westminster Tea-Room, or an intellectual wrestling match over lunch at the *Gay Hussar*. As the going in the election got rougher, and his patience with the media wore thinner, Foot grew more determined to get his points across rather than just respond to questions. But there was no suspicion of a well-conceived plan to pull the wool over the interviewer's eyes. Television journalism will not see his like again.

In 1983 the television election was, as ever, controversial. As a new recruit to full-time broadcasting I was surprised by the politicians' sensitivity to what went on the screen, compared with the shrugs with which they greeted the slings and arrows of outrageous Fleet Street. Broadcasters make strenuous efforts to maintain fairness and balance, and the more unreasonable complaints seemed like a simple determination to fire shots across bows for party advantage. Not for the last time.

Labour's defence policy always looked likely to cause dissent. In an essay in April Denis Healey staked out his position. He knew the dangers of losing working-class voters, as a passing flick at Marxist theory demonstrated: 'The working class is often more patriotic and nationalistic than the capitalist class. That is why capitalist multinationals are more effective than socialist internationals.' He proceeded to argue a detailed multilateralist case, aimed at a defence strategy that would make NATO no longer dependent on first use of nuclear weapons, but simultaneously warning the Labour Left that it might not like the consequences of failures in American leadership: 'Opinion polls show that the European reaction is more likely to be towards unilateral nuclear *re*armament than towards unilateral *dis*-armament – towards greater nationalism rather than towards neutralism, which is simply chauvinism with an inferiority complex.'

So the position on which the Healey wing of the Labour leadership would take its stand was now clearer. Labour might be committed to unilateralism and a non-nuclear strategy, but it was also committed to NATO rather than to neutralism, which Healey was ridiculing as 'chauvinism with an inferiority complex'. The Manifesto, with ostentatious even-handedness, said: 'Unilateralism and multilateralism must go hand in hand if either is to succeed. It is for this reason that we are against moves that would disrupt our existing alliances, but are resolved on measures to enable Britain to pursue a non-nuclear defence policy.' The stumbling block for the Healeyites was a later commitment to 'carry through in the lifetime of the next Parliament our non-nuclear defence policy'. This included not only resistance to Cruise missiles in Britain, but the removal of all existing nuclear bases and weapons. Trident would be cancelled, though Polaris would only be included in negotiations.

During the campaign, as public and private polls suggested defence was damaging Labour, Michael Foot and Denis Healey cobbled together a formula for a Foot speech which said that Labour would 'move towards' a non-nuclear policy and the removal of nuclear bases. But the former Prime Minister, Jim Callaghan, had been angered by the vacillations. Speaking in his own constituency a fortnight before polling, Callaghan declared that Polaris had still a dozen years of life, and should not be abandoned unilaterally.

Meanwhile, the Alliance was fighting for survival as a major third force in politics. It was the unpredictable element in the otherwise stable mixture of a Labour North and a Tory South (with the South stretching further North

in good Conservative years). One of the ironies of mid-eighties politics was
that the SDP, born to replace Labour after the Gang of Four had departed
that nest, now relied for its healthy survival into the next Parliament on
being able to cut substantially into Conservative support.

Any third party in the British system has an uphill task in making sure it is
treated seriously. The Alliance had to hold its press conferences first.
Journalists, never at their best in the early morning, found themselves
assembling at the ungodly hour of 8.30 a.m. in the marble splendour of the
National Liberal Club. Some grizzled faces emitted a groan when faced
with yet another shopping-basket of inflationary groceries, yet David Steel,
Roy Jenkins and their carefully chosen teams succeeded each day in getting
the election day off to a lively start, seizing the initiative and putting the
larger parties under pressure. But the general perception of their chances
was reflected in the questions: the Alliance's own programme was not put
under the same critical interrogation as those of the Government or
Labour Opposition, because the questioners could not really make themselves believe in the possibility of an Alliance or Alliance-led government.

Half-way through the election, when the surge the Alliance needed
showed little sign of appearing, a council of war was held at Steel's home in
the Scottish borders. Liberals and Social Democrats emerged from this
Ettrick Bridge summit ostentatiously unbowed. They were determined to
talk up their support, but the real objective now was damage limitation,
saving seats, and exploiting Labour's obvious difficulties. Polls had shown
Steel to be more popular than Jenkins, but the conference decided the dual
leadership must not be altered in midstream. Roy Jenkins' governmental
'bottom' would be useful in the search for Conservative votes, but David
Steel would play the more prominent part on television.

What Jenkins needed on television was more space. He treated it as
civilised conversation and, provided interviews were conducted in that way,
he could perform well, but not if the atmosphere was too querulous. Steel's
performance was not as frank as it looked: he seemed relaxed, but was in
fact well disciplined, with meticulous attention to detail and irritation at any
distraction from vote-getting. In his appearances art concealed art: he
succeeded in pretending to go along with the interviewer, while carefully
working through his mental list of points he was determined to make. David
Owen was another man determined to use his television appearances to
best advantage. Sometimes viewers might detect that a short fuse lay just
below the surface; Owen dispelled any thought of the SDP as the 'Wine
and Cheese Party', one of its opponents' jibes. He was in deadly earnest.

In the final ten days, as Labour quarrelled and its challenge to the
Government became hopeless, Alliance leaders claimed to be catching up,
or even overtaking, Labour. That did not happen, but in the final stretch
their surge at last came and they achieved a remarkably good third place,
though with a disappointing number of MPs.

The Prime Minister dominated the Conservative press conferences. Indeed, the whole campaign to re-elect the Government was concentrated on her, with other ministers only in supporting roles. Her advisers worked hard on 'photo opportunities': the famous incident of holding the calf on the farm, for example, when Denis Thatcher was rumoured to be nervous about the animal's mortality. It was all more Madison Avenue than British electors had previously seen. From time to time politics broke through, and not always comfortably. Mrs Thatcher ran into trouble at an early press conference over an incident largely based on a misunderstanding. Francis Pym and she were actually attempting to say the same thing in answer to a question on the Falklands, but when she over-fussily endorsed what he said, there was laughter among the groundlings of Fleet Street and the media, who are not accustomed to having the Prime Minister as their quarry. Thoughts raced back to the uneasy relationship between her and her Foreign Secretary.

With his move to the Foreign Office in 1982, after the Falklands invasion, Francis Pym began to look like an alternative leader, the king over the street, if not over the water. The Foreign Office may be isolated from the political mainstream, but it is a place where a man can keep out of trouble better than at the Home Office or the Treasury. It is a convenient waiting-room for Number Ten, as Jim Callaghan had recently proved. With Carrington gone and Whitelaw prepared to lead the Lords after the election, Pym became the senior figure on the wing of the Conservative Party that Mrs Thatcher did not fully command. Yet he was not an out-and-out 'wet'; he bridged the gap between Right and Left more obviously than Jim Prior or Peter Walker. Even though Margaret Thatcher had inherited a Heathite party, her leadership had inevitably changed its complexion. If she were to lose the election Francis Pym would be conveniently placed in the Centre.

Not that Pym carried a loaded revolver when he visited Number Ten. Unsheathed daggers were not his constant companions, but that did not help him. Prime Ministers and their entourages are notoriously sensitive to potential rivals: uneasy lies not only the head that wears a crown, but also the heads with all those little coronets and tiaras that depend on the crown remaining on the same neatly coiffured brow. So when Francis Pym subsequently uttered his Butlerian remarks about how undesirable land-slides can be, Whitehall knives and Fleet Street typewriters flashed and crashed. He had merely mused about indications in the polls that a Tory landslide was certain, and doubted whether that would be good for the country or the Government. Mrs Thatcher sought to laugh it off as a typical ex-Chief Whip's remark, implying that such men were a race apart, but she neither forgave nor forgot.

Margaret Thatcher is a well-disciplined and strictly programmed Prime Minister, but her swift rebuke to Pym threw interesting light on what can happen when she encounters the unexpected. Sitting in a traffic jam on the way to an interview with her during that election, I noticed an unattributed remark by a Tory MP that she had 'a headmistress image'. It seemed a possible way to ventilate a series of interviews which were becoming too stuffy, so I asked her about the remark. It was like bowling a long hop to Ian Botham, which is not a bad thing to do if your sole objective is to see the great all-rounder in full flow, eyes flashing, nostrils dilating, bat swinging. The Prime Minister reacted in much the same style. She gave viewers to understand quite forcefully that some of her best friends had been headmistresses, that she knew her own mind, and what was wrong with that? And that anyhow she was unlikely to change at her age. I was happy enough to have a flash of real feeling 'in the can', but she was quite nervous about the passage until her image adviser, Gordon Reece, assured her it was good.

Mrs Thatcher had a good election. The polls indicate she was a considerable asset to her party. Her performances on television, at press conferences and on public platforms had been formidable, within the guidelines that she, or her genes, had set: usually sure-footed, impassioned, convinced even to those who did not find her convincing. An academic who knew both Margaret Thatcher and Shirley Williams when they were students said that 'one was all head and the other all heart – but not the way you would think'.

This paradox was, of course, an unashamed piece of smart Oxford chatter; and as a cynic remarked, God wouldn't have put Oxford at the end of the M40 if he hadn't meant it to be a dormitory for Lime Grove. Like most such remarks intended for media after-life, it contains only part of the truth: Mrs Williams also has considerable heart, and Mrs Thatcher has a strong, if not a strongly speculative, intellect. What is true is that the Prime Minister does have strong emotions. This showed when journalists questioned her persistently about the *Belgrano* sinking. She seemed near to breaking down. Her eyes flashed with anger as she spoke, but in quieter moments she looked hurt, playing uncharacteristically with an ear-ring. It was the only time in the election that her composure slipped just a little.

The assumption that Margaret Thatcher is 'all head' probably arose from her possessing dual qualifications as an industrial chemist and tax lawyer, the latter acquired while she was bearing and rearing twins. She also fitted in Parliamentary, Cabinet and Opposition front-bench responsibilities, which certainly vouched for her single-mindedness. Yet she was clearly far removed in character from Aneurin Bevan's famous jibe about 'a desiccated calculating machine' – some said directed at Hugh Gaitskell, Bevan's rival, others at Harold Wilson, his supporter.

During the election campaign a printer's error in the *Sunday Times* made her 'the Prim Minister'. Such errors occasionally have a manic truthfulness, but this time the slipping finger got its subject wrong. To watch her anxious aides when she cuts loose in conversation or interview makes the observer suspect that what they fear in her is not primness so much as impulsiveness, which occasionally makes Cabinet and Cabinet committee discussions more complicated than they need be. Yet it is often a self-conscious show of impulsiveness. There was a revealing moment during her election interview with Brian Walden. As his precious minutes ticked away she was giving a very long answer. He tried to slip in a final question. 'Don't interrupt me, I'm in full flow,' she shouted, in what must surely have been a rare moment of self-satire.

It is when she is in 'full flow' that some of Margaret Thatcher's more memorable remarks have been made. She does go on a bit, but when emotion takes over from her political auto-pilot, the talk becomes more interesting. If the interviewer insists too rigorously on his right to guide the discussion, he risks being taken back into the deserts of arid statistics in which she is happy to wander. On this occasion Walden left her in 'full flow', but was rewarded, alas, only with the plangent, remorseless Thatcher, fitting in the six or seven points she had not yet made fully enough to satisfy her.

It is such aggressive self-assurance that bewitches her admirers and repels her critics. Sydney Smith once said of a Cambridge head of college that if his forte was science, his foible was omniscience. There is a touch of that about Margaret Thatcher: she is 'armed so strong in honesty' that she finds it difficult to countenance divergent views. Yet this is mixed with a streak of caution, a concealed tentativeness that, for example, left the Tories' 1983 Manifesto less definite about rates, education vouchers and spending on the Welfare State than her own radical instincts dictated.

The Prime Minister's social attitudes also arouse controversy. A leading SDP figure says: 'It's not her Victorian values so much as her suburban values that I hate.' There is matter for a doctoral thesis in that remark: what people mean by 'suburban values' is not always clear. Tony Crosland, in the years before he came to recognise Harold Wilson's virtues, used to be hypercritical of his life-style. Once, when I was putting Wilson's more positive qualities to him, he interrupted with the words: 'No! The bloody man plays golf.' I felt obliged to confess that I occasionally swung a tennis racket myself. 'Yes,' said Crosland understandingly (for he also played tennis), 'but at least I assume you don't like talking to the bloody people.'

Whether Margaret Thatcher's values could be called suburban, or whether they merely represented a currently fashionable reaction against the equally fashionable liberal intellectual culture of the post-war years was a moot point. By 1983, whatever her own pretensions might be, her main claim to political leadership lay not in the moral or social fields, but in having transformed the national economic debate. She was the most ideological prime minister Britain had had in modern times. With a few kindred spirits at the top – most notably Keith Joseph and Geoffrey Howe at the beginning, Norman Tebbit and Cecil Parkinson later, Nigel Lawson all through – she imposed her own vision of a market-dominated economy on her party and, she hoped, on the country. Others, of course, had believed in the merits of private business decisions and the market economy for as long or longer. The names of Enoch Powell and John Biffen spring to mind.

But what she had uniquely done was to turn a point of view into a crusade. She stamped the decisions all governments take across a huge field of economic and social policy with a variation of the Good House-keeping Seal of Approval – private provision, good; public provision, suspect. It was a political mood she developed in the following parliament with her privatisation programme – a programme her Conservative predecessor-but-two was to describe as 'selling off the family silver'.

Before the election was over Conservative victory seemed so secure that speculation began whether Margaret Thatcher's mood would mellow in a second term. She had more than half of this generation of ministers now speaking her language: Geoffrey Howe, Patrick Jenkin, Leon Brittan, Nigel Lawson, Cecil Parkinson and Norman Fowler had reshaped their oratory along Thatcherite lines, some earlier, some later. Jim Prior was in terminal exile in Ulster, Peter Walker at peripheral departments – Agriculture before the election, Energy afterwards – Francis Pym soon to be on the back benches. Everything seemed to be going the way she had predetermined. Yet Britain faced a difficult period. The world and domestic slumps were not nearly over; the problems of competitiveness and wage levels were not settled, even amid such devastating unemployment. Third World countries kept joining the queue for industrialisation, suggesting our domestic troubles would grow worse rather than better. Britain's population was ageing, so the cost of public services would continue to rise. Fewer people in work provided a smaller tax base.

There were two ways in which Margaret Thatcher could respond to this: aggressively or emolliently. In 1979, on the steps of Number Ten after becoming Prime Minister, she had quoted St Francis, in favour of harmony and against discord. Perhaps St Francis would prove to have been just a little delayed in the Whitehall traffic?

Whatever direction she was about to take, the voters gave her a strong parliamentary position. The Conservatives, with 397 MPs, had a majority of 144 over all other parties combined. Labour, supported by 27.6% of those who voted, had 209 seats, while the Alliance, with 25.4%, had only 23. Even more woundingly for the Social Democrats, seventeen of these Members were Liberals, leaving the new party reduced to a rump of six. Two of the original Gang of Four, Shirley Williams and Bill Rodgers, were out. It was a disaster for Labour, and left the Alliance in a tantalising but powerless position. Both Opposition parties would have to begin fundamental re-building in the middle of appalling problems.

CHAPTER 10

A BANANA SKIN OUT OF EVERY CANDLE END

After the election Margaret Thatcher bestrode the political world like a colossus. While opponents licked their wounds and changed their leaders, she set about changing her Government. On the Friday and Saturday the Prime Minister indulged in her own kind of genteel butchery among her Cabinet. By Sunday at Chequers the Mistress of the House was busy with the delicate business of pruning: not the roses, which would have needed to be done before the spring buds; she was pruning junior ministers.

Mrs Thatcher had delivered the electoral goods to the Conservatives, and might expect a period of undiluted loyalty, even sycophancy, from a freshman generation swept to Westminster on the hem of her skirt. But little apples grow again, and so do political discontents. When the Government's second term began, the end of the world recession was tentative, the prognosis for unemployment remained uncertain, demographic factors were unfavourable, and the ability to pay for public services, including the much-loved NHS, had a large question-mark over it.

The Prime Minister's determination to have a Government more in her own image was revealed at once by her dismissal of Francis Pym. Only when victory was an accomplished fact did she tell him: 'Francis, I want a new Foreign Secretary.' During the campaign they had travelled home together from America, but she gave no hint of her dissatisfaction. Their relationship was always star-crossed, but the dismissal came as a great shock to him. Even before his famous campaign remark about the dangers of a landslide victory, he had never concealed his doubts about her economic and social philosophies. She had only made him Foreign Secretary, at the nadir of her fortunes after the loss of the Falklands, Lord Carrington and the Foreign Office team, because she could not afford to leave such a powerful political figure discontent at such a perilous time for her leadership. Having reached the post he had cherished for so long, he slipped into the shared values of the Foreign Office like an old, familiar jacket. The Prime Minister does not share those values, and that added to the personal strains.

In his book the following year, Francis Pym described Margaret Thatcher's leadership as being inimical to the spirit of Conservatism. She had a black-and-white view of politics, unwilling to take notice of opponents', or even colleagues', opinions, intolerant, narrow-minded, suffering from tunnel vision. The Government had become overcentralised, he argued, because of 'the Prime Minister's tendency to think that she is always right'. He added this damaging description of her attitude to Ministers:

> To be loyal means 100% acceptance of Government thinking: any dissent, or even the admittance of doubt, is treachery and treason. After nine years as party leader and five as Prime Minister, Margaret Thatcher still asks the question, 'Are you one of us?', by which she means, 'Are you completely free of any doubt as to the utter rightness of everything we are doing?' It will come as no surprise that I am not 'one of us'.

It will come as no surprise to the reader that this is a view of the Prime Minister which is fervently denied by her admirers. On the contrary, they argue, she relishes argument, has great respect for people who stand up to her, admittedly takes much persuasion to abandon a position she has taken up, but is ultimately willing to be influenced by someone who can match her in debate, or whose knowledge of the subject is greater than hers. Example: Carrington on Rhodesia.

Her new economic team, the core of the Government, was certainly in her own image. She had a tough-minded Chancellor, Nigel Lawson, the only minister during the election, incidentally, who predicted that unemployment would fall. The new Industry Secretary, her Party Chairman, Cecil Parkinson, was personally close to her. Norman Tebbit stayed at Employment. There were rumours that he would have liked the Home Office, to tackle law and order; these were denied, but what was true was that Willie Whitelaw, who had agreed to go to the Lords as its leader while remaining Deputy Prime Minister, had not wanted Tebbit, or any other pro-hanging minister, to succeed him.

Whitelaw would have preferred Francis Pym to be kept in the Cabinet by an offer of the Home Office. Pym says he would not have accepted. The same high office figured in an anecdote from that lapidary political commentator, Margot Asquith. When she heard that Campbell-Bannerman was trying to palm Haldane off with the Home Secretaryship, instead of the Lord Chancellorship which he coveted, she recalled what George Eliot once said: 'When a man wants a peach, it is no good offering him the largest vegetable marrow.' In the event Leon Brittan became Home Secretary. In promoting two comparatively junior ministers, Lawson and Brittan, to these senior jobs, Mrs Thatcher strengthened her own grip on the government through men whose careers she had created, but she risked signalling to others that the paths to promotion were becoming blocked for years ahead. There was a rumble of discontent among older disappointed or rejected men.

Sir Geoffrey Howe moved from the Treasury to the Foreign Office. His ambitions had been widely misunderstood. Because he is a Right Honourable and *Learned* Member – Westminsterese for a Privy Councillor (usually a Cabinet member, past or present) as well as a lawyer – many assumed he had a lawyer's approach to politics: have brief, will travel, so to speak. People thought that after 1983 he would become Lord Chancellor, thus crowning the legal politician's career as the highest judge in the land, better paid than the Prime Minister and with a seat both on the Woolsack and in the Cabinet. Definitely not to be sneezed at. But Howe did sneeze at it, because he never could face a lifetime on the bench, which was one reason for going into politics. Perhaps when his hair has turned greyer than even unruly money supply figures or South African crises can turn it, and when the famous suede shoes have made way for Hailsham-style boots, a spell on the Woolsack will be welcome. In 1983 his prayer was an adaptation of Augustine's: 'Make me judicial, Lord, but not yet.' For the Foreign Secretary remains an ambitious politician. No one could imagine him wading through slaughter to a throne; on the other hand, if he found a crown hanging on a hawthorn bush he would not be above trying it on for size, while watching with owlish shyness to see if some pretty Young Conservative curtsied.

Sir Geoffrey was the Heath survivor who has lasted best through the Thatcher years. In the eighteenth century, when they favoured nicknames, he would have been called Durability Howe. He specialises in being unruffled, inexorable, keeping at things. Like Andrew Aguecheek, he 'cannot sing, nor heel the high lavolte, nor sweeten talk, nor play at subtle games'. But then he does not have Falstaff's fickleness either. When arguing a case he is hard to stop; there is a conviction that is impervious to the jibe of time-serving often levelled at lawyer–politicians. His mild manner misleads many. History will judge Sir Geoffrey to have been a quiet zealot.

His reputation, despite problems over the American invasion of Grenada, banning of unions at GCHQ, the Libyan bombings, and sanctions against South Africa, grew steadily throughout this Parliament. The Foreign Office is a rather special political niche. Once in Cleveland, Ohio, when I was being shown over old people's flats, an ancient lady with a twinkle in her eye confessed that the residents called the estate 'God's waiting-room'. Nowadays, with Britain's world role diminished, the Foreign Office is a waiting-room, not outside the Pearly Gates but conveniently close to the only slightly less desirable residence, No. 10 Downing Street. It is a place where a politician may hope to keep out of trouble and let time erase memories of more turbulent days. A suitable post for ex-Chancellors who believe they have something left to do. Harold Macmillan and Jim Callaghan had both proved its merits.

John Biffen, who continued as Leader of the Commons, is more interested in politics, as distinct from administration, than almost any other minister. He had taken over during the Falklands crisis, and had used bipartisan affection for him to smooth the Government's paths. He and

Margaret Thatcher came from the same grammar school/Oxbridge background, but he found her narrow in her sympathies. He began as an economic 'dry' but, after he joined John Nott in opposing some spending cuts in 1981, his thinking diverged from that of the Prime Minister and he worried about her style.

So Margaret Thatcher had now gathered the real economic power into a tight inner circle of ministers who thought like her. Her pre-eminence was unchallenged, but as Harold Macmillan ultimately discovered, the power of dismissal is not enough to keep a Prime Minister free of troubles. Such a landslide victory had brought to Westminster Tory MPs from constituencies they never expected to win. A promising career in business or the professions was interrupted for a seat in Parliament that seemed almost to be on loan from the Opposition. But this did not reconcile the surprised victor to losing next time: he wanted his Government to be careful, not to do silly things, to avoid banana skins. His nightly prayer was 'May the tide never go out', Canute in reverse.

This was a tall order for the Prime Minister. She had too many disappointed old-stagers on her back benches and too many youngsters waiting on the edge of their seats for office. The Cabinet was in her ideological image, but not, consequently, as well balanced as Tory Cabinets have been. Many Conservatives had the uneasy feeling she was not working with the grain of their faith, a Tory faith, but rather with a monetarist ideology. Sir Ian Gilmour, sacked from her first government, spoke for this group:

> The dominant traits in the Conservative intellectual tradition, to be found in Halifax, Hume, Burke, Coleridge, Disraeli, and Salisbury, are scepticism, a sense of the limitations of human reason, a rejection of abstraction or abstract doctrines, a distrust of systems, and a belief instead in the importance of experience and of 'circumstances'.

Or as Burke himself put it, when reflecting on the French Revolution and on the limitations of metaphysical abstraction: 'Circumstances (which with some gentlemen pass for nothing) give in reality to every political principle its distinguishing colour and discriminating effect. The circumstances are what render every civil and political scheme beneficial or noxious to mankind.'

Well, 'some gentlemen', and at least one lady, did not agree. They thought a political party that was going to change the direction of an unsuccessful economy and effect a political, almost a moral, revolution needed the stiffened backbone of theory to keep it straight, and never mind 'circumstances'. Or as Sir Ian, more sceptically, put it: 'Disbelief was suspended; credulity took its place; monetarism was enthroned in the Conservative Party.'

The centenary conference at Blackpool that year was marred by the resignation of Cecil Parkinson, Mrs Thatcher's right-hand man in the election triumph, after it became known that Sara Keays was to have his child. But less personal difficulties worried many Tories. One MP indulged in gallows humour at the hotel bar: 'Eat, drink and be merry, for tomorrow Nigel Lawson will announce the public spending cuts.'

How had the Tories contrived to sink from euphoria to testy unease, if not gloom, in four months? Even though demoralised, Opposition MPs were saying the Government's dilemma over public spending derived from shameful lack of frankness during the election. Labour returned to its charge of 'a hidden manifesto': that Ministers had draconian plans for trimming the NHS and other services, which they had concealed from voters. 1982 had been lollipops year and that had run into the election campaign, but now hard choices had to be made. How, without spectacular economic growth, did Britain pay for pensions and benefits for a growing number of old and unemployed people? The Treasury called attention to an approaching gap between probable revenue and near-essential expenditure.

The 1984 Public Expenditure Survey did not increase the popularity of Peter Rees, Chief Secretary to the Treasury. Its early pains began to be reported in the overexcited vocabulary of Billy Bunter school stories: 'I say, you chaps, quick! Fight behind the bicycle-shed. Bruiser Heseltine is tearing into Peter Rees, the School Swot. And little Norman Fowler's taking his jacket off. Even Patrick Jenkin, the Owl of the Remove, is looking almost belligerent. Whitelaw, the Head of School, is trying to separate them, but he's far too much of a gentleman. Anyhow, the Head herself thinks a bit of a scrap's what's needed, get rid of bad blood.'

The Public Expenditure Survey is now among the most important functions of government, purporting to shape Whitehall's and local councils' spending plans quite precisely for the year immediately ahead, drawing sketch-plans for the more distant future, and providing a framework for the Chancellor's tax changes the following April. That is what PES purports to do. But nothing in politics, as in life, is quite as cut and dried as that. Spending programmes move more quickly, or slowly, than planned, so the bills come in sooner or later than expected. Projections of unemployment, revenue, wages, all prove inaccurate and throw things out of kilter. For Nigel Lawson and Peter Rees it was like steering a yacht whose rudder had broken, in a simultaneous storm and fog (which is meteorologically improbable), with the charts constantly drenched in sea-water. The skipper and mate, who were more personally distant from each other than Chancellor and Chief Secretary ideally should be, had not been wholly frank with the rest of the crew about their precise destination. The Treasury sometimes keeps its deepest thoughts to itself, on a 'need to know' basis.

Some Tories suspected Lawson's political *nous*. He did not have the personal coterie that senior Ministers accumulate during a more gradual ascent. Nor did his style encourage such loyalty. The word 'arrogant' is tossed around too freely. It is difficult to tell when a public figure is really arrogant, rather than just affecting that quality/defect. In private the Chancellor has charm and humour, but he holds his opinions tenaciously and rarely lets his bone go with the dog. At Treasury 'prayer meetings' – the gatherings of senior and junior ministers held weekly or more often in larger Whitehall departments – he tends to 'shoot the messenger' who brings news that Treasury policy is being criticised. Yet the Chancellor was often used simply as a whipping-boy for the Prime Minister. Most Conservative MPs, when pressed, believed the Government had no alternative but to stick to its guns. So the irritation with Nigel Lawson was partly frustration at the perceived absence of an alternative that would produce the long-awaited economic miracle.

Alternatives were on offer. In Cabinet and out Peter Walker argued a species of Macmillan Toryism, based on higher public spending to mop up unemployment. John Biffen and Michael Heseltine favoured more of the public money available going to capital spending rather than revenue, particularly benefits. But Tory opinion did not rally round any particular alternative. Rather it blamed bad public opinion polls and anxieties about unemployment on 'bad presentation'. If Conservative MPs and conference representatives had been present at the destruction of Sodom and Gomorrah, they would have blamed the troubles of the Cities of the Plain on 'bad presentation'. If only, they would have murmured, the City Fathers had had the wisdom to change their public relations agency in time. Lot's wife was never up to the standard of the Saatchis . . . It is difficult to persuade them that times are sometimes hard, news often bad.

Nigel Lawson's presentation is far from perfect. At party conferences he has made several poor speeches, and suffered the dreaded punishment of 'Withholding of Standing Ovation', the Tory equivalent of the Death of a Thousand Cuts. Lawson is not without political ambition, and fought back successfully at the 1986 conference, but in this Parliament he has been cast as Wicked Uncle in the pantomime of taxes and benefits.

Mrs Thatcher came to power in 1979 believing that a sharp cut in taxes would produce the Enterprise Culture, a spurt in growth that has eluded Britain throughout the post-war period. This plan has proved more difficult in execution than in conception, and some Tories suspected an intellectual weakness in the analysis, deriving from the British people's incorrigible propensity to consume more than they produce. The argument went like this:

The British are determined to live higher on the hog than their own efforts justify. Blame it on failure to adjust to the loss of empire, or socialism, or management, or workers, or simply the implacable gods. Whatever reason you choose, no political party ever risks confronting voters with the consequences of driving towards a brick wall. Each invents a plausible escape road, which is really always the same escape road although each party and age paints its entrance pillars in different, more attractive colours. The escape road is economic growth.

It could be argued that once the 1979 hope of a swift economic revolution receded, and as unemployment hugely increased the amount spent on benefits, Thatcherite philosophy required a sharp cut in the real level of these benefits. But in the 1983 election the Prime Minister avoided a commitment to such a course. Some highly-placed Tories believe that when the history of the Thatcher years is written, the Government's historic mistake will be seen to have been over public spending. They maintain that, while North Sea oil provided a cushion, ministers ought to have weaned the nation away from its worship of consumption, whether in higher personal incomes or welfare spending, and diverted money to New Deal schemes to provide jobs and regenerate capacity to produce wealth. Others clung to the belief that the Government should cut public spending in order to cut taxes, and then sit it out until the economic breakthrough came. Other Tories still saw their duty as the protection of the unfortunate: in the present state of the nation and the world why cut taxes? To allow us to buy more video-recorders to watch more Ethiopian children starve?

What gave political edge to these doubts was the Government's large majority. The 1983 influx represented one-sixth of Tory strength. In time the discipline of ambition might work its ancient magic and lick them into docility, but the mid-eighties turned into the years of rebellion. MPs' blood-pressure rose at the political risks of radicalism, and there were rebellions over MPs' pay, the GLC, the Welfare State, proposed removal of tax concessions on pension lump sums, and many other issues.

One meeting of the 1922 Committee of Conservative backbenchers just before Christmas 1984 may stand for the new ferocity of Mrs Thatcher's MPs during this Parliament. As a site for revolution, or counter-revolution, Committee Room 14 at the House of Commons does not rate with the Bastille or the Finland Station. Nor is it as luxurious as the Carlton Club, where the 1922 Committee was born out of the death throes of the Lloyd George coalition. But Room 14 has desk-tops for banging approbation, usually after an end-of-term speech from the Prime Minister. The desk-banging at the student grants meeting, almost unprecedentedly, was to support the Government's critics. The victim of this rage, which swept from Tory constituency associations into the parliamentary party, was the gentlest of ministers, Sir Keith Joseph, a holy innocent who took the Government's philosophy seriously. He was engulfed, and eventually swept away, by a revolution of rising expectations among the foot-soldiers of the Conservative Party. True, the intellectual colour of the revolts was not always clear, and the rebels wanted to bend the regime not break it. But the Prime Minister feared her whole economic strategy was being subverted and the word went out that the line had to be held against various pressure groups and in favour of cutting public spending and taxes.

But critics doubted the Government's political subtlety. Terence Higgins, an ex-Treasury minister from the Heath years, said the spending cuts were so finicky that ministers were 'making a banana skin out of every candle end', surely an inspired mixing of two contemporary metaphors. Ministerial anxiety grew when the student grants revolt succeeded. A *Daily Telegraph* leader put this starkly: 'A party which advocates correction of the balance of responsibilities between the individual and the state has shrunk from applying the logic of that correction to those best able to absorb it', i.e. middle-class parents. This was the most blatant example of a radical government's troubles with its middle-class supporters. Ministers who supported that radicalism thought the surrender on student grants, though politically inevitable, was intellectually wrong. They accused many backbenchers, shuddering at their bulging postbags of protest, of not understanding what Thatcherite economics were all about. It was intended to be a revolution, wasn't it?

What shocked ministers was the breadth of support for the defence of student grants. Knights of the Shires were muttering in the Smoking Room that they weren't even consulted about the length of the Christmas Recess nowadays. Solid men of the Centre said ominously that they were getting nearly as many letters about taxing pension lump sums as about students. Such men were not habitual rebels, and governments always have to worry when what Proust calls 'the anaesthetic effect of habit' is removed. You need a bit of ether drifting around a well-drilled back bench. But for MPs defending marginal seats the argument was now electoral rather than doctrinal.

The longest-running argument in Conservative governments of the seventies and eighties came to a head in local government legislation. Patrick Jenkin drew the short straw, not for the first time in his ministerial life, by having to fight through a measure that the Prime Minister wanted in order to redeem an ancient promise, but which was unpopular with many of the new local-government intake of Tory MPs. Kenneth Baker, who was emerging as the Panzer Grenadier of this Administration, was drafted in at a crucial moment as No. 2 (and eventual successor) to the shell-shocked Jenkin. The Bill got through, but created more scar-tissue in the Party.

Another running sore was the miners' strike. The quarrel between Margaret Thatcher and Arthur Scargill looked as if it had been written in both their stars. To some Tories Scargill seemed a second-term equivalent of Galtieri, cast as their election winner. A government elected, *inter alia*, on a law-and-order ticket might seem politically fortunate to face a strike in which violence became an issue. Ever since police authority had crumbled during the Heath years, at Upper Clyde Shipbuilders and the Saltley coke depot, Conservatives had been preparing for just such a challenge.

By the autumn of 1984 the Prime Minister was talking of sustaining the strike for a year, referring to 'the enemy within'. Not every Conservative was ecstatic about her tone. 'If the choice is between Margaret and Scargill,' said one doubter, 'then we haven't got much choice. That's why we've been so mute and inglorious.' ('Wets' are well-schooled in their Thomas Gray, a kind of early, honorary 'wet' himself.) As the strike dragged on the commanders on either side were not fully in control, and Tories wondered whether the electoral results would be favourable.

For the Conservative balance-sheet on the strike was more complicated than that of the new Labour leadership under Neil Kinnock. A corner-cutting accountant could have dealt with Labour's balance in one sharp footnote: 'Your company has lost a year's trading.' For the Government, on the credit side was the pleasure of its own supporters in the facing down of a major union with a bogeyman leader. Ministers also hoped for economic benefits from their victory: no urgent queue of other unions gasping to take on the Government; wider acceptance of the new trade union laws; perhaps even greater moderation in wage claims. But there was a down side also. Infuriatingly for the Prime Minister, the public opinion which damned Scargill and blamed Kinnock was now dissatisfied with her also. A MORI poll suggested voters were unhappy at any hint of triumphalism: 60% were dissatisfied with her handling of the miners, only 29% satisfied.

Radical Conservatives still believed that 'a social security time-bomb' was ticking away. The Treasury thought that a slimming in welfare spending, preferably by as much as £4 billion, was a prerequisite of the low-tax economy the Chancellor believed would produce the Enterprise Society. But Norman Fowler had a highly political view of his task in creating 'a new Beveridge'. He wanted to make changes without pulling the roof in. He hoped Tory backbenchers would resist cuts that made their Party look too hard-faced at a time when their Government was presiding over the worst unemployment for fifty years. Fowler shrewdly sought to cast Lawson and Rees as men whose political antennae were too insensitive to keep the Conservatives out of electoral trouble.

Social security has always aroused political passions. In 1911, when Lloyd George introduced the original National Insurance Bill – based on the Kaiser's Germany – duchesses and their servants joined in denouncing him as 'a benevolent busybody', 'mongrel' and 'tyrant'. When Northcliffe's *Times* advised people to defy the law and not pay the new contributions, Lloyd George foreshadowed our modern quarrels. Was there, he asked, to be one class of citizens which could obey the laws if they liked and another which must obey whether they liked or not? He added that some people thought the law was 'purely a weapon to keep the working classes in order'.

Beveridge's reforms, which emerged from the wartime coalition to differential enthusiasm from Churchill and Attlee, created the modern Welfare State. But to insular-minded critics of British feather-bedding Fowler pointed out that Britain's provision for the poor and unemployed was now anything but generous by modern European standards. The Prime Minister, who took the chair of the Cabinet committee considering the Fowler proposals, had radical instincts, but was cautious politically. Defenders of the Welfare State pointed out gleefully that 60% of Fowler's benefits were protected by pledges she had given or authorised. These covered basic pensions, widows' benefits, industrial injuries, invalidity and supplementary pensions. She was reported to have said privately that any attempt to reduce the real value of unemployment benefit would be electoral suicide. Right-wing critics were already calling the Fowler review a damp squib, but conceded that the 1983 election pledges had undermined the Government's authority to introduce the more radical changes they wanted.

Fowler's ostensible aim was to direct money more accurately to where it was needed. Critics thought this begged Bernard Shaw's paradoxical question about the Deserving and Undeserving Poor, but nevertheless the Prime Minister wanted this Doolittle Syndrome tackled. Fowler believed he could slash through the byzantine complexities of the system. He sought to create new bands of benefit, cutting a ready-to-wear suit to clothe the poor but ending tailor-made bonuses for such things as heating, diet, furniture, Christmas – and death: an incongruous grouping, perhaps, but the Welfare State by now was not just the original Beveridge blueprint but a pattern of organic growth. Some would be better off, some worse. Sceptics feared claimants would be pleased at first, but would recoil when they found a once-off grant for a new cooker or Aunt Edith's funeral was no longer available.

Ministers slowly realised they were walking on eggshells. A proposal to phase out the State Earnings-Related Pensions Scheme was watered down. Robert McCrindle, a Conservative backbencher who is an expert on pensions, had warned the Government that the pensions industry was neither equipped nor especially keen to attract the business of those who relied on SERPS, and that abolition might simply add to the cost of supplementary benefits.

Despite the disappointments over the Fowler review, the radicalism of Margaret Thatcher's natural supporters in the Conservative ranks remained undimmed. Indeed, it will probably remain that way until the Young Turks of the New Right fray into Knights of the Suburbs. The less radical Tories, however, began to think the Prime Minister had a fundamental problem: no less than Class and Conservatism. This provoked one young MP, Michael Brown, to speculate that she might be prepared to risk offending middle-class supporters in order to consolidate the blue-collar vote she raided so successfully in 1979 and 1983. Brown reported in a *Guardian* article that, instead of Christmas cards from his Conservative supporters, he had received 'an avalanche of letters' on overseas aid, student grants, taxation of lump-sum pension payments, and possible VAT on books and newspapers (which almost got into several budgets during this period). Brown argued that it was the Conservative middle classes who now felt threatened by the Thatcher Revolution, whereas industrial workers had been pleased by her sale of council houses, trade union legislation, and privatisation. Brown, a Northern MP, added: 'Conservative supporters in the southern heartlands of the stockbroker belt went along with the Thatcher philosophy until it began, earlier in 1984, to threaten their suburban tranquillity.'

Yet the Prime Minister and her Chancellor wanted to broaden the tax base sufficiently to reduce rates of income tax, and so create in Britain the Enterprise Culture that they admired in the United States. But they had to contrive to do this without alienating either her middle-class base, at which the Alliance hoped to chip away, or the newly-won support among the working class, which was Labour's target. The new coalition she had created in 1983 was an uneasy one. Perhaps because most Tories are more conservative with a small 'c' than the Prime Minister, it was middle-class erosion they feared most. A disillusioned minister confessed to Roy Hattersley about this time that the Government had raised its self-destructive potential to new levels: 'We can now hit a Tory constituency chairman from five miles up in the atmosphere.' That might be egging the pudding, but it reflected a Tory suspicion that the middle classes might not be in altruistic mood in 1985. For the first time since before the Falklands war in 1982, Labour began to feel it might have the Government on the run.

The other issue that put the Government on the defensive was the Health Service. The Government persistently said there were no cuts but more doctors, more nurses, more patients treated. The Opposition parties and the medical and nursing professions were equally constant in complaining about reduced services. It is a complex argument, not susceptible to pat answers. One problem is demographic: more old people who require care. Another is the advance in medical techniques – from hip replacements to kidney transplants – which add to costs. The Government made its comparison with what happened yesterday, or rather pre-1979 when Labour was in power, while the Opposition and NHS professionals talked about what was happening abroad. My cardiologist once astonished a minister by revealing that France and Germany are each doing four times as many coronary artery bypass operations, the surgical procedure which has benefited, among others, Len Murray, Sir Michael Havers, Lord Fitt, Sir Robin Day and myself.

CHAPTER 11

LABOUR BUYS ITS DREAM TICKET

On a wintry February night in 1985, I was driving from the Television Centre to Broadcasting House, via the House of Commons, when the car radio – 'that last infirmary of noble minds', as someone wittily called the House of Lords – produced a familiar voice. It was Michael Foot on Radio 4, talking with marvellous gusto about Byron. Surely he must be the first leader of a political party since Arthur Balfour who could have given such a talk (and Balfour predated Marconi). Foot confessed that the best way to read *Don Juan* was to have two or three days in hospital, which he had recently done; but if you were not prepared to go that far, you should at least carve a decent gap in your life to enjoy the poem.

As I came out of the House with an overnight case, I saw the former Leader of Her Majesty's Opposition himself, striding through Palace Yard to take part in a vote, his stick swinging happily. The cares of leadership had passed from him and the relief showed. Michael Foot had been deeply depressed by the 1983 disaster. He knew at once that he must resign, but wanted to give Neil Kinnock the best possible chance to succeed him.

The general election of 1983 was another revolution in British politics. The Labour Party was deeply wounded, perhaps mortally, and what any new leader had to discover was whether he could guide it through a period of convalescence to renewed strength, or whether his was to be the melancholy task of presiding over the obsequies of a party that would have lasted just the first eighty-three years of the twentieth century. A change in direction was overdue, for great political parties rarely commit suicide.

On the Sunday morning after polling day I returned from church to find a series of messages from BBC producers and one from Denis Healey. The office calls were to report Michael Foot's announcement that he would not be standing for re-election in October. Denis Healey's call was to confirm to me that he was giving up the deputy leadership and would not be seeking the leadership. It had long been Healey's intention that, if Labour lost, he would withdraw from its top leadership and remain only as foreign affairs spokesman. He was entertaining his 94-year-old mother to lunch that day, and some observers wondered whether a 65-year-old stripling from such a long-lived family might not still have a 1988 victory in him. But after Michael Foot's defeat septuagenarian generals were out of fashion. Labour's worst mistake in its modern history must be its failure to give Healey a spell as its leader.

No sooner was the announcement made that Sunday morning than Neil Kinnock, Roy Hattersley and Peter Shore were up and running. Within forty-eight hours of the election disaster they were outlining their policies for the Labour Party on radio and television. Soon Eric Heffer's hat was in the ring also. The far Left had faced a problem in finding a candidate since Tony Benn had lost his Bristol seat: so quickly does a political generation pass!

From the outset, the contest for the leadership was a better-natured affair than when Benn challenged Healey for the deputy's post in 1981. Kinnock and Hattersley, who emerged as the leading candidates, gave the impression that they quite liked each other, even if they could not avoid occasional barbed comment on their rivals' idiosyncrasies. They were open-eyed in their ambition, and each recognised that the other had to go for the job. Neither would have subscribed to the view of the Dickens character who said that 'ambition wasn't made to rhyme with Perdition for nothing'.

Peter Shore was the most experienced candidate, both in service and in ministerial posts held – Economic Affairs, Environment, Trade. Before entering Parliament he had been Research Secretary at Labour head-quarters; his strength was as a conceptual thinker who had put a personal stamp on Labour's policies in the sixties; his weakness was a lack of common touch. He had shown a gift for impassioned oratory in the anti-Common Market cause, but there was a gap between his public speaking and assiduous committee work on the one hand, and his weakness in party in-fighting and rough-house broadcasting, of which so much modern politics consists.

The leadership election was being held under the new electoral system. The trade unions had 40% of the vote, the constituency parties and the Parliamentary Labour Party 30% each. The election was formally due to take place on the opening evening of the party conference in Brighton at the end of September, but once the major unions declared themselves the result would be a foregone conclusion. From quite early on it became clear that Neil Kinnock's supporters in these unions had the election sewn up for him.

So the political interest in the campaign lay in the leading contenders' plans for saving the Labour Party from extinction. How far did they realise the depths of their failure in 1983? Did they see a need for internal revolution – or, as the Left would have seen what eventually happened, counter-revolution – reversing the change in direction of the seventies and early eighties? In this the campaign of Roy Hattersley, although he knew from early on that he would lose, was significant.

Hattersley's aim was to recall Labour to its historic role and attitudes as the principal voice of working-class Britain. He articulated the views of many Labour people who believed they must change course or die. At the same time he wanted to conduct his campaign in such a way as to avoid the fate for Labour that a Washington wit once predicted before a Democratic Party convention: 'a good, clean fight from which no survivors will emerge.' The question Hattersley posed was this: was it wiser to stick to policies evolved since 1973 – unilateral nuclear disarmament; withdrawal, or at least Gaullist detachment, from Europe; an economic policy relying on centralised planning of everything from external trade to investment policies of major companies – yet stop short of a plan for incomes? Or was it necessary to reposition Labour nearer to the known views of those who had supported it since the war but had deserted in droves in 1979 and 1983?

In Labour's most successful years, from the second world war to 1970 when it had occupied power for about half the time, it had the support of a voting coalition consisting of the industrial working class and those members of the middle and professional classes whose views were socialist or reformist. All movements for change in politics need such a coalition to sustain them. In the United States in the thirties Franklin Roosevelt built up a three-sided coalition which gave him the muscle to extract America from the Great Depression – the South, ethnic groups in the northern cities and organised labour. It was the crumbling of that coalition, during the civil rights struggle in the South and the national anguish over Vietnam, that ended the Democrats' period as the natural party of government and put a Republican in the White House for all but four of the past eighteen years.

Roy Hattersley's case was that a new coalition of voters was available for mobilising in support of a moderate Labour Party within the Attlee–Gaitskell–Wilson–Callaghan tradition. He set out to show that a majority of trade unionists could be won back for Labour; that former council-house tenants were not irretrievably lost because they had bought their own homes; and that Labour could compete with the SDP and Liberals in universities and among professional, administrative and business people of progressive tinge.

Hattersley was in the Crosland tradition of socialism. What offended him most was the British class system, as he saw it expressed in education, housing, the world of work, even in what was then his front-bench responsibility, law and order, where the rights of a young black man stopped by the police at night often seemed less equal (in the Orwellian sense) than those of a middle-aged, middle-class white citizen. He sometimes described himself as a gas-and-water or municipal socialist. That label covered the Sheffield tradition from which he came, with its ameliorist thrust acquired in the hard times before the war. But it did not quite capture the evangelical fervour of his campaign to turn the Labour Party round, in the hope that it could again capture the whole Centre-Left segment of the electorate, which was divided between Labour, the Alliance and abstention. His charge against his own Party was that it was letting its working-class supporters down by failing to adopt policies that would bring it to power. As far as Roy Hattersley was concerned, that was the ignominy of 1983.

What Hattersley believed divided people like him from at least some of his former social democratic colleagues was an empathy with those born and living below what was now a moving, but still steep, social precipice. Despite his own affluent life-style his friends maintained that no one could justly apply to him what President Lyndon Johnson once said of his fellow-Texan, Governor John Connally: 'That sonofabitch has forgotten he was ever poor.'

That was the agenda Roy Hattersley contributed in Labour's new era. The electoral mountain the Party had to climb was now sinking into its consciousness. To achieve an overall majority in the next election, Labour would have to gain almost 120 seats. It would have to do this in face of an Alliance challenge which, after a 25.4% national vote in 1983, was certainly not going to fade quickly. Detailed analysis of the results showed that Labour had lost a sizeable proportion of its old constituency in the manual working class, without building alternative support strong enough to give much hope of power; while the Alliance had swept up many of those unhappy with Labour, without either replacing Labour as the principal opposition to the Tories or taking enough Conservative votes, even during an economic recession, to enlarge its own Westminster bridgehead.

The only reasonable hope for Labour was that it could squeeze the Alliance parties, leaving them to garner ex-Conservative supporters, as the Liberals on their own had successfully done in periods of Tory unpopularity during the previous quarter-century. Meanwhile, in this scenario, Labour would itself win back from the Conservatives many of the working-class voters it had lost in 1979 and 1983. But this presupposed a more open minded dialogue between Labour and its traditional supporters than had taken place for more than a decade. The Party would have to face its own weakness, recognise the scale of its 1983 defeat, and acknowledge that even greater disaster was probable unless it grew back towards the people who had voted for it in the past. A second possibility was that people determined to cast an anti-Thatcher vote might conclude that the Alliance now had a better chance of replacing her. A third possibility was of further realignment on the Left of British politics. But the depths of bitterness reached during the general election between the Alliance and Labour's Right made that seem impossible. Both groups had burned their boats, as the Alliance were drawn to the Right and Labour's moderates to the Left by the exigencies of electioneering.

Each of the Opposition parties had to rely on the eclipse of the other if it was to have a realistic chance of power. The most impassioned defence of Labour's future during the election had come from a surprising source: Margaret Thatcher said on television, 'The Labour Party will not die. The Labour Party will never die.' Alliance leaders saw this as the most blatant

Tory self-interest, aimed at their jugular. No doubt there was an element of that, but I happened to be the interviewer whom the Prime Minister fixed with her most penetrating gaze as she said it, and I have no doubt she believed what she was saying, as most leading Tories do. They note Labour's strong roots through large areas of Britain, and they think – and hope – that one day it will change back to something more Gaitskell-like (or Alliance-like), and so become an acceptable alternative from a Conservative point of view.

As the gravity of the election results sank in during the summer of 1983, few Labour people were complacent about the future. Trade Unions for a Labour Victory (TULV) produced a report that was devastatingly frank about the unions' efforts to help Labour and about the Party's own campaign. Trade unionists, who had appeared to be moving back to Labour after defecting during the Alliance launch or the Falklands war, had fallen away again during the election campaign itself. By polling day union support for Labour was 12% below that in 1979, which was itself not a good year. Most of them had switched to the Alliance. According to the TULV analysis of the election and of public and private attitude studies, Labour still seemed to be the party to which most working-class people instinctively looked first, while Alliance support was more middle-class. But were old loyalties beginning to slip permanently? Certainly voters appeared to be more footloose than at any time since 1922, when the Lloyd George coalition broke up and the Liberal Party lost its way.

Indeed, the ten years which followed 1922 were the most obvious guide that history offered to the Labour Party after 1983. The question was whether Labour was fated to decline, as the Liberals had done then, and to be replaced by the Alliance as the alternative to semi-permanent Conservative rule. The 1920s' precedent suggested that such a switch took a political generation to complete, even if the tide flowed steadily in one direction, which was by no means certain.

It is worth examining this precedent. At the end of the Great War in 1918, Labour had had 39 MPs, and raised this to 59 when the Coalition held its 'coupon election' that year. When Conservative MPs abandoned Lloyd George in 1922 at a famous meeting in the Carlton Club which gave their 1922 backbenchers' committee its mysterious name, the Coalition broke up and a divided Liberal Party faced a bleak world. In the 1922 election the Tories gained 5.5 million votes and 345 seats, Labour had 4.2 million and 142 seats, and the Liberals 4 million and 117 seats. Labour was in second place and its Long March had begun, although it was not to form a majority government until almost another quarter-century had passed.

However, by 1924 Ramsay MacDonald was forming the first minority Labour Government – 'that insane miracle', he called it, and George V wondered what his grandmother would have thought. The Liberals were more suicidally divided then than Labour was in 1983. The Asquithians had not forgotten and were never to forgive what they saw as Lloyd George's treachery to their leader during the war. That quarrel ran, with malign effect, through the slow, lingering death of Liberal England, making the Montagues look emollient towards the Capulets and the Martins forgiving towards the McCoys. Lloyd George wrote to Margot Asquith in an attempt at reconciliation, saying Liberals' quarrels were 'largely petty and personal'. He added: 'If we can genuinely decide to forget past grievances – and, believe me, the grievances are not all on one side – Liberal revival is a certainty. If not, then neither of us will live to see the day when Liberalism will become again a dominant force in national life.' It was a letter Michael Foot might have written to Tony Benn in 1981. But do politicians ever learn such lessons either through history or their electoral misfortunes?

Even when I began to write about British politics in the mid-fifties the Asquith–Lloyd George quarrel was still there, in posthumous travail. Pale shadows of those 'past grievances' still flitted across what was now a Conservative–Labour world. Churchill had recently given a free run against Labour to Asquith's daughter, Lady Violet Bonham-Carter; but Lloyd George's daughter, Lady Megan, left the Liberals to fight a Carmarthen by-election for Labour. She summoned me to her hotel to explain to the *Manchester Guardian*, the ancient organ of Liberalism, why she believed her father, if still alive, would by then have joined Labour.

The lesson to be derived from those frustrating years for modern politicians of the Left was that a party that fights itself cannot defeat others and will ultimately destroy itself. This was a lesson that might apply to modern Liberals as they quarrelled spasmodically with their SDP allies, but the more fundamental lessons were for Labour, which had already lost its social democratic wing.

There was also a lesson on policy. Lloyd George had foreseen the risk that Liberal policies would come to seem less relevant as those of the new party, Labour, became more so. The war had diverted him in his most creative years from tackling unemployment and poverty, but as late as the 1929 election he produced, with the aid of J. M. Keynes, a programme of public works to reduce unemployment. This was before Keynes had fully developed his ideas, and three years before Roosevelt's New Deal. In David Lloyd George the Liberals had a seer and a genius, but by 1929 too many of them had lost interest.

Now Labour, in the year of its greatest electoral disaster and facing a first leadership election under its new rules, had to decide whether its 1983 programme would look relevant four or five years ahead. The trade union research showed that on an important tranche of policies – Europe, law and order, defence, nuclear arms and taxation – trade unionists put Labour behind the Conservatives. On nuclear arms union members were actually more hostile than other voters. Yet there was some evidence in the survey by TULV that a '1920s in reverse', with the Alliance replacing Labour as the principal party of the Left, was not probable. The bad news for Labour in this survey was its poor showing among new voters, among working-class house-owners and in the South. The good news was that the Alliance vote was heavily white-collar, weak in the North and in Scotland, and above all extremely volatile: 28% of those who voted Liberal in 1979 had gone elsewhere by 1983, although this was more than made up by an influx of new Alliance voters. But even if Labour people comforted themselves with the belief that the Alliance 1983 vote was monstrously swollen by protest against both Tories and Labour, they still faced an awesome task in checking the tide.

As the summer passed, it became certain that Neil Kinnock would be the man chosen to inherit this task. Union votes piled up during their conference season: his own transport workers, the railwaymen and footplatemen, public employees, health service workers, printers, postmen, steelworkers, shopworkers, and many more. By midsummer even Hattersley supporters acknowledged privately that Kinnock would win and that Hattersley would be his deputy. The phrase 'dream ticket' began to be used about the two men who were to head a new partnership of the pragmatic Left and the Centre-Right. For Kinnock was revealing himself as pragmatic: he was determined to take head-on what he saw as the lunacies of recent years, and he warned local Labour parties that they must speak *for* the public as well as *to* themselves'. Labour views on his prospective leadership ranged from ecstatic support to 'He'll be a total disaster' and 'To hell with the issues – Neil will compromise so long as it wins votes'. (Politicans' private judgements of their colleagues do not err on the side of charity.)

Kinnock made three moves that pointed to his future pragmatism. He quickly acknowledged that withdrawal from Europe might look an anachronistic commitment in 1987 or 1988. Already he was establishing stronger links with European socialists and renewing his musical memories of *Bandiera Rossa*. Second, in a seminal speech at Wandsworth he warned Labour that it could only win consent to help the disadvantaged if it again engaged the loyalty of the relatively advantaged. This might seem like a truism, but it served warning to David Steel and David Owen that a new Labour leader of their own generation would be competing for the same voters. Kinnock urged his Party to win support from 'the home owner as well as the homeless, the stable family as well as the single parent, the confidently employed as well as the unemployed, the majority as well as the minorities'.

His third move was on defence, but it was a limited one. Kinnock worked on a document which said that Polaris should be included in the Geneva negotiations on intermediate-range missiles. But it was Britain's role in NATO, and specifically his opposition to United States nuclear bases in this country, which divided Kinnock from Hattersley, Shore, Healey and the Centre-Right. It was an internal problem that was to remain as insoluble under Kinnock's leadership as under Foot's. Neil Kinnock cares passionately about nuclear weapons. The first lunch we ever had together was dominated by a discussion of what he regarded as the apostasy of his boyhood hero, Aneurin Bevan; and on the day when he himself was to be elected Labour leader, I had tea with him and an excited group of constituency supporters from South Wales, and noted that every one of them, apart from the Kinnocks, wore a CND badge. There was not much room for him to compromise on this subject, as he had on many others. In private Kinnock would say to multilateralists: 'Don't worry, kid; it'll be all right when we're in government.' They were not sure what he meant, and all they could do was exercise a Micawberish instinct that something would turn up.

Lloyd George quoted Churchill as saying once, 'Success in politics depends on how well you can control your conscience.' If accurately remembered, that was a devastating piece of cynicism. Yet it contained an essential, paradoxical truth: at the heart of democratic politics lies the necessity to compromise, a willingness to sacrifice some desired goals in order to achieve power to reach others. But was compromise to be contemplated on such a fundamental subject as a politician's attitude to nuclear weapons?

Neil and Glenys Kinnock had both joined CND as students at Cardiff. When Bevan made his famous speech at Labour's Brighton conference in 1957, urging delegates not to send a Labour Foreign Secretary 'naked into the conference chamber', Kinnock had regarded it as a betrayal. In any examination of Kinnock's political roots the comparison with Bevan is irresistible. It is not just the Welshness, though nationality has something to do with the eloquence and the 'hyperbolical tongue' that both men have relished and suffered from. Both were also fated to wrestle with one of the great issues of this century's second half, nuclear weapons.

Bevan, the undisputed leader of Labour's Left, in his endeavour to heal old divisions with Hugh Gaitskell's wing and make a Labour government possible, offended old friends. As they subjected him to unprecedented heckling, Bevan's combative instincts took over, and wounding phrases flowed from his quicksilver tongue. After the 'naked into the conference chamber' taunt, he added: 'And you call that statesmanship! I call it an emotional spasm.' He accused them of dismantling the whole fabric of Britain's international relationships without putting anything in its place, and of driving the country 'into diplomatic purdah'. Michael Foot has an anguished account of the Brighton speech in the second volume of his biography of Bevan. It reveals his own bewilderment at his change of stance. Neither he nor Neil Kinnock has ever fully understood why Bevan did it, though Foot has been readier to forgive. But he records this sad indictment of his hero's style in that speech: 'He could be possessed by

Lloyd George's terrible urge to claw down an enemy, and on this occasion the enemy was his friends.'

The parallel between Kinnock and Bevan runs deep, because this accurately described *daemon* can possess them both, yet both have the redeeming gift of wit and fun. Once, at a by-election in Wales, I found myself alone in a hotel breakfast-room with Bevan, whom I scarcely knew. He was suspicious of journalists, except those who were old friends, so he regaled me with an admonitory tale about the *Western Mail* in Cardiff which, he claimed, kept a critical leader about him permanently in type. When I expressed mild scepticism about this he offered anecdotal proof. Once, in a health debate, he had made a speech which drew on his experience as founder of the NHS and was moderate in tone. This was praised by several Conservative MPs, and the Parliamentary Correspondent of the *Western Mail* wrote on the front page: 'Mr Bevan made what, for him, was a remarkably benign speech, and this was well received on all sides of the House.' 'But when I turned to the leading article,' he said, his voice rising to the falsetto which always heralded laughter, 'what do you think I read? "Mr Bevan delivered himself of his usual envenomed piece of class hatred." They keep it standing in type, I tell you.'

Kinnock's two great Welsh predecessors, Lloyd George and Bevan, had both gone straight into the Cabinet from the back benches. But if he wins an election Kinnock will be the first man since Ramsay MacDonald to move into Downing Street without having held any government office. Those who criticised his position on defence believed that this inexperience was part of the problem. One senior Labour man ruminated on the shock Neil Kinnock would receive in his first week at Number Ten: 'The American Ambassador would be there within days, wanting to know the score. The Chiefs of Staff would jib at losing the American nuclear umbrella.' Even then some American officials were murmuring that Labour's call for withdrawal of American nuclear bases would destroy NATO. The new leader faced major problems.

Roy Hattersley had been on Labour's front bench, in government and opposition, since 1967. Relations between him and Kinnock were certain to be crucial to Labour's future. Although the way in which union block votes were piled up for Kinnock made the result a foregone conclusion, Hattersley had said two things during the campaign that bore on that relationship. One was to serve notice that people like himself did not intend to abandon Labour, but would stay in despite all disappointment to reassert the radical, Centrist strand in Labour thinking and policy. That message was for the SDP. But the other was for Kinnock. It recorded Hattersley's belief that, however willing he himself might be to compromise to reach agreement on policy, his were views the Labour Party must accommodate if it was ever to win power again. This seemed in tune with what Kinnock said in his acceptance speech: 'Our purpose is the government of Britain . . . Every interest – sectional, factional, regional and personal – is secondary to that major aim.'

Cynics on the Left jeered privately that this meant he would do whatever proved necessary to get Labour elected and himself installed as Prime Minister. It was, again, the agonised question of the legitimate place of compromise in democratic politics. Neil Kinnock believed he spoke for the majority of the shell-shocked, post-1983 Labour Party in saying that the pursuit of power was the only proper activity for a democratic party. Only the 'Vinegar Tendency', he said privately, wanted to continue the internal strife that had done Labour so much electoral damage. Certainly his acceptance speech, perhaps the most effective he has ever made, caught the mood of that first post-election conference, when he said: 'Remember how each and every one of you felt on that dreadful morning of June 10, and think to yourselves: "June 9, 1983: never again will we experience that." Unity is the price of victory.'

Kinnock was elected with 71% of the votes in the electoral college, to Hattersley's 19, Heffer's 6 and Shore's 3. Hattersley won the election for deputy leader. By the time it happened most Labour people, even those who did not vote for him, thought Kinnock would make a good job of the leadership. He had pleased the Centre-Right by acknowledging that Labour's worst mistake in June had been to underestimate the Alliance, particularly the SDP. So he realised that Roy Hattersley and the ideas his wing of the Labour Party espoused were essential to the fight for that segment of voters. The worries being expressed privately about him were less on his policies, which those Labour people who were unhappy seemed to have buried in their collective subconscious, but his lack of experience, what Margaret Thatcher might do to him in the House, and what his own rhetoric might do to him. One critic applied to Kinnock the sly remark of J. K. Galbraith about Joseph Schumpeter: 'Given the choice between being right and being memorable, he never hesitated.'

Yet both the new leader and deputy leader were men whose whole lives seemed to point them to their new responsibilities. Each was an only child, and bore the stigmata of parental ambitions for him. Perhaps some university psychology department might offer as a thesis subject: 'Influence of the absence of sibling rivalry on the political careers of only children'. The paper would be a certain success at a British Association conference. Kinnock's wife, Glenys, is quoted in Robert Harris's biography as saying that her husband was always very conscious of his parents, who had both died by the time he became Labour leader: 'He's a great believer in roots and background and decency and clean shoes and looking smart and all those aspirations for their children which his parents and my parents represent.' Her remark catches a part of the Kinnock enigma. One part of him is dominated by the Freudian super-ego she describes; the other is more self-indulgent. The former drove him up the shaky ladder of Labour politics – MP at 28, Leader at 41 – and has produced a tough party disciplinarian. The latter raises suspicions that he is intellectually supine, quick but not deep in mind, inclined to substitute Welsh rhetoric for the real world: in fact inebriated – as Churchill once said of an opponent – by the exuberance of his own verbosity.

Yet it was the exuberance of Neil Kinnock's politics which won him the Leadership of the Labour Party. For years past, while rivals like Roy Hattersley and Peter Shore had been concentrating on their standing in the Commons, Kinnock was stumping the constituencies and union branches with his evangelistic oratory, with an eye on the NEC elections and another on the future. At times his voting record at Westminster had been poor, but when he fought the Devolution Bill of his mentor, Michael Foot, he had displayed appetite for the grind of long committee stages. Paradoxically, but some said typically, when the collapse of the devolution legislation had undermined the Callaghan government and it lost a vote of confidence to an alliance of Conservatives, Liberals and Nationalists, it was Kinnock who led the defiant singing of the *Red Flag* by Labour MPs below the gangway. Many of his choir that night did not survive the electoral defeats of 1979 and 1983. Now Neil Kinnock was leader, and he must win back those seats if Labour was to hold power again.

CHAPTER 12

OWEN, TOUGH AND TENDER

The Alliance emerged from the 1983 general election with 23 seats – 17 Liberals and 6 Social Democrats – but 25.4% of the national vote. The contrast between this encouraging support from a quarter of those who voted and the disappointing fall in representation at Westminster reflected not just the existing electoral system, against which the Alliance railed. Less encouragingly it demonstrated that the Alliance had failed in its original aim: to break the class mould of British politics. Labour and Conservative heartlands, though nibbled away at the edges, seemed generally impregnable. The Alliance could only break through if public attitudes to class and politics had changed radically and permanently. After June 1983, no one knew whether such a seismic shift had begun. That would have to wait for an answer until 1987 or 1988. Shirley Williams, with that academic's honesty which keeps overcoming a politician's canniness, pointed out the Alliance's weakness: although it now occupied second place in nearly half the seats in Britain, its vote was within 10% of only twenty-one Conservative MPs and five Labour ones. A major swing of opinion would still be needed next time if the Alliance was to win enough seats to change the face of politics.

After the election Roy Jenkins decided to resign the SDP leadership, and David Owen, the only other member of the original Gang of Four to survive the election, succeeded him without a contest. Meanwhile, David Steel had a long rest at his Borders home, to recover from a virus infection and from post-election frustration or depression. But Steel soon found himself engaged in a sharp internal row. Partly because of his own mood, partly because colleagues soon exercised their liberal, almost anarchic pre-dilection for vigorous internecine quarrelling, he emerged from his rest in fighting stance. The leading critic was Cyril Smith, supported by David Alton, who is from the Liverpool community-politics tradition, and Simon Hughes, victor of the Bermondsey by-election and soon to be a thorn in Steel's flesh over defence. Smith's political objectives are not always pellucid, but often in the past he had distanced himself from Steel and he now described him as 'too authoritarian'. Within Liberalism that is a serious charge, though Gladstone, Asquith and Lloyd George, each in a unique style, were not averse to having their own ways. Steel faced a new phenomenon.

The urban and local government strand in the modern Liberal Party drew its considerable strength from the maxim that you find out what the grass roots want and, within reason, give it to them. Steel was sceptical how many votes community politics delivered compared with the influence of the party nationally. But his quarrel – subsequently repaired – with the Association of Liberal Councillors and its maverick leader, Tony Greaves, raised important issues. Critics attacked Alliance policy-making and demanded abolition of the leader's veto on future manifestoes. More significant, some critics raised the defence issue, which was to plague the Alliance throughout the new Parliament. Two years previously, at their Llandudno Assembly, Liberals had defied their leaders and opposed Cruise missiles. But it was that same week, at an emotional fringe meeting which was among the most exciting occasions in the politics of the eighties, that the Alliance with the SDP was born, and this overshadowed the Cruise decision. Since unilateral nuclear disarmament was one of the issues that drove the Social Democrats out of the Labour Party, Steel put his Assembly's decision on the back-burner, and later agreed to a collective defence policy with David Owen. That, after all, was what both believed in anyhow.

The quarrel illustrated a fundamental problem for the Alliance: that at least in Left-of-Centre parties the rank and file are more and more determined to have a significant voice in policy. There is a great and growing gulf between the conviction of parliamentary leaders, that they know best what the public will vote for, and the belief of grass-roots activists, that they know best what is right. Liberal Assemblies have grown more and more like Labour Party conferences. The radical wing is more self-confident in its rebelliousness than it used to be. There is no comparison between the unyielding Young Turks of today and the first, mild Liberal revolt I witnessed, when in 1956 the Grimond supporters – Young Turks in their day – had persuaded the party leader, Clement Davies, that it was 'time for a change'. I can still savour the thunderbolts of loathing that flashed from their eyes on two aged Liberals, innocent of this persuasion, who greeted Davies' announcement of his retirement with strangled cries of 'No, Clem, no!'

That occasion could not rival in its fervour the full-throated roar of the Liberal Left when it defeated David Steel in the defence debates of the eighties. For conference buffs there is a difference between applause for attacks on rival parties and for a victory within one's own. Those roars of defiance symbolised a new spirit, as Liberals sniffed the possibility of at least shared power. David Steel knew he would face more Liberal revolts in future, and he learned, as Labour leaders have done, to avert them, skirt them or thole them.

David Owen made clear that he did not intend to dodge the defence issue raised by his Liberal allies. He said in a *New Democrat* interview: 'We must not be frightened of a debate on unilateralism, but had we in the SDP gone down that road the Alliance would have polled nearer 13% than the 26% it achieved.' He added that he detected 'certain anarchical tendencies in the Liberal Party which make it difficult for them to stand firm on key policy issues'. This looked like a sentence which would go into the Conservative Central Office compost heap for recycling.

1983 had produced an unhappy summer for the Liberals, what with Steel's absence, the arguments after the election disappointment, and the silly season in Fleet Street. The lost souls of the Westminster press corps, left to keep the dog-watch in that depressing first recess of a new Parliament, were hard put to it to consume another forest of newsprint. So the salty exchanges between Steel and his critics came as a boon and a blessing to them. Even the ranks of Tuscany – where Neil Kinnock, Roy Hattersley and other Labour aspirants to leadership were on holiday – could scarce forbear to cheer the Liberal disarray.

Nor were the events of that August without longer-term significance. These were the first breezes of a great and important debate about the future of Liberalism and the Alliance, even of British politics. The political landscape was misty in 1983 and no one had a clear idea of what would emerge. Even the new Alliance was afflicted – or blessed – by the revolutionary instinct of the eighties. What made Alliance people testy was that, although their electoral support had been better than seemed likely when the campaign began, it was still a let-down from the heady days of 1981 when the new party thought it had a good chance of forming the next government.

The Social Democrats had faced a harsh election, their first outside the warm womb of an established party. Before 1983 their new party had experienced only the euphoria or disappointment of by-elections, the soufflés of politics. General elections were about the red meat of power, and the sobering fact was that the SDP had lost most of the seats held by MPs who had come over from Labour: they had entered the election with 29 MPs and emerged from it with only six, one-third of the number held by Liberals. Only the Alliance national vote, so near to Labour's, sustained their morale at this moment when it finally became clear that 'breaking the mould' would be a long job.

What was daunting was a sense of missed opportunity. It was hard to imagine a better electoral climate than existed in 1983 for a party aiming to replace Labour. True, the Falklands factor and the Prime Minister's overwhelming popularity made it difficult to pick up the dissident Conservative votes Liberals traditionally relied on, but Labour had been tearing itself apart for four years and was losing much of its working-class support, and the Alliance had hoped to establish a larger Westminster bridgehead.

In every Alliance speech between June and October, while Labour was effectively leaderless, one sentiment was *de rigueur*: a blunt statement that they had replaced Labour as the real Opposition. The principal evidence was the current state of the polls, which seemed a transitory basis for such an historic assertion. But if the evidence was meagre the intentions were clear: to embarrass and demoralise Labour, and to propagate the case for proportional representation. Much midnight oil had already gone into calculating what the results might have been if one or another system of PR had operated. Among Alliance supporters PR was now a crusade with strong emotions behind it. A radio listener wrote rebuking me for reporting that the Government had had an overwhelming victory in the election. What I meant, the writer told me, was 'an overwhelming parliamentary victory, which is a very different matter'.

This letter reminded me of an incident involving the late Tom Henry, editor of the *Manchester Evening News*, who knew how much his paper's prosperity and circulation depended on the resilience in adversity of the city's two great football clubs. On one occasion when Newcastle defeated Manchester United by six goals to one, the chief sub-editor wrote the uncompromisingly truthful headline 'Newcastle thrash United'. When Henry saw it in proof, a frown clouded his face and he altered it to 'United in seven-goal thriller'. Another of the many faces of truth. Clearly I should have said 'Thatcher in split-vote thriller'.

When all the mathematical sophistries about election results had been exhausted – including the mischievous thought that fewer than one in five of those entitled to vote had supported parties advocating PR – the Tories still enjoyed a majority that would last them five years if they wished. The divided Opposition faced a herculean task at the end of the Parliament if they were to overturn that majority and form an alternative government. For whatever the pros and cons of PR – and there are both – its introduction would depend not on abstract judgements of right and wrong but on political strengths and advantages. Margaret Thatcher opposed change; so would any likely Labour leader. Against such opposition those seeking change, even the strong business lobby whose fear of a Left-wing government provided most of its financial muscle, were unlikely to prevail, unless an Alliance holding the balance of power forced the issue.

David Owen's leadership meant a change in relations with the Liberals. Among the original Gang of Four he had remained the most aloof from them. In 1983 his instincts were strongly Left of Centre, even though he was alienated from old allies on Labour's Right. But so far as some Liberals were concerned the problems with Owen were less ideological than personal. They thought he made little effort to bridge the gap between the two parties.

Owen was more interested in evolving the SDP's own policies. He claimed they were offering the most radical and realistic programme against poverty, and promised 'a major redistribution of income to the poorest'. This was to be a continuing theme with him, while outside Parliament Shirley Williams was working on new ideas to counter unemployment. Bill Rodgers, though enthusiastically behind an assault on poverty, was suspicious of Owen's 'radical' tag; he wrote in *Political Quarterly*: 'Among Social Democrats, there is a clear majority of problem-solvers, committed to a practical programme of conscience and reform. They may call themselves radicals, but their preference is for cautious change.'

Roy Jenkins had always been the nearest of the four to the political Centre and keenest for closer ties with the Liberals. Jenkinsites hoped that by the next election the gap between the separate parties would have diminished almost to vanishing point. If there was a merger before then, so much the better. Bill Rodgers and Shirley Williams favoured organic growth, and Rodgers thought what appeared to be parallel lines might confound Euclid and converge. David Owen, however, was convinced a merger would bring defections neither party could afford.

Owen's personality remained, for many Alliance supporters, a conundrum encased in an enigma. In a new political period he enjoyed many advantages: his age put him in the same generation of leaders the Liberals already had and Labour was soon to get; he had good looks and charm and when free of moodiness – what a friend called his 'black periods' – could be amusing company, with the pervasive aura of a reasonable man. Yet at forty-five he still seemed a personality whose complexities were concealed even from himself – Dr Owen and Mr Hyde, some presumed. He has a sharp mind, whose range he constantly pushes out. As leader of a small party he was having to adjust to the change from his life with Labour, where he was able to deal with restricted fields – earlier health, more recently foreign affairs. The quality of judgement on which he prided himself cannot be infinite in range, and nothing would harm him more than seeming to take pot-shot decisions. A friendly critic saw both a strength and a potential weakness: 'David is best when his convictions are flowing freely. He has a capacity for saying something with great clarity and certainty – and something different not long afterwards. I don't think his political calculations are yet sound, and they sometimes vitiate his instincts.'

Yet most Social Democrats believed their new leader was a great asset. Any apparent rashness was a fault of his virtue: a remarkably open and frank approach that is unusual in a senior politician. Perhaps it was political traditions learned from his American wife, perhaps his medical training, but Owen never seemed reluctant to make up his mind, never stuck for an opinion. Sometimes these opinions were brusquely stated. Before the election he had become more scathing about former Labour comrades than had other Social Democrats. The split has widened since then, but he had avoided a position where working with Labour would be impossible. In 1983 that seemed prudent, for the mathematics of a divided Opposition made the next general election look a hazardous one for both Alliance and Labour.

Social Democrat leaders had great respect for David Steel, but they were astonished by his handling of the summer quarrel with Liberal critics. One, deeply versed in the conspiratorial world of Labour politics, said that in future Steel would have to watch his back: 'David has an extraordinary style during his Assembly week. He holds court in his suite, goes out to lunch and dinner with journalists, and shows a certain distaste for his followers. He needs a wider circle within his own party.' Many Liberals knew that beneath Steel's charm he had that single-mindedness common in some able Scots which does not always leave enough room for the social graces. Most political leaders nowadays could learn something from the way in which Arthur Balfour won friends (as described by Winston Churchill):

> He possessed and practised the art of always appearing interested in any subject that was raised, or in any person with whom he was talking . . . All who met him came away with the feeling that *they* had been at their very best, and that they had found someone who, whether he agreed or differed, understood their point of view. Very often they remembered the thing they had said to him, which he had welcomed or seemed to agree with, better than what he had said to them . . .

Few modern politicians could live up to that billing. Churchill thought Balfour 'the best-mannered man I ever met', and from the other side of the political fence Beatrice Webb in her diary describes him as 'aloof from all the greed and grime of common human nature'.

Both Alliance leaders needed tact to handle the evolving relationship between their parties. Liberals who believed in community politics found themselves in uneasy harness with politicians of quite different provenance. Liberal attitudes to the SDP were varied and ambiguous. One Steel friend pointed out that, although there had been no votes cast against the Alliance in the Association of Liberal Councillors, the cradle of community politics, some members of that body would 'like to gobble the SDP up for breakfast, and then get ready for lunch'.

Such ideas were not without parallel in the SDP. One of Owen's critics thought he was not so much determined to keep the parties separate that he did not dream of absorbing the Liberals. Other Social Democrats, noting the Liberals' raucous troubles after the election, which reminded them too painfully of the quarrelsome atmosphere they had left behind in the Labour Party, were cautious about their allies. They believed they were helpful electorally but otherwise somewhat embarrassing and to be kept at a safe distance. However, the years proved that such arm's-length friendship was not feasible: the Alliance would grow closer because its whole electoral hopes lay in unity. They were bound to each other with hoops of Steel, and necessity.

That did not deter David Owen from recognising publicly that the relationship was subtle, and one that he hoped to adjust. At the Liberal Assembly Glee Night he and his wife sang a specially composed song,

'Tough but Tender'. It did not dodge the issues that worried him:

> Let's be tough on defence,
> And mean what we say;
> No use sitting on the fence,
> There's no other way.

Not poetry, perhaps, but to the point. Or again:

> At the next election
> We must all agree
> Not on joint selection,
> But joint policy.

In other words, no more constitutional fiddling and no more fudging and mudging on policy, Owen's pet political aversion which he trounced so severely during his final Labour pains. The chorus of his ambiguous love song was more emollient:

> Love us tender, love us true,
> All our dreams fulfil;
> Truly, Liberals, we love you,
> And we always will.

Sceptics passed lightly over the final line. Dr Owen, as a man of the world, doubtless knew the Breach of Promise which so cruelly afflicted that earlier political thinker, Mr Pickwick. When the 1983 conferences of Social Democrats and Liberals had held their election inquests, betting men might have been reluctant to put their shirts on that 'and we always will'. The path of true love never did run smooth, but divorce was even more perilous. Anyhow, the song did Owen a bit of necessary good with the Liberals, who like a laugh.

While the internal relationships needed careful nurturing, the real question was whether Alliance chances of replacing Labour and defeating the Conservatives in 1987 or 1988 looked better or worse after their conferences, and after Neil Kinnock had succeeded Michael Foot. Their hope was that strains in the Alliance would be eased by events in the Labour Party. If even after the election of a new leader Labour were to plough disastrously into the sand, the Alliance would ride a wave of success. But suppose – as was to happen – that the Kinnock–Hattersley Dream Ticket had a prolonged honeymoon in the opinion polls? This would accelerate the self-examination within the Alliance that David Steel's sabbatical and David Owen's succession had begun. These two leaders were tenser and tougher, and perhaps less tender, than their predecessors, Roy Jenkins and David Steel the Younger. In such circumstances would the Centre hold?

CHAPTER 13

'EVERYONE'S MOTHER-IN-LAW'

The bomb at the Conservative conference in Brighton in October 1984 was a shattering reminder of the mortality of politicians. It left all who were there with poignant memories. Two nights before Norman Tebbit and his wife, Margaret, received injuries from which she will never recover, I sat with him on a settee outside his room while she went to bed. We were discussing the conference, and as always his conversation ranged from the hyperbolically outrageous to the quietly commonsensical. As I left around 1 a.m. he delivered a final grinning rebuke: 'You've run me into trouble again; I'll have to wake up Margaret to get into the room now.' In his more relaxed moments Norman Tebbit has the wistful charm of Stan Laurel.

Less than an hour after the explosion I interviewed the Prime Minister at Brighton police headquarters. She did not then know there had been serious casualties, and was concerned to get her 'business as usual' message across to the nation at breakfast-time. It was nearly four hours later, talking to Lord Whitelaw outside the *Today* caravan-studio, that I learned how bleak the casualty list was becoming. By the time we had finished the Nine O'Clock News that evening, eaten a hasty supper and left for London at 11 p.m., the whole misery of what had happened was sinking in. A few yards from our studios firemen were still digging, with fading hope of finding anyone else alive. You could read how forlorn that hope was in the face of an MP who was staying overnight because a friend was still missing. Political conferences would never be the same again, for their informality is now greatly diminished by security precautions.

Just a couple of weeks before the Brighton tragedy the Prime Minister undertook her annual autumn reshuffle. Eleven months into her second government Jim Prior had told her he had been long enough in Northern Ireland. He would have taken another post, but only a more senior one than he had already held in Edward Heath's government and hers. Geoffrey Howe, Nigel Lawson and Leon Brittan, only recently into the three great offices of state, could not be moved. Prior made it easier for the Prime Minister by saying he had no intention of leading a backbench revolt. She made no substantial offer, and her most effective critic within the Cabinet left office, became chairman of GEC, and decided to leave politics at the next election.

His resignation letter expressed sadness at leaving colleagues with whom he had developed lasting friendships: 'We came into the House together, and have worked together ever since, not always in complete harmony, but with a frankness that is characteristic of both of us.' The Prime Minister replied: 'I take your point about frankness. That's what Cabinets are for, and lively discussions usually lead to good decisions.' This might seem a far cry from the 1979 Kenneth Harris interview and the era of 'not wasting any time having internal arguments', but even five years on that phrase from the interview came nearer to reality. Margaret Thatcher still believed her job was to choose a course, give a lead, and not let dissension in the crew divert the captain from the mark. Her letter contained a warm tribute to Prior's work in Northern Ireland, although he had sometimes felt she was frustrating his policies there. The Prime Minister included in her tribute his wife, Jane, whose opinion of her has always remained well short of unqualified admiration. Politics is not always as straightforward as it seems.

Douglas Hurd succeeded Prior in Northern Ireland, but the most significant new appointment was David Young, chairman of the Manpower Services Commission, who became Minister without Portfolio then, and was made Employment Secretary the following year. He had no faith in Government macro-economic measures against unemployment, preferring supply-side measures bearing directly on the labour market. People must be prepared to move from manufacturing to service trades, he declared, echoing one of the Prime Minister's own obsessions at the time. But although unemployment was the issue which, according to the opinion polls, worried voters most, the dominant issue for many politicians halfway through Margaret Thatcher's second term was her style of leadership. Her name was synonymous with the revolutionary form of Conservatism for which she proselytised. This was true in a way that it had not been true of any recent Prime Minister. Thatcherism, yes. But Macmillanism? Douglas-Homeism? Heathism? Surely not.

The reason for this pre-eminence is what her admirers call Mrs Thatcher's certitude and detractors describe as stubbornness. By 1985 she was at the peak of her political powers: she had grown steadily in parliamentary skill, seizing and demolishing critical points with demonic energy, hammering home her own case with no trace of doubt. In her Cabinet she had all but rooted out dissent and finally had an administration in her own image. Her self-confidence as a broadcasting propagandist was unsurpassed. Saving death or ill-health nothing could now prevent her leading the Conservatives into a third election. Yet a sense of her political fragility occasionally creeps into unexpected mouths. A fervent admirer on her staff said: 'She enjoys a lot of respect for her ability, but not a lot of affection. If things go wrong, she wouldn't have a lot to rely on.'

That remark was made before the storms of 1986, beginning with the Westland affair, broke around her. The criticisms of her took many forms. One minister complained that, with her own creations – he seemed to stop just short of saying 'creatures' – in the senior jobs, she lacked independent advice. Another worried about her habit of arguing *ad hominem* rather than logically. He dismissed any suggestion that he might be complaining of a difference in style natural to a woman; with a shout of 'Chauvinism!', he declared vehemently: 'There are dozens of blue-stockings with Margaret Thatcher's qualifications who would squirm at her method of conducting an argument.' When asked for an example, he said the PM would see a Whitehall paper presented to a Cabinet committee, glance at the civil servant's initials on it, and exclaim: 'Ah, that's Snodgrass. I knew him at Education. He's unsound, definitely not one of us.' Again that phrase which so offended Francis Pym.

Another anxiety in Tory mental filing-cabinets came under the heading 'Margaret/*hubris*'. Her occasional Churchillian echoes caused shudders. One backbencher said: 'It's all right for other people to draw such parallels, but when you start believing your own . . .' A senior minister drew a parallel with Harold Macmillan after his 1959 election triumph which he found worrying. Even with lieutenants as talented as Butler, Heath, Maudling and Macleod, each with an independent party base, Macmillan had floated so far above his party that he had dissipated its energy and his government died of inanition.

Despite such criticisms, Margaret Thatcher's hold on the Conservative Party was more secure than ever. She worked hard at this, although sometimes her attempts at the human touch were spoiled by an all-too-human weakness. After one all-night sitting her bleary-eyed troops were pleased to see her arrive at their breakfast table in the Commons Tea-Room. It was an imaginative gesture that not many Prime Ministers would have thought of, but instead of flattering them by listening to their views she could not stop herself giving them hers.

As is the case with prime ministers, her frequent deeds of kindness – inquiries about sick wives, adjurations to get more sleep, ability to remember children's names and educational progress – do not go unremembered, but Mrs Thatcher's deficient sense of humour is an acknowledged handicap. She once looked incredulously at a television interviewer who was asking about the atmosphere between political opponents and said: 'Do you ever say to Mr Kinnock: "You did very well today, Neil"?' Mrs Thatcher replied tartly: 'No, I've never had occasion to say that.'

What keeps coming up in colleagues' conversation about her is her attitude to those with contrary views. Admirers maintain she likes to be joshed by subordinates and to be stood up to by other ministers. The story is told of a diminutive ambassador of a minor country, coming for a first meeting, who was expected by her staff to be totally overawed. Instead, he dived straight into an argument with her. They both enjoyed themselves greatly. But a Tory MP puts a brutally contrasting view: 'She's like everyone's mother-in-law, talking and not listening. [Apologies to half my readers, but MPs *do* sometimes talk like that.] She doesn't hear adverse views unless they are more or less shouted. Of our 400 MPs, 100 are total loyalists [a less benevolent phrase was used], 200 will support her so long as she delivers the goods. Of the remaining 100, a majority would like rid of her, only they know that's impossible, while a small minority would like some time to try a plot.'

That remark was made in the autumn of 1984, and the 'plot' has still not occurred. Margaret Thatcher has held doubting Conservatives in line by a mixture of unrelenting leadership and a formidable reputation as a vote-getter. But it is not only the open critics who think her revolution is not permanent. Quite early in her first government, a minister whose loyalty is not open to doubt astonished me by saying that, when she passed from the political scene in the fulness of time, the Conservative Party would be 'as if she had never been': in other words, that the waters would close over Thatcherism, and that historical Conservatism would flow towards a sea, a political Ganges or Thames. In his view, the Conservative Party is dedicated to the proper objective of seeking and retaining power, and therefore struggles constantly to be regarded as a party of the whole nation, impatient of all dogma.

The criticism of Margaret Thatcher from within Conservative ranks may result simply from the passage of time. In modern politics leaders seem to have a shorter shelf-life than before. A junior minister in Harold Wilson's government once astonished his opponents with an assurance that when his Rt Hon. Friend formed his fourth administration, he would still only be as old as Mr Gladstone was when he formed his first. Or was it his second? The details scarcely matter. The point is that this piece of Question-time rodomontade was based on a fallacy common among politicians: that the present is likely to stretch unchanged into the future. Harold Wilson himself said to me in 1966: 'Ted and I are going to be facing each other for as long as Gladstone and Disraeli. If you don't relish the prospect, you'd better emigrate.' Finding the prospect less daunting than some – for as a boy I enjoyed reading about the long-running Gladstone and Disraeli show – I never took passage for Philadelphia. It proved prudent to save the fare, for within ten years Wilson was at work on his memoirs, and Heath had been painfully removed from his leadership by the Thatcher revolution.

Much has changed since the days of Gladstone and Disraeli. Newspapers today may not devote millions of words a year to reporting speeches in Midlothian and elsewhere, but they do sell millions of copies a day that expose most aspects of politicians' public and private lives to the vulgar gaze. In the days of Gladstone and Disraeli many of the vulgar neither read newspapers nor, indeed, had the right to vote. Then there is radio and television. When Franklin Roosevelt mastered the wireless, the new medium seemed ideal for fireside chats from the President to his adoring public. Even television – in its early days when Michael Foot and Bob Boothby shone intellectually, in black-and-white, in our living-rooms – seemed likely to win politicians great loyalty. But the iron law of politics is that nothing ever turns out quite as expected.

Press, radio and television have all changed beyond recognition in the past quarter-century. On the positive side they put the people and policies of government under a microscope beyond the dreams of the nineteenth century. More negatively, their new forms, and particularly the insatiable appetites of television, render even admired political figures more quickly shop-soiled. The same set of ideas can be repackaged just so often without inducing boredom.

Nor can the strains of modern government be ignored. Mrs Thatcher's instinct to intervene in decisions and her puritan work ethic both add to the strain that any prime minister undergoes. Gone are the days when Arthur Balfour (according to Churchill) could stay in bed till lunchtime, 'un-approachable, transacting business, reading, writing, ruminating . . . he seemed carefree, even at the head of a tottering government, even in the darkest hours of war'. Gone, too, is the possibility of conducting political leadership from Biarritz. Nowadays state papers have to be read far into the early hours; there are Cabinet committees to chair soon after breakfast; and a gruelling day before the next supply of red boxes.

Since the Thatchers bought a house in Dulwich, speculation about how long she would want to go on has increased. With her usual political caution she has detected the danger of becoming a lame-duck leader, so has inserted the thought that she wants to continue into the nineties. To find the answer, it may be better to look not only at the likely result of the next election, at the economic entrails, at who Mrs Thatcher would like to succeed to the Conservative leadership, but also at what is called the Denis Factor. On this theory there would come a time when Denis Thatcher would indicate, courteously but firmly, that he had done his stint for the Conservative Party and wanted a quieter life, and that this would be more influential with the Prime Minister than anything else.

The sterling crisis of January 1985 reminded the Prime Minister and Nigel Lawson that this water-walled bulwark can never be as secure and confident from foreign purposes as Shakespeare imagined. The markets did not like Britain's economic situation. According to political or economic taste the villain might be a strong dollar, oil-price instability, public borrowing, the miners' strike, run-down infrastructure, or interest rates. A combination of sterling's troubles and continued backbench rebel-lion left Nigel Lawson with a grotty choice. One minister said he could either risk being left as the boy on the burning deck, with everyone else fleeing from the rigours of his Medium Term Financial Strategy, which would be carrying conviction politics beyond the threshold of stubborn-ness; or he could bend subtly to please Tory critics. Lawson seemed – as

Peel once said of himself – to lack 'the patience to listen to the sentiments of individuals whom it is equally imprudent to neglect and an intolerable bore to consult'.

The Chancellor had had a miserable six months. His conference speech had been a failure, which both hurt and harmed him. As the Treasury grip tightened on public spending, and with few painless cuts now to be made, the scar-tissue began to show. The pound's troubles damaged his reputation for omnicompetence. As pre-Budget speculation about VAT on books, newspapers or children's clothes, or taxation of pensions, set Conservative MPs' letter-boxes rattling with protest, some wondered whether they really wanted a radical Chancellor.

In the event the 1985 Budget, although it was judged to have made any genuine fall in unemployment before the next election improbable, was by no means apolitical. Lawson remained the High Priest of Thatcherite economics, but he sniffed the warning smoke from his back benches and postponed his ambition to be a radical in tax matters. No more VAT changes in this Parliament; no interference with occupational pensions. The Prime Minister liked the Budget, though she may not have relished Julian Critchley's joke about the Government's radicalism having stumbled over its own middle-class supporters.

Lawson had bound the Prime Minister to him, both through his political flexibility and his adherence to a tight borrowing requirement, the criterion of the new orthodoxy. After this Budget she would find it hard to dismiss him, even though the Party was not sure that it loved either the orthodoxy or the Chancellor. He seemed to have provided a new safety belt, in the form of exceptionally large reserves in each year between then and the general election. Perhaps he recalled a couple of amusing articles Harold Wilson, then Shadow Chancellor, wrote during the Macmillan government. These explained the Electoral Cycle. Wilson maintained that governments could keep themselves in office by careful manipulation of demand management – stop–go – so that goodies came in election year and blotted from the public's fickle memory the horrors that had gone before. The size of Nigel Lawson's contingency reserves for the rest of this Parliament suggested that he intended to wear the belt of Thatcherite orthodoxy and the braces of flexible response, to keep the Government's trousers safely in place.

Tory sceptics took this flexibility as a belated acknowledgement by the Treasury of the imprecision of their forecasting. Even Treasury ministers have shared this scepticism. Joel Barnett, the Labour Chief Secretary, wrote that he had some experience as an accountant of juggling with figures, but that he had discovered he was a babe in arms when it came 'to the sort of sophisticated massaging and fudging I learned as Chief Secretary: it is a case of changing this or that "assumption" and *abracadabra!* – the public-sector borrowing requirement is about the figure you first thought of.'

His chief, Denis Healey, was equally sceptical. He used to greet his statisticians as 'entrail-gazers' or 'soothsayers'. His doubts arose from personal experience during the war. He was injured in training, so was given as light duty the task of counting the soldiers who boarded or left trains at a railway station. His side hurt, so he did not feel like running up and down the platform and decided the best way to gather statistics was to ask the ticket collector to do half the job. The future Chancellor then made up his part of the statistics. He subsequently found that the ticket collector did the same thing, so he has never had undue reverence for statistics since.

Nigel Lawson's freedom of manoeuvre increased also because of the Government's privatisation programme. The sale of assets like British Telecom gave him more money in his books because the accounting conventions allow such asset sales to be classed as 'negative public expenditure'. When Lord Stockton, in a characteristic coup-de-théâtre on the first day television cameras were allowed into the House of Lords, described this as selling the family silver, ministers could only smile through gritted teeth.

It was a bad summer for Conservatives in 1985, with third places in the Brecon by-election and some opinion polls, but the Prime Minister's end-of-term speech to her backbenchers followed Marshal Foch in the darkest days of the Great War: 'Mon centre cède, ma droite recule, situation excellente. J'attaque.' She admonished faint hearts to remember 1984's gloom, with the miners' strike raging, public order at risk, the pound slipping. Now, she claimed, the economy was stronger than since she took office, and she gave them a list of Opposition targets to attack: defence, union ballots, workers' shareholdings for Labour; disunity and defence for the Alliance.

She also revealed how she planned to square the circle of controlling public expenditure, while rejecting Opposition charges that she was cutting services. The buzz-word was 'relevant'. She planned to assert her priorities – defence, crime, the NHS, pensions and cutting income tax – and take the credit. The Keep Calm faction was fortified; Old Hands rubbed their noses and murmured: 'Micawber lives, and politics rules, ok?' Margaret was, after all, a politican who wanted to win a third term more than she craved a martyr's fate at some Friedmanite stake. But the presentation was difficult. While the Prime Minister talked of tax cuts and Norman Tebbit chastised the media for mistaking what he called 'planned reallocation of expenditure' for spending cuts, the Treasury was still playing its more austere tunes. Bruised by January's sterling crisis, the Knights of Great George Street were still opening their hair-shirts to beat on their chests a hymn of financial rectitude. Pity the poor Chancellor, who has simultaneously to address high-spending ministers and low-thinking markets, not to mention wage-earners and businessmen, housewives and taxpayers, all of whom would be transformed, one day in the next two years, into voters. No wonder the trumpet occasionally gives an uncertain sound.

The reshuffle in 1985 was a careful balancing act. Conservative canvassers in the local elections had caused alarm by bringing back the whispered message that on the doorsteps Margaret Thatcher was no longer the assured vote-winner of 1983. The Cabinet was too much in her own image now, for although she had never had a Night of the Long Knives like Macmillan, her first term had been a Parliament of the Long Knives. But in 1985 caution prevailed. True believers were still in charge of the Treasury, Employment, and Trade and Industry (where Leon Brittan replaced Norman Tebbit, who took over the party chairmanship). The more independent spirits – Peter Walker, John Biffen and Michael Heseltine – remained isolated in posts where the Prime Minister felt she had their measure. But Douglas Hurd, Ted Heath's former political secretary, who had entered the Cabinet just a year earlier, was promoted to Home Secretary, and Kenneth Baker, Kenneth Clarke and John MacGregor (who was once in charge of Heath's office) joined the Cabinet. Patrick Jenkin and Peter Rees were sacked. The new men, because they owed their preferment to Mrs Thatcher, were unlikely to attain quickly the collective influence that a like-minded group in her first Cabinet – Whitelaw, Carrington, Soames, Prior, Pym, Walker, Gilmour and St John-Stevas – had. MacGregor was not, any longer, a wet. Yet the Prime Minister had made her gesture.

By the autumn statistical battle had been joined on unemployment. The Government claimed Britain was producing more new jobs than the rest of Europe put together, though not yet enough to match our demographic trends (more young people joining the labour market than were leaving it on retirement). The Opposition said most of these new jobs were only part-time, that the figures were being doctored by special schemes, and that the dole queues were not diminishing. Renewed rioting provoked controversy about how much unemployment, especially among young black people, was an influence. Even before these inner-city troubles ministers had turned their minds more to public order, because of disturbances during the miners' strike and at football matches. The Prime Minister had quietly determined it was in her interests to diversify the political debate and to concentrate less single-mindedly on the economy, where she could not be sure whether she was winning or losing votes. Anxiety over aggro and arson shown on television offered her the cue.

Mrs Thatcher regarded Leon Brittan, Home Secretary since 1983, as a competent, even brilliant administrator. But she accepted what Lord Whitelaw had been telling her for some time: that he was not at his best in front of cameras, where a Home Secretary spends even more time than such doughty boxophiles as Norman Tebbit, Neil Kinnock or David Owen. Douglas Hurd was a more emollient public performer, with a safe pair of hands, and therefore more suited to handling such newsworthy subjects as drugs, football troubles, inner-city riots, even animal experiments. He was also offered the poisoned chalice of Sunday opening of shops, a subject he quickly disposed of – whether by subconscious intent or not – by losing the Commons vote. Tom King replaced Hurd in Ulster, making way for Lord Young at Employment.

Douglas Hurd was the Cabinet's enigma. He was a Heathman who had made the transition with slow dignity from the wilderness of his new leader's frown to the Cabinet table. But where did he stand politically now? The disputed relationship between deprivation and rioting divided Peter Walker and Michael Heseltine from the Thatcherites. Hurd took the stern view. He maximised Labour's embarrassment over some in its new generation of local politicians who took an anti-police line, including one who marked a policeman's murder by proclaiming that the police had been given 'a bloody good hiding'. Neil Kinnock accused Hurd of dodging his own responsibility to seek the real causes of the riots. It seemed that the 1985–6 session might be dominated by Home Office issues, and that party stalwarts were in belligerent mood. John Biffen coined the happy aphorism that MPs had returned from their summer break eager to 'beat their ploughshares into swords'. As it turned out, the Opposition were given more exciting material to chew on.

In October 1985 Westland was still in the future and Tories were encouraged by a partial recovery by the Prime Minister from her springtime unpopularity. The MP who first alerted me to criticism on the doorsteps now revealed that no such iron had entered into the souls of party activists. The Tory army marches on its stomach, and in that stomach is wine and cheese. With a shudder of retrospective anguish this MP recalled that, during the edgy weeks when politicians return from beaches, grouse moors or party conferences, he had consumed more political wine and cheese than hot dinners. The Tory rank and file, he asserted with relief, still began every conversation with the words: 'Of course, *she's* marvellous . . .', even if some added the minatory thought: 'But *you* know the policy's got to change, don't you?'

Noel Coward once described Churchill as 'a great man with more Achilles' heels than are usual in a biped'. Some Labour people hoped the description applied to Margaret Thatcher, but even doubting Tories now believed she would lead them into the next election, and most thought she would do better for them than anyone else who could possibly get into the job in time. But she and Norman Tebbit, then as near to an *alter ego* as such an individualist could tolerate, continued to believe there were few votes for a radical government in Quiet Life policies. They decided to follow their star in persuading people they would be better off if they did more for themselves rather than relying on the Government; if more of the economy was in private hands; if the individual citizen made more of his own choices than the make of his car or the destination of his summer holiday. Both

Prime Minister and Party Chairman wanted to fight in 1987 or 1988 on this Luther-like stance: Hier stehe ich; ich kann nicht anders.

This sent shivers through what Right-wing Tories called 'the nervous Nellies'. Even some senior ministers thought it was a high-risk strategy, and did not feel it would be followed to the bitter end. Murmuring behind hands continued: 'All is not as it seems.' Politics is often about where you place your emphasis. The present Government has always taken credit for running a tight ship, for controlling and, where necessary, reducing public spending. But now it began to realise that there was potentially great political damage in charges by the Opposition and pressure groups that it was cutting the NHS, education, housebuilding and other desirable services. So the emphasis changed. No U-turns, of course, but a little more flexibility, a little less radicalism between now and the election.

John Biffen, so often the philosopher of dissent in this Cabinet, warned his party about the criticism that it had no genuine interest in schools or health, was passive about unemployment, oblivious of urban decay, and had enthusiasm only for income-tax cuts to help the better off. He called this 'an absurd caricature', but said it would be believed unless they themselves presented 'the true face of social Toryism'. All this was in the hallowed tradition of coded dissent, but it went down like a lead balloon with Cabinet radicals. Yet Biffen was merely arguing publicly what Whitelaw, Walker, Heseltine, Fowler, Younger, Hurd, Baker and Clarke would urge in Cabinet: that they must make a virtue of their spending as well as their economies; and, by implication, where more needed to be spent the money must be found.

Politically, however, the Conservative mood was for greater unity. During 1985 they had looked into the abyss of unfavourable opinion polls and reduced public support for the Prime Minister, and they did not like what they saw. One side-effect of having the largest parliamentary majority since Attlee's forty years before was that many Tory MPs in marginal seats had the strongest reason to put personal interest in retaining these seats ahead of any personal reservations about Government policy. All they asked of the Government was that it took no electoral risks, and avoided banana skins like the plague.

That was before the Westland affair.

CHAPTER 14

KINNOCK CLIMBS
HIS SNOWDON

In the first two years of his leadership, Neil Kinnock sometimes seemed to be on the same impossible roller-coaster that had destroyed Michael Foot. After the shortest of honeymoons he had been plunged into three apparently insoluble dilemmas: the miners' strike, the rows involving far Left Labour councils, and the grumbling dispute with Militant. Yet early public opinion polls suggested people were willing to give the new leader a chance. So in November 1983, after brief courtesies, the Prime Minister engaged him in battle at their first question-time. Kinnock asked what was the purpose of having a Star Chamber as part of the public-spending survey: 'Can it be nothing more than a clumsy cover-up for the divisions that exist in the Cabinet, and the indecisions that exist in the Prime Minister?'

The lady was not having that, but her problem was how to handle her new opponent. She knew his inexperience worried some Labour people, and this thought must have been bubbling around in her subconscious as she awaited his attack, for it burst forth in this remarkable passage in Hansard:

> I appreciate that the Rt Hon. Gentleman has asked a *well-studied supplementary question*, but had he consulted *his Rt Hon. Friends* and colleagues, he would have known that *all* public expenditure annual surveys cause problems. That is well known, and to refer to my noble friend, Viscount Whitelaw, as a 'Star Chamber' *carries no weight at all*.

In the italicised phrases the Prime Minister was (1) implying that the new boy's question reeked of midnight oil, thus showing over-eagerness; (2) reminding MPs that he'd only just been made a Privy Councillor (Rt Hon.) on becoming Leader of the Opposition, and therefore had no ministerial experience; (3) suggesting that, unlike her and Hattersley and Healey, he hadn't been living with Public Expenditure Surveys for years past; and (4) calling him a lightweight. Their relationship had begun in the querulous snappiness that was to continue throughout the Parliament.

The shelves of the Commons Library groan with blue books in which committee after committee asserts that the object of Prime Minister's question-time is to extract information. But everyone knows that what most MPs really want is a great political dog-fight, in which Government and Opposition leaders seek to damage each other, to the benefit of their egos, their supporters' morale and, in time, their standing in the polls. Plus a bit of fun.

A Leader of the Opposition who has not been Prime Minister has a problem in establishing himself at question-time, not least because his opponent always has the last word. (No, this does not apply only to women Prime Ministers.) The two crowded quarter-hours on Tuesday and Thursday are now more hit-and-miss than ever, because a rowdy House makes it difficult to hear. The new Speaker, Jack Weatherill, was uncertain in his early days how often he ought to call Kinnock. Below the gangway an entirely separate battle was going on between Labour's Left, led by Dennis Skinner, and the SDP MPs whom they had tortured verbally before 1983, when there was no electoral mandate for the new party alignment. The Alliance were now beginning, in the words of a British Lions rugby captain, to 'get their retaliation in first'. But Tory back-benchers, who like their diamonds rough, were on Skinner's side in these tussles.

Neil Kinnock was advised not to rely on question-time to establish himself at Westminster, but he made only two set-piece speeches in his first year. One, on NHS cuts, was successful. The other was in what John Biffen, the Leader of the House, called the end-of-term 'up-market knockabout'. Few modern orators succeed both in the House and on platforms outside. Even when Harold Wilson was the darling of West-minster, in his wittiest period as Shadow Chancellor, his conference speeches were not outstanding. Michael Foot, who was good on the platform, lacked the precision to shine at the despatch box. Nye Bevan could handle both House and public meeting: at the height of Bevan's powers Churchill once ordered his whips to stop Tory backbenchers interrupting him because he scored points by making fools of them. When Kinnock made his end-of-term speech a number of Conservatives were willing to be foolish to his advantage. But Kinnock had been much criticised for prolixity, so that day he had memorised a briefer text and ploughed through it, refusing to allow the interventions that might have brought the speech alive, rattled by a well-drilled Tory fusillade of 'Scargill'.

This was another way in which Kinnock suffered from not having held office. He had only been at the despatch box before as Shadow Education Secretary. Unfortunately the traditional training method of the British textile industry, 'standing next to Nellie', is only available to those in the lower reaches of politics. Neil Kinnock was having to learn at the top, and as many a managing director's son has discovered, this can be a painful experience. Yet the balance sheet on his leadership as he entered 1984 was favourable. An opinion poll at the turn of the year suggested he had already restored Labour to a position hard on the heels of the Conservatives, with the Alliance far behind.

His friends believed he had earned his good luck by the common sense and vigour with which he had tackled a daunting task. Government misfortunes at home and abroad extended his honeymoon with the public. Labour's new-born sense of fraternity produced better results in opinion polls and in European elections in June 1984, so it might become habitual, with Labour people learning again to like one another. Many MPs who had not voted for Kinnock began to think he would prove a stronger and more effective leader than they had bargained for. But as that shrewd observer of the Westminster scene, Anthony Trollope, once observed, 'a man is only as strong as his weakest moment'. Soon enough Kinnock would have to turn from apprentice into journeyman, to sort out the perplexing differences on policy and in tone that still divided Labour. It was then that the public would judge whether his learning curve was rising sharply enough.

The first, impossible, hurdle Neil Kinnock faced, less than six months after he became leader, was the miners' strike. This did both him and the Labour Party great damage. Kinnock had an atavistic affection for an industry in which his family, friends and constituents worked, but he disliked and distrusted Arthur Scargill, and hated the way in which the miners were being led. The dislike was reciprocated. Kinnock's loyalties were divided, and it showed in an uncertain performance.

The two most agonising issues were the way in which the strike began and the violence which disfigured it. Kinnock was hesitant in handling both. Scargill's failure to hold a ballot vote before calling the strike eventually led to its defeat, and Kinnock was blamed for not making his disapproval known early enough. Mass picketing led to bruising encounters between strikers and working miners and police. Half-way through the dispute, as Kinnock gloomily noted how Labour's recovery had been retarded, he also observed that from time to time his party's popularity took an unexpected turn for the better. When television showed police horses charging pickets, the public mood changed in his favour. It changed also when Labour's energy spokesman, Stan Orme, was mediating in the dispute. But overall the strike was extremely bad news for Labour.

Kinnock believed that, if the strike had not taken place, Labour's standing in the polls a year after his election might have been in the low forties, five or six points ahead of the Government. In the event it had still not reached that level two years into his leadership. His own popularity also suffered from this unrewarding baptism of fire. While the Prime Minister, David Steel and David Owen all saw their personal ratings gaining or holding steady, a slide in Kinnock's damaged Labour morale. His own mood remained ebullient, though that is perhaps as much a statement about his own personality as about external circumstances. He sometimes joked that, if some of the polls were to be believed, Labour would race ahead if he were not its leader. He still hoped his political convalescence after the strike ended would be short. That hope was fulfilled, for public memories are short and those of the strike seemed to fade with remarkable speed; but it was damaging to him because, at an already delicate moment in its history, Labour was deprived of a desperately needed year for recovery from the débâcle of 1983.

This was a year in which Kinnock ought to have established himself as alternative Prime Minister, and built on the new mood of political realism and on the appetite for power that his first months as leader had re-created in the Party. The end of the strike left him with as little as two years till polling day, and with a Snowdon to climb. He had to achieve another revival in support, with a trade union movement that was badly demoralised and divided by the miners' defeat. Union leaders were angry with each other because of support given or withheld during the strike: lorry drivers and others had ignored their leaders and continued to work. Len Murray, the TUC general secretary, retired early, ill and in despair of achieving the new mood he knew was essential. In impossible conditions his successor, Norman Willis, struggled to find his feet and create a new style.

Kinnock had positive achievements in the early years of his leadership, however. He circumvented the quarrelsome forum of the National Executive Committee by switching much of the policy-making to joint working parties in which Labour MPs had a substantial voice. In any event the NEC was now more manageable, since Tony Benn and Eric Heffer, Kinnock's two principal critics there, had been removed from the chairmanships of the key committees. Many Labour people had come to regard Benn as a symbol of their troubles during the past decade, yet it was a perverse reading of his character and actions to think that securing the Labour leadership was his motivation. Had that been so he would have done better in the early seventies to cling to the Wilsonist political position he once held, on Labour's instinctive Centre-Left. Instead, his aim through fifteen years had been to achieve an irreversible shift in the Labour Party itself, as well as in British society, as the largely Bennite programme of 1973 had proclaimed. Although it was a shifting alliance of activists and apparatchiks that had brought about the revolution in the Labour Party which led to the breakaway by the Social Democrats, Tony Benn was the figure round whom they revolved. He was deeply hurt in Labour's bleakest years after 1981 to hear himself and his policies described as 'loony'. He would say sadly that commentators (and colleagues) who used such language might, in a different atmosphere, have treated him with the respect his seniority deserved. He attributed this change in his treatment to resentment against his own anti-media campaign.

What made Benn a difficult team-mate was a streak of blinkered independence that forced him to follow his own convictions – critics said the star of his ambition – well beyond the limit of prudence imposed by the modern party system. His Labour opponents – and the phrase included, although it did not reflect the venom of, most leading Labour figures –

maintained that the course he had taken had done their party immeasurable damage.

A fierce struggle took place within Labour's ranks between those like Benn, Scargill, Ken Livingstone and Dennis Skinner who rejected 'revisionism' and believed in the mobilisation of the working class; and the Labour leadership, which saw the electoral battle in less ideological terms. Indeed, the word 'electoral' begs a question and entangles us in another argument: whether Labour's counter-counter-revolution against Margaret Thatcher's brand of Conservatism could be conducted solely, or even principally, by parliamentary means. One shadow minister, impatient of the far Left's behaviour, argued that the real division was between those who really wanted a Labour Government again, and those who in their hearts preferred a Labour Opposition and the unblemished atmosphere of the wilderness. In this division there is no doubt where Neil Kinnock's instincts lie. He has no time for what he regards as daft demands for revolutionary leadership. These became common during the miners' strike and as the row between some Labour councils and Whitehall grew more bitter.

In his New Year message for 1985 Kinnock scoffed at 'false promises of dramatic action that might sound thrilling, but will look tawdry and self-indulgent when lack of power or support prevents them from being carried out'. He is against general strikes, illegal action by councils, the belief that laws can be changed except through Parliament. In this he represents the views of most Labour MPs and most people likely to consider voting Labour. The Kinnock revolution within the Labour Party was un-ashamedly a parliamentary one. So while he fought his week-by-week battles on the miners' strike and various council disputes, Kinnock was trying to educate Labour in his own ethos of democratic socialism. Simul-taneously the rows over Militant, reselection and Labour's other constitu-tional diversions were subplots in what could still be regarded only as a political tragi-comedy.

The 1984 party conference had demonstrated, yet again, that Labour's is the most unpredictable of all these assemblies, because of its democratic intentions. Some would write 'democratic structure', others 'democratic pretensions', but the middle way is most just: Labour does *intend* to be democratic, and its conference certainly does matter. The block vote is an unsatisfactory instrument of democracy, yet it grows with apparent inevitability from Labour's history and federal structure, with trade unions forming the original nucleus, and individual membership as an afterthought. Neil Kinnock learned painfully that year how conservative a party Labour is. He wanted to extend participatory democracy by intro-ducing, just permissively, the principle of 'one member, one vote' in the reselection of MPs, which might have taken the power from sometimes wildly unrepresentative caucuses. But this tentative step was complicated by the wish to preserve the rights of local union branches. The days when many Labour seats had been the rotten borough of a major union were sliding swiftly into history. Kinnock himself is a symbol of that passing, for as a young man he seized Bedwellty, in the heart of the Welsh coalfield (and the predecessor of his present constituency, Islwyn), from the National Union of Mineworkers.

But 'one member, one vote' perished, not through democratic decision, but in a Byzantine confusion in which all motions were defeated in a bewildering battle of ambuscades, forays, sallies and escalades by the leader's friends and enemies, all exercising their military skills. A Labour leader no longer enjoys an easy ability to fix a conference decision by judicious massaging of elbows and egos.

The nearest to a mid-term test of national electoral opinion came in the shire council polling in May 1985. Rival interpretation of these results, alas, left the prospects for the next general election looking no clearer. Lies, damned lies, and statistics indeed! In the first twenty-four hours detailed voting figures for the whole country were not available. This provided the media with headaches and the political parties with an irresistible – and unresisted – opportunity for selective statistics-mongering. By Friday evening all three believed, or said they believed, that they had done well, and consequently deserved the prize of higher public support in succeeding opinion polls.

A few things were clear. The Conservatives had lost the unquestioned political dominance of 1983, and for the first time Margaret Thatcher was being widely criticised on election doorsteps. The Alliance had blasted the hopes of opponents who thought it a transitory phenomenon; it was now well established as a third force in British politics, though it looked no nearer than before to replacing either of the older parties. Labour, although these elections did not include its most favourable electoral test-beds, the big cities, Scotland and London, did surprisingly well. It had recovered from the 1983 disaster and from the threat of slow extinction, but it still had much to do if it was to construct a reliable winning constituency of voters. Nevertheless Labour had most to be cheerful, or at least relieved, about for it was firmly re-established, in share of votes, as runner-up to the Tories.

Labour was encouraged particularly by its revival in what had seemed, after 1983, to be the party's Southern wastelands. The Tory vote in the South dropped by 12.1%, Labour's rose by 9.4, the Alliance's by 2.6. After a general election in which it had been almost wiped out in the South apart from London, Labour now believed it could be a national party again. But the hot breath of the Alliance still blew uncomfortably on its neck, and many Conservative MPs in the South were still more nervous about the Alliance than about Labour.

Neil Kinnock was irritated that the Alliance had been more successful than Labour in having their interpretation of the results accepted, for this had the effect of improving the Alliance's standing in the polls. Alliance spokesmen pointed simply to their number of new councillors, though they still had only about half as many as the Tories or Labour. Kinnock accused the media of 'following the Alliance into a fantasy world', and quoted instead changes in percentage share of the poll, which showed Labour gaining heavily, the Conservatives falling heavily, and the Alliance vote drifting slightly lower.

The complexity of interpretation was confirmed when the former Conservative chairman, Cecil Parkinson, suggested that Conservative Central Office might have taken the wind out of Labour's sails by comparing the results not with the general election in 1983 but with the 1981 council elections, and delivering one insistent message: Labour under Kinnock had slipped back from its local government high-water mark under Michael Foot. Parkinson's moral, of course, was that Labour's prospects had not improved; but a House of Commons Library projection of the results suggested that, on the 'very rough' estimates possible of likely parliamentary gains and losses, Labour would have gained 82 seats against the Alliance's 25.

How well was Kinnock's attempt to revolutionise the Labour Party going? Like so much in politics the answer depended on when you started. Measured against its standing when he became leader, the answer in mid-1985 was 'remarkably well'; but compared with previous Oppositions in mid-term it was 'rather badly'. The three-party split changed the mathematics and made judgements more tentative. What did look quite silly by 1985 was the 'Labour is finished' school of journalism that flourished after the 1983 disaster. Labour had tiptoed through some well-advertised marshes since then. Reselection of MPs had at least avoided the crop of spectacular casualties that had been predicted, although some moderate or ageing MPs decided not to stand again, and the complexion of a future Parliamentary Labour Party would be more Left-wing.

Militant, with five of its leading figures expelled during Michael Foot's leadership, had run into that logical quagmire which engulfs humourless, unelectable factions in an elective system. Labour's Right traditionally takes the view, originating from Machiavelli, that 'men must be either pampered or crushed, because they can get revenge for small injuries, but not for grievous ones'. On this analysis, to expel only five Militant leaders was to stir up a hornets' nest; some Right-wingers would have liked Kinnock to abandon all caution and crush the Tendency. Militant was still to earn Labour much unfavourable publicity, and its Trotskyist affection for resort to 'capitalist courts' forced Labour's new general secretary, Larry Whitty, to advise the NEC to be circumspect in expulsions. But local Labour people were alerted to Militant, and its influence seemed, though still troublesome, to be past its peak.

In 1985 Labour MPs who had once despaired at their Party's follies became more cheerful. A shadow minister who had contemplated leaving politics said he now believed Labour had a valuable election asset in Margaret Thatcher; his own supporters, he reported, would end internal strife in order to replace her. Jim Callaghan, celebrating forty years in Parliament, claimed her attitudes might give Labour its largest victory since 1945. This optimism might be premature, but reasons for the change of mood were evident. These were not just the favourable movements in the polls and the Government's greater propensity to stumble. Within Labour's ranks the constituencies began to react against Militant and other far Left groups, a chastened mood developed on the Livingstone wing of local government, and some suspected Neil Kinnock had been more right in his reservations about the miners' strike than they cared to admit. They also began to think the Alliance would hurt the Conservatives more than Labour. One insider murmured enigmatically: 'The Alliance is our can-opener in the South.' His argument was that Alliance erosion of the Tory vote might give Labour a scattering of southern seats on a three-way split, but more importantly the Alliance itself would win enough seats from the Conservatives to leave Labour as the largest party – less ambitious than Callaghan's view, but well beyond Labour expectations only a few months earlier.

Another anxiety had been about the new legal requirement for trade union ballots on political funding. When it became clear that Labour's financial windpipe was at risk, redoubtable backroom figures like Bill Keys in the TUC, and John Golding, then at Westminster, showed their organisational skills. No union voted itself out of the Labour fold, and in the process of winning the ballots union leaders developed organising muscles that had long been flaccid.

Neil Kinnock's strength was in licking his Party back into shape. His Westminster performances remained patchy, although the best were more effective than at the start. He attracted the same criticism that Lloyd George once made about Churchill (in a 1936 conversation with Ribbentrop, and therefore before Churchill's great years): 'He was a rhetorician and not an orator. He thought only of how a phrase sounds, not how it might move or influence crowds.' But Kinnock made a speech in the debate on Norman Fowler's Welfare State review that was more architectonic, and more calculated to win a wider argument. He linked Labour's attack on Fowler with his general critique of the Government over unemployment, housing and the NHS. He persisted in his attack on the paucity of vital figures in the Fowler proposals, which some Conservative MPs clearly found infuriating. But Kinnock was learning that hardest of parliamentary skills – how to allow opponents to intervene during a speech without losing the thread. He shares the Prime Minister's tendency to convince himself as he goes along, and this tempts him into verbosity, for he also has a Welsh rhetorician's love of epithetical pyramids. His strength is that people like his warmth and humour. Labour's improved spirit in 1985 derived in part from a feeling that it would be churlish to allow factionalism, however enjoyable, to douse the bubbling enthusiasm of their young leader.

But Labour MPs worried that their poll rating was going to stick at 35 or 36%, which in a bad Conservative period was four points too low for comfort. Some attributed this to lack of gravitas, or 'bottom', in the leadership. To some extent gravitas is in the eye of the beholder: the fact that Kinnock has never held office and that his deputy, Roy Hattersley, was in the Cabinet only during Labour's three final years made them look less experienced than their opponents, who had now been in power for six years. Once again Kinnock was urged to copy Harold Wilson in 1962–3, and establish Labour's credibility through major policy speeches.

This argument from precedent has some weaknesses. Wilson's speeches were valuable to Labour chiefly to impress what we may call the Leader-writing Faction, which – under the influence of President Kennedy – was hungry for a whiff of British New Frontiers. By the summer of 1985 leader-writers were more sceptical, not to say cynical. They had witnessed Labour and Conservative revolutions in 1964 and 1979: neither had produced paradise on earth. They had been through the satirical sixties and the iconoclastic seventies; their newspapers' owners were more interventionist, so the leader-writers were often less influential within their own offices, and therefore with the public. Kinnock was right to doubt how modern Fleet Street would treat a Wilsonian campaign.

On policy, Kinnock was tenderly cultivating a plant new to the modern Labour Party: flexibility. He was not likely to rival the flexibility of the first Lord Rothermere who, when Baldwin unexpectedly embraced Protection in 1923, had announced in the lunch edition of his *Evening News*: 'An article by Lord Rothermere, "My Plea for Tariffs", will appear in next Sunday's *Sunday Pictorial*', only to amend the promised title in the 6.30 p.m. edition to 'Should Free Trade Have Another Chance?' But Kinnock did begin to try to switch Europe from Labour's debit to profit columns. He began to discuss unemployment with French and German socialist leaders, and no more was heard of the 1983 threat to withdraw.

Roy Hattersley was using his Shadow Chancellorship to make new policy, which was then incorporated in joint Labour–TUC documents. By a process of steady drip, he was moving Labour and the unions back again to the study of incomes. Since the Winter of Discontent incomes policy had been 'the sin that dare not speak its name', even in the party of planning. Whether Hattersley could get a commitment from the TUC that would impress voters as realistic remained to be seen. A prolific journalist, he attracted a criticism common in puritanical Labour circles: that he is too much renaissance man, and should concentrate solely on politics. Among his friends, however, there was only the same affectionate criticism that Churchill made of F. E. Smith: 'He seemed to have a double dose of human nature: he burned all his candles at both ends.' But Hattersley found his writing therapeutic. Belles lettres must certainly be a pleasing contrast with the hassled life of a modern Labour politician.

Kinnock was criticised in 1985 for directing too much of his fire directly at Mrs Thatcher, rather than at Government policies. Based on experience in 1983, many Labour MPs regarded the Prime Minister as their opponents' strong suit. Kinnock agreed that she was a huge plus to the Tories, but concluded from this that his primary task was to loosen her hold on the public. Labour's private polls early in 1985 suggested she was being damaged in her reputation for economic and crisis management by sterling's troubles in January, higher mortgage interest, and unemployment, and was regarded by many as being 'out of touch' and 'talking down'. Labour strategists claimed they led among the young and among skilled workers, whose defection had magnified their 1983 defeat.

Even before Westland the next election looked more open than the last. In the thirties my father once briefly took to backing horses on a system based on the phases of the moon. He did this for modest stakes and for laughs, for I like to think I inherited from him a steak of self-mockery, rather than of credulity. The moon is not a reliable guide to horses' form. By 1985, however, it might have been as useful in predicting a three-horse election as any other system. With public opinion polls all over the place, pundits and politicians began to crave the kind of by-election that would give them some clue.

Brecon and Radnor was not the constituency Labour would have chosen. From the start, all three parties privately suspected the Alliance would win. There might be more sheep than people in this picturesque area of prosperous-looking farms, tucked into fertile valleys against the dramatic backdrop of the Brecon Beacons. But there were 47,000 people, varied by region, class, occupation and attitudes: not a cross-section of the British, or even the Welsh nation, but a useful test of mid-term opinion.

The Conservatives had gained Brecon from Labour in 1979, and fortified their hold in 1983 when redistribution deprived Labour of some industrial strongholds in the constituency. The Tories then had nearly half the votes, with the other two parties almost equal. Yet at this stage in the Government's fortunes they expected to lose. Labour hoped but did not quite believe it might win. The Alliance knew it could scarcely afford anything but a morale-boosting victory. But the three-party split makes forecasting perilous: in by-elections, as distinct from general elections, some voters seem to want to back the winner rather than their own opinions. That is why national party headquarters focus full attention on a single seat. Confidence is all.

The tidy little towns of mid-Wales, with their euphonious names – Llandrindrod Wells, Builth Wells, Crickhowell, Ystradgynlais – sleeping gently under the early summer sun, scarcely knew what had hit them when the caravans arrived. Each party seemed determined that someone on their behalf would speak personally to each voter, and probably to most sheep, on a principle analogous to that for VIPs' visits to the Services: 'If it moves, salute it; if it doesn't, paint it white.' With saturation canvassing and a constellation of political luminaries the voters felt like VIPs.

And then there were the media. They descended on the decent pubs of Brecon, a swarm of opinionated young men wearing their ideologies on the sleeves of their Young Fogey suits or suede jackets, to torture the candidates at daily press conferences in the hope that one – or, better still, all – would break under interrogation. The most vulnerable was the Conservative, Chris Butler, who eschewed any suspicion of being 'on the pinker side' of his party. But the Tories were nervous about unemployment, although they displayed a tight-lipped determination to tough it out. One formidable lady at party headquarters was heard exhorting another with doubts: 'Don't be apologetic, dear.'

The Liberal, Richard Livesey, who had stood in 1983, and his Party's election wizard, Andrew Ellis, tried to convince anyone who would listen that Labour's vote was confined to the old industrial areas of Ystradgynlais and to Brecon town, and that it had little support in the small market towns and villages where most people lived. This was denied by Richard Willey, son of the former Labour minister, who pointed to their good showing right across the constituency in the shire council voting in May. Such hypeing and counter-hypeing is common in knife-edge by-elections nowadays. Contrary to the proverb, the race is often to the swift (of tongue, in this case): the party that can persuade voters it is going to win becomes more likely to do so. As Lord David Cecil once observed, our party system has much to be said for it but it does not provide a natural home for the detached thinker. Particularly at by-election times.

The Liberals won, but by only 559 votes over Labour, with the Conservatives a bad third. It was a valuable boost for the Alliance before the summer break, and the message on the doorsteps confirmed that Margaret Thatcher might not be the certain vote-winner she once was. One Tory MP complained that the Government had 'got its rhetoric in an ideological twist' and needed to be more pragmatic. However, another, reflecting a mood that was to grow stronger, admitted that as a card-carrying 'Wet' he 'wouldn't have started from here', but said retreat now would be damaging. So backbenchers like himself, in a soldierly way, must remain steady under fire, plump for the tax cuts the Prime Minister craved, and keep both powder and policies dry for the general election. In other words, no more whingeing or rocking the boat. As Conservative morale sagged in early 1986, this was a mood the whips encouraged.

For the Alliance the good news from Brecon and Radnor was that many Conservative voters were willing to defect, at least in by-elections, and even more when they saw the Liberals as the only way of stopping Labour winning. The bad news was that Neil Kinnock's revival was working in even less obvious Labour areas, so that the Alliance had a desperate fight on its hands if it was to break through on what had once seemed the most vulnerable sector of the political front – as a replacement for a dying Labour Party.

For Labour the good news was that, in a constituency which no longer had a strong industrial base but with public services offering Labour a foothold in agricultural areas, it could take votes from both Conservatives and Alliance. The bad news was the growth of that 'stop Labour' sentiment which had made many Tories abandon their colours because they thought the Liberals were the lesser evil. The feeling grew that, unusually, the next election would be fought less on a pro- or anti-Government choice than on a pro- or anti-Labour one.

Labour's leaders detected this message. Neil Kinnock and Roy Hattersley blamed Arthur Scargill for the Liberal victory, saying his behaviour had lost the 280 votes which would have turned the election for Labour. Kinnock had concluded that if he was to arrest the 'stop Labour at any cost' mood which affected some voters, he must be tougher with his supporters and win the right to enter the general election nimble-footed. He walked a narrow line between reigniting Labour's internal rows and responding to what voters wanted. But in Neil Kinnock's mind the die was cast. He began to prepare for Labour's 1985 conference in Bournemouth. After his speech there, nothing between him and his Party would be quite the same.

CHAPTER 15

MORE THAN A REFUGEE CAMP?

The year of 1984 was a difficult one for the Alliance. It thrives on by-elections and, although there were some, including Portsmouth South where the Social Democrats registered a gain, not enough winnable contests came to restart the bandwagon that rolled immediately after their launch in 1981. The dearth of winnable seats was no accident. The Prime Minister joined the Grim Reaper in a reluctance to send anyone upstairs – to the House of Lords in her case, to even Higher Service as far as the other gentleman is concerned.

So the Alliance's principal test was in elections for the European Parliament. This, with 78 constituencies instead of the 650 in a Westminster election, further emphasised the disadvantage to the Alliance of having its support spread so evenly through the country. Some optimists hoped they might win ten seats, but after the election the Alliance remained without a single Euro-MP.

By the end of 1984, the key question about the future remained unanswered: Was the mould of what Alliance people called 'class-based politics' being broken? There was some evidence of a revival of support for the principle of political consensus, on which Margaret Thatcher and Tony Benn had poured such scorn in the early eighties. Tory 'Wets' still looked with distant admiration at the SDP. One minister privately said of their policies and tone: 'That's what the people want, you know.' But when I questioned him, it turned out that he hoped pressure of Alliance success would help him and his friends to pull the Conservative Party back to the centre ground in which their own hopes rested.

One thoughtful Conservative said that, if you looked at the broad acres of the South and at the suburbs, you might conclude that the mould was cracking. But in the North and in the cities, Gilbert and Sullivan's rule, slightly adapted, still prevailed: four out of every five little boys and girls that are born into the world alive were either little Labour folk or else little Conservatives.

Professor David Marquand, an unshrinkingly honest prophet of social democracy, wrote in the *New Democrat*: 'Labour cannot win, but it can – and on present form almost certainly will – prevent the only other anti-Conservative force from winning instead ... As in the 1920s, anti-Conservative England is divided against itself, and Conservative England is running away with the spoils.' This had been Roy Jenkins' original dread.

Marquand had earlier pointed out that if the Conservatives in 1987 or 1988 were to match even their worst post-war vote of 36% (in October 1974), and if another 5% went to Nationalist or Unionist candidates, Labour and the Alliance would be left with 59% to divide between them. At that time it seemed that both Labour and Alliance would do well enough to frustrate each other.

This was Margaret Thatcher's safety margin. After all the revolutions that had taken place in the eighties, the key to the new Parliament was this: Could either Neil Kinnock and Roy Hattersley on the one hand, or David Steel and David Owen on the other, forge far enough ahead in public support to make their party look convincingly like an alternative to the Conservatives? As they fought to prove that they could, no Olympic final that year produced more bumping and boring than the deadly struggle on the Opposition benches of the House of Commons. Some Labour thinkers saw the mirror-image of Marquand's case, but with the Alliance cast as the spoilers of course. Their electoral conclusions were not substantially different from his. Few in either party were willing to contemplate the Marquand solution: another realignment of the Left, leading to a broad-based coalition of all democratic anti-Thatcher forces, with party labels having to be sacrificed, including what he called 'the narrow organisational interests' of the Alliance.

A hard-headed Liberal who accepted this black analysis of the non-Conservative arithmetic reached a different conclusion: the Alliance had no alternative but to 'elbow Labour aside'. But had it not taken Labour twenty-five, or arguably forty-five years to do precisely that to the Liberals in the first half of the century? He came back with a briefer version of the Decline of Liberal England, making it stretch merely from 1915, and Asquith's last wholly Liberal Cabinet, to 1924, when only 40 Liberals were elected. But if we leave aside the stimulus to change provided by the cataclysmic Asquith–Lloyd George vendetta, and the even more cataclysmic effect on domestic politics of the Great War, that still leaves a gap of thirty years between that last Liberal government in 1915 and the first majority Labour government in 1945 – a long gap in the slow march of the non-Conservative forces in British public life.

To more optimistic Alliance supporters Labour still looked ripe for plucking. They hoped to reap a harvest of discontent after reselection and the defeat of the miners. But the Alliance had its own problems of policy and organisation: Liberal and SDP grass roots continued to show how different their instincts were, on subjects as diverse as defence and Northern Ireland. The fight over candidates went on, and the argument about whether they should be chosen by open or closed selection – to outsiders a recondite subject – was conducted with the fierce conviction of Medieval Schoolmen (or the late-twentieth-century Labour Party). At the close of 1984, as Margaret Thatcher contemplated an implacable economy, revolting students, parents and MPs, and her unpalatable choices over taxes, spending and welfare benefits, the state of the Opposition parties provided some of her happier moments.

The SDP aspired to be a classless party. They rejected the 'Volvo, claret and credit card' image foisted on them by commentators, and eschewed the idea of representing a class interest, although David Owen characteristically defended middle-class values against fashionable jibes. Critics regarded this classless aspiration as hypocritical. About this time Norman Tebbit had a party piece which he performed at more up-market Conservative functions: 'I am a Social Democrat. I believe in preservation of the Green Belt; I live in a newly built house on the very edge of town. My wife and I are passionate supporters of state education; Jason and Cressida go to a coeducational prep school, where the headmistress has progressive views. We think revival of British manufacturing industry is essential; we drive a Merc. and a Volvo Estate.'

Opponents were also sceptical about the solidity of the Alliance 1983 vote. John Smith, Labour's industry spokesman, believed the Alliance was 'a refugee camp'. The phrase contained an element of self-accusation, assuming that 1983 Thatcher supporters were so disillusioned as to flee that coop but still not prepared to vote Labour. And with increasing stridency Tories implied that the Alliance would betray these 'refugees', by letting in what Central Office persistently called 'a hard-Left Government'. Both the Alliance's opponents believed it lacked positive appeal and lived off temporary disaffection with one or other of the older parties. But the gloomy prognostication for the Alliance that opponents built on this belief ignored the most certain psephological fact in recent elections: a modest but significant melting at the edges of the huge icebergs of traditional party support. The key question remained: Would many voters who deserted Labour for Mrs Thatcher, either in 1979 or 1983, return to support Neil Kinnock? Or would they turn to the Alliance?

The uncertainty about these questions has made campaigning methods throughout this Parliament difficult for the parties to settle. Which opponent do you attack? My physical education teacher at school, a retired RSM in the Grenadier Guards, had a novel form of boxing: he would put three little boys in the ring together, urge two of them to attack the third, and then, when signs of victory developed, shout at them to change sides. This caused confusion, to say the least. The sergeant-major, long since departed to a Higher Parade Ground, had discovered the existential question of three-party politics: Who is my enemy?

The Social Democrats were a party in search of a philosophy, and Owen believed that search should be adventurous. His followers soon learned not to underestimate his radical instincts. Just as the formation of the SDP set off a revolution in British politics, so the switch in its leadership from Roy Jenkins to David Owen set the Party off in a new direction. At each of the many assemblies required by the new Party's baroque constitution, the faithful wondered anxiously What David Would Say Next. Although his leadership was acknowledged to be exciting and brave, some of them would have preferred a quieter life, a period of consolidation of both their own Party and the Alliance. But Owen is not a man for the quiet life. Oscar Wilde was once approached by a poet with pretensions to the Laureateship, who alleged that there was a conspiracy of silence against him. Wilde's advice was terse: 'Join it.'

This was not advice that would have appealed to David Owen, who often worries that there is a conspiracy of silence against his Social Democrats at Westminster and in the media. He has an instinct for stirring things up. He often complains about the treatment of the Alliance in allocation of debating time, seats on committees, and other matters controlled by the two larger parties. Once, when he was raising these subjects in the House, Conservative and Labour sides ganged up on him and began a series of noisy interruptions which eventually drowned Owen's voice. The Speaker, Bernard Weatherill, then new to the job, had a distressing habit, when the noise grew intolerable, of asking the MP on his feet to wind up his remarks more quickly. On this occasion he showed little disposition to protect Owen from the barracking.

A combative gleam appeared in the Doctor's eye and he stood his ground. When the noise subsided enough for his words to be heard, he indicated to the Chair that he proposed to stay on his feet until he had made his points, and it seemed clear that he would not mind greatly if this meant the rest of the day. The House wisely suspended its bully-boy tactics, which at times like this leave MPs with little authority to lecture university students who refuse to give a hearing to politicians. The incident passed because Owen had displayed a touch of steel. He has had to do this several times. His view is that, as a party leader, he should not behave in such a way as to have himself suspended, but short of that he stands and fights for his Party's rights.

The Social Democrats needed a distinctive economic posture. Even aided by a Labour Party which had taken a more Left-wing stance, and a Conservative Party which, since 1976, had been leaning Right, it was difficult to cut a convincing swathe down the middle that would not look too much like what one cynic described as 'unreconstructed Keynesianism'. The Prime Minister, predictably, did not help them: as David Owen and Roy Jenkins advocated policies similar to those the latter had followed as Chancellor, she taunted them by standing on its head that unwise remark about the infant Soviet Union: 'I have seen the past, and it does not work.' The future, for Margaret Thatcher, did not consist of any variety of Keynesianism.

A thoughtful Social Democrat professed himself undismayed by a slump in the Alliance's standing that worried his friends. This coincided with the spurt that Kinnock's election as leader gave Labour. The Social Democrat believed, with a determinist view of history that any Marxist would envy, that Labour was suffering from inability to adjust to the changing nature of British society, decline of the trade unions, bourgeoisification of the working class, and so on. On this reading, Labour's replacement by the third force was an inevitable step in the evolutionary process.

For this man political revolution had turned into evolution, but not for David Owen. The outstanding revelation of his radicalism was the emphasis he put on multi-party coalition. In a *Guardian* article he presented this not simply as a strategy for the SDP, but as a political future for Britain. His resistance to anything that might lead to merger with the Liberals was part of that game plan. This was to keep his own Social Democrats light on their feet, ready to take part in a coalition with anyone, particularly anyone who could be forced by post-election arithmetic to concede proportional representation. The key passage in his article was this:

> We will prosper or perish on our ability to convince the electors of the virtues of multi-party government. Most people know that the voting system is not fair; we must go beyond that. We must convince them that it is not merely unjust, but unsound in practice as well as in principle. We must constantly reiterate that the British voting system creates bad government: secretive, partisan, narrowly class-based, frequently authoritarian, and usually excessively ideological government. Throughout the country we must confidently assert the virtues and strengths of multi-party government.

Even before he left Labour Owen had argued that European countries with varying voting systems had been much better governed, or at least not worse governed, by coalitions than Britain had been by its single-party administrations. He even seemed to include Belgium and Italy in that claim, so his belief in coalitions had roots in his past. But of more immediate political significance was his open abandonment of the pretence that the Alliance was likely to form a government on its own. Before 1983, when Jenkins was leader, Owen had been irritated by talk of a Prime Minister-designate, which he thought contributed to the sham nature of so much political infighting. His thesis was that after the next election the Alliance would hold the balance of power, and would demand that the largest party should negotiate on what was included in its Queen's Speech, that there should be no dissolution of Parliament for three years, and that negotiations should be held to create a coalition. Many observers saw his acknowledgement that there would not be an Alliance government as realistic. But what would the Liberals make of this new strategy, Liberals whose hopes had been kept alive through sixty drab years by successive leaders urging them to march towards the sound of gunfire, or advising them to go home and prepare for government?

David Owen had set himself as mammoth a task as the creation of the

Alliance had been: to convince Social Democrats that his strategy made sense; to take Liberals at least some way along the same road, so that the Alliance did not go sour; and to persuade voters to elect enough Alliance MPs to force a coalition. After that, he and others would try to persuade one or other of the larger parties to pay the price, proportional representation. That might make coalition Britain's normal form of government. It was a tall order.

He began this task at once, at a time when there were more imponderables in British politics than might have been expected after the Conservatives' election triumph. The questions were these: By 1987 or 1988 would Margaret Thatcher's economic achievements have convinced voters that eight or more years spent shivering in a hair shirt outside the Headmistress's door had been worth it? Would Labour allow Neil Kinnock to obliterate the memory of its earlier lunacies? Or would the two Davids be able so to exploit the difficulties of the two major parties that the political revolution they began in 1981 would be completed?

In the first year of the new Parliament Owen outshone Steel. He possesses one capacity essential to a politician of the first rank. Some call it arrogance, others the ability to suspend disbelief and imagine that 649 other MPs, most of them either politically or congenitally egocentric, will want to listen to you. Steel looked modest by comparison. This was partly because he had never held office. When you have once stood at the despatch box to make an announcement of Government policy, even as Parliamentary Under-Secretary in the Department of Odd Jobs, it is easier to believe that people are hanging on your every word. Having been Foreign Secretary helps even more.

However, Steel had special reasons for being self-effacing during 1984. He took a conscious decision that a party leader of eight years' standing must not 'batter the ear-drums of the public' in the first year after a general election. He had also been concerned about his long-suffering wife and children: he is the only party leader in recent times whose family have lived away from London. While Debbie Owen, an American literary agent, is a natural metropolitan, Judy Steel stands firm in their Scottish Borders base, which is what David Steel prefers also. But his peripatetic leadership imposes strains. Steel said sadly that he missed too much of his children's adolescence, and he was now trying, in a fallow political year, to make up for it by being at home more often. The conscience, or super-ego, of a Scottish Presbyterian makes him more vulnerable than most to such anxiety. But grass-roots Liberals, who are relentless in their demands on their leader's time, did not ease up, and Steel is an obliging man.

By contrast, David Owen has developed a tough skin. His break with Labour contributed to that. If in old age he compiles a list of those to whom he feels grateful, Dennis Skinner, his chief Labour tormentor below the gangway, might perversely figure on it, rather as Malcolm Marshall should be on Mike Gatting's list. Playing bouncers, in politics as in cricket, is a maturing experience. But Owen's critics say it has also been a coarsening one. There was an undertow of criticism within the Alliance even during this vintage year. The thrust of the charge was that the obverse of his dash, energy, decisiveness and courage was a political rootlessness; that he was stronger on tactics than on strategy. Even the notorious Foreign Office reservations about his period there were being rewritten into a division between the young, who admired his willingness to 'have a go', and the more senior, who had to live with the aftermath of his inconsistency. Some quotations from colleagues in 1984 illustrate the kind of criticisms that were made:

'He's a cavalry commander, Rupert of the Rhine. But which direction will he charge in next? And what's it got to do with the battle anyhow?'

'He worries about not being macho more than any politician ought to do. He once told an SDP feminist: "What this party needs is balls."'

'Which direction is he moving in? In the direction of opportunism, of course.' (This was said mainly in admiration by a Liberal who believed the Alliance would live or die by grabbing the ten per cent of voters who were afloat and not being too scrupulous about the means.)

'David holds ideas strongly, but for a very short time. One day he's sitting beetle-browed, almost sulking, because people won't agree with him. A couple of weeks later the same subject is peripheral to his interests.'

The criticism, in parts, resembled that made against Mrs Thatcher, that she made policy 'on the hoof'. A despairing Liberal said of Owen: 'The SDP has battalions of vice-chancellors, professors and economists on its working parties. It's really the small-L liberal Establishment in exile. But David Owen just gets together with a few henchmen, and decides what he wants to say.' Yet the problem for a third party, he added, is to prove that it has intellectual clout, and is more than a vehicle of protest against an unpopular government and an unproven opposition.

Owen, however, had taken aboard another fact about third-party politics: the need for instant reaction to events. His staff had orders to keep an hour-by-hour watch on the MPs' news agency tape-machine, conveniently sited near his office. When he phoned in to discover what the news of the world was, he was ready, at the drop of a radio or television producer's hand, to give his opinion. If the Fleet Street obloquy of 'instant quote' – slightly less offensive than 'rent-a-quote', which is used of some backbenchers – were thrown at David Owen, it would simply produce that boyish, disarming smile which reminds people that within the tough façade is a more engaging human being. But it was this quickly acquired popular touch, this willingness to react, which made Owen's mark in SDP politics. This had happened not just since he became leader but during the Falklands campaign, when his career came alight, on television and in the House, for the first time since he left Labour.

Owen's overt brashness conceals his sensitiveness. Even in that summer of media success, when some Gallery correspondents were praising him as the most effective party leader at Westminster, he was wryly aware of the immanent danger of *hubris*. The general election had left him as something of a one-man band, at least as far as heavyweight politics was concerned. He had only six MPs, most of them inexperienced, and with Roy Jenkins ill for a time. This compared with Steel's seventeen. But it was a handicap that Owen turned into an advantage. Neil Kinnock, the other novice leader, had to share the Labour limelight with a large front-bench team, and therefore performed principally under the Prime Minister's shadow during her 15-minute question-times on Tuesdays and Thursdays. Owen, though deprived of a place at the Opposition despatch box, was constantly up and down in the House, and frequently appeared on radio and television.

The relationship between Owen and Steel is nothing like so close as that between Jenkins and Steel. But then the ages of the present leaders are inconveniently close, and neither is without ambition. They find it easy to work together, but Owen's political posture as well as his buccaneering style make him a more controversial figure within the Alliance than Steel. One theory of Alliance politics was that the Liberals should mobilise discontented Tories ('Orpington man', after a famous by-election in the sixties) as well as what one Social Democrat scathingly called 'the green and furry vote'; while the SDP would bring in Labour people who had grown steadily more unhappy since Hugh Gaitskell's time. Yet in 1984 Owen was accused of alienating Labour voters the Alliance needed to win, especially in the North.

There is a queue of people waiting to tell the earnest inquirer how daft such notions always were. A radical Liberal: 'Anyone who thought the Social Democrats were to the Left of us is out of his mind'; a Northern Liberal. 'Their *leaders* were Labour, but the rank and file are mostly uncommitted or ex-Tories. The credit-card system of paying subscriptions was bound to affect their social mix.' Owen denied that his emphasis on the social market economy represented a sharp move to the Right. His version was not so much Sir Keith Joseph's as the Bad Godesberg Manifesto of the German Social Democrats in the fifties, when they abandoned nationalisation. He acknowledged that the Gang of Four would have been wiser to make it clear when they left Labour that they were rethinking their economic positions. Now he felt himself freed from what he called 'Clause IV socialism'.

A less theoretical problem arose between the two Davids in the summer of 1984. It concerned the miners' strike. Owen's instinct was profoundly anti, and he made this clear publicly; but Steel concentrated his fire on Margaret Thatcher, for having appointed Ian MacGregor chairman of the Coal Board in the first place, and for talking about the strike in terms of 'victory' and 'defeat'. The two Alliance leaders failed to co-ordinate their pronouncements in a crucial period while Steel was at the Democratic Party Convention in San Francisco, which Owen skipped because he thought the miners' strike was more important.

Privately Steel was sometimes critical of Owen. He shared the worry that more Alliance support was coming from ex-Conservative than from ex-Labour voters. This had helped the SDP to win the Portsmouth South by-election, but it deprived the Alliance of other victories, in by-elections and the European elections, which would have kept their bandwagon rolling. Part of the problem was that Neil Kinnock's leadership had arrested the Labour decline, but Steel also blamed the hostility among Labour supporters to David Owen. He worried about the danger that, at a time when there was some reaction against Thatcherism, Owen risked becoming a hero to her most loyal supporters in the *Daily Express* and the *Sun*. A harsher critic commented: 'David Owen is creating a bull market in "Thatchers" when others are selling them.'

Alliance optimists maintained that Owen's more aggressive instincts made the two leaders more complementary in their talents than Steel and Jenkins had been. They praised Steel as a long-distance runner with the patience that Owen lacks; in a hung Parliament he would be a shrewd negotiator. That was the role that David Steel saw for himself in British politics: to transform Britain into a country in which governments are negotiated between parties, a view that harmonised with Owen's latest thinking. The Lib-Lab Pact with Jim Callaghan had been a valuable apprenticeship for Steel. Callaghan was not the only Labour man who could conceive of a government that would include Kinnock, Steel and Owen, although the present Labour leadership persistently claimed that in a hung Parliament they would simply form a minority government, and challenge the Alliance to bring them down.

But it was David Owen's role that constantly fascinated politicians of all parties. One younger Conservative 'Wet' said he sometimes could not remember what divided him from Owen. Another complained that Owen should be taking over from the Labour Party, whereas he was proving himself 'the best Conservative leader we haven't got'. Politically and personally, the two Davids remain different animals. Steel is emollient, with few enemies. Owen sometimes appears to be a man at war with himself, uncertain whether to rely on toughness or his personal charm. He does have political enemies, even though most people who know him better can recall some kind deed he has done. But envious voices keep whispering 'too big for his boots' and 'pride comes before a fall'. Being made Foreign Secretary on Tony Crosland's death – at thirty-eight the youngest Foreign Secretary since Anthony Eden – was certain to rouse the dragon of jealousy. Perhaps the real fear of his critics is that fortune will one day deal him again too favourable a hand, and that he will, as Churchill enviously said of Arthur Balfour, 'pass from one Cabinet to another, from the Prime

Minister who was his champion to the Prime Minister who had been his most severe critic, like a powerful, graceful cat, walking delicately and unsoiled across a rather muddy street'.

In 1985 a fundamental debate developed about the nature of social democracy. Roy Jenkins, the most perceptive of political essayists, published a book which contained the following quotation from Keynes:

> Ought I to join the Labour Party? Superficially, that is more attractive [than joining the Conservatives]. But looked at closer, there are great difficulties. To begin with, it is a class party, and the class is not my class. If I am going to pursue sectional interests, I shall pursue my own . . . I can be influenced by what seems to me justice and good sense, but the class war will find me on the side of the educated bourgeoisie.

Jenkins used this in an elegant argument that Keynes, who became a Liberal, had rejected 'the ugly sisters' of Conservatism and Labour, and would have been enchanted if Cinderella (Liberals-with-a-partner) had existed in his lifetime. David Owen was now leading the SDP away from its Labour roots and in the direction of Keynes's 'educated bourgeoisie'. Owen believed, and with evidence to support him, that the majority of his Party's members, by contrast with its London élite, had no political affiliation before the SDP was formed, and had no hankering after traditional Labour policies. A touching moment at the Party's conference was when Shirley Williams, the President, confessed rather sadly that the phrase 'traditional Labour values', used in a motion, although it had resonance for her, clearly had none for the majority of Social Democrats.

The arguments were complex. They were bound to be in a party aspiring to break the mould rather than building on the well-established foundations the larger parties had, foundations the Alliance called 'class-based' and others would call 'representative of the interests of the nation'. Jenkins found Owen's attitude to Labour paradoxical. Originally he himself had been regarded as the most Right-wing of the Gang of Four, but he maintained he had always seen the SDP as a Left-of-Centre party, a radical alternative to the Tories and replacement for Labour. He now feared what others had long worried about: that it might get most of its votes from Conservatives. But Owen argued that people who happened to vote for Mrs Thatcher in 1979 or 1983 were not all 'cradle Conservatives'; they had simply grown fed up with Labour and should now be ripe for the Alliance to harvest. He believed such harvesting is best done by a party which he aspired to make more redistributive than Labour, and yet which put a little iron into the Liberal tendency to preach populist radicalism.

Modern Liberalism also has a formidable task in defining its identity. Under David Owen the Social Democrats' patron saint seemed to be Lot's Wife, who was turned into a Pillar of Salt for looking back at the sinful Cities of the Plain. But when Liberals looked back they saw two traditions, in the Whiggery of Asquith and the radicalism of Lloyd George, which had performed a disastrous gymnastic splits. After the second world war successive leaders had tried to carve out a middle way between Tories and Labour, but they had only limited influence over electoral tides which swept in and out, for Liberals depended on the unpopularity of others. Success has been most frequent in rural Scotland, Wales and the West Country, with forays into Tory suburbia and, less often, bridgeheads in Labour's industrial heartlands. The theory that the SDP could reach the industrial parts of Britain that Liberalism could not reach did not produce early results. Candidates in working-class seats had found how difficult such Heinekenism was in practice. For better or worse the Social Democrats under Owen had abandoned what one of them called 'hand-me-down Labour philosophy', but Roy Jenkins continued to argue that 'we should keep our radical edge well honed, and endeavour to cut as deep in Durham as in Devon'.

The two Alliance parties were slowly growing more like each other, although there was a difference, which one cynic called Arsenic and Old Lace. The Liberals are an old-fashioned party, proud of their history, the most glorious moments of which were now seventy years in the past. In their long march through the wilderness they had found several potential Moseses, but still were not in the Promised Land; yet their refusal to abandon hope during the dark years gave them a certain dignity now that the sun was shining again. The SDP is an altogether less emotional institution, preoccupied greatly with effectiveness and the mechanics of government and politics. This does not mean its leaders lack idealism; they have, after all, made heavy sacrifices in their own political careers. But they reacted against the conversion of idealism into ideology in the Labour Party they left.

In 1985 the Alliance filled a slight hiatus in its policy-making by launching a debate on the Sovereign's role in a hung Parliament. The tactic was, presumably, to talk up the possibility of such a result in the next general election, in the belief that, as Tin Pan Alley once put it, 'wishing will make it so'. There had been similar discussion before the 1983 election, but it withered under the sun of Margaret Thatcher's triumph. The Alliance took an activist view of the Queen's powers. David Owen said in one broadcast that she had a totally free hand. This was different from the conventional view, expressed, for example, in Asquith's 'Memorandum on the Constitutional Position of the Sovereign', written during the Home Rule crisis. The Liberal leader had begun this with a chilling reminder that the Stuarts 'pushed matters to extremes, with the result that Charles I lost his head and James II his throne'.

The real issue was how the Alliance should conduct itself in a Parliament in which it held the balance of power. Neil Kinnock, like Michael Foot before him, made clear that, if Labour were the largest party, he would form a minority government and challenge the Alliance to bring him down. But David Steel argued that in such circumstances Kinnock, or anyone else, might be refused a dissolution and second election. Norman St John-Stevas challenged this. According to Bagehot's editor, no British sovereign for more than a century has refused a dissolution to the incumbent, and he cited a Canadian precedent in warning of the danger that the Palace might have to grant an election to a *second* defeated Prime Minister after refusing it to the *first* – a sure way for the Queen to be dragged into party controversy.

The precedents, and the assumed attitudes in the Palace, began to be discussed. It was said that Harold Wilson owed his chance to hold the second 1974 election, which fortified his grip on power and eventually drove Edward Heath from the Conservative leadership, to the fact that Heath had devoted a weekend after the first election in the spring to attempting to form a coalition with the Liberals. On this theory, where no party has a majority the Queen allows 'one go' to each man. Thus Heath had his 'go' when he tried to persuade Jeremy Thorpe, David Steel and John Pardoe to sustain his Government, although it had lost its majority. Therefore when Wilson decided seven months later that his Government could not carry on with a majority of 34 against it, he was entitled to his 'go' – a fresh election.

This precedent might be relevant if Mrs Thatcher were to lose her overall majority but remain leader of the largest party. If the Prime Minister could not get enough Alliance, or conceivably Ulster Unionist, support, the Queen might grant her a dissolution. On the Wilson precedents – 1966, October 1974 – this second election helps the incumbent, though in 1951 the exhausted Attlee government found that, once the tide had begun to flow out eighteen months earlier, it was now doomed to be swept from office.

Alternatively, the Queen might be made aware – but how? – that another Conservative Prime Minister would be acceptable to the Alliance, even that he could obtain his Party's support for proportional representation. Or Neil Kinnock might be asked to form a government. He would have the advantage over any Conservative leader of having gained ground in the election rather than lost it, but the disadvantage of more policy commitments which the Alliance does not like. Labour's chance of being granted a second election might be strong.

In all such hypothetical circumstance the Crown has a dilemma. Basically the Queen's choice is either to accede to the major parties' preference for minority government followed by another election, or to make coalition inevitable by refusing a dissolution. Either course would involve the Palace more actively in political choice than contemporary attitudes to the monarchy make prudent. In the twenties King George V was not averse to seeing minority governments formed. In 1923 Baldwin had, as he inelegantly put it, 'dished the Goat' (Lloyd George) by adopting Protection while the latter was abroad. But Baldwin's minority government lasted only a short time, and the King then sent for Ramsay MacDonald as leader of the second largest party. Sixty years on it is hard to realise what a shock this must have been. The King wrote in his diary: 'Today 23 years ago, dear Grandmama [Queen Victoria] died. I wonder what she would have thought of a Labour Government!' But a few weeks later he wrote to Queen Alexandra, the Queen Mother: 'The new Ministers have different ideas from ours, as they are all socialists, but they ought to be given a chance and ought to be treated fairly.' King George, it should be remembered, had been on the throne when just six years earlier his cousin, the Tsar, and his family were overthrown and murdered. The cousins, incidentally, looked so much alike that when Nikita Khrushchev dined at the Carlton Club forty years later, he took umbrage at a portrait of George V, whose display he took to be a studied insult to himself.

In a hung Parliament, the Alliance's dilemma would also be acute. Liberal and SDP leaders hope that, if the difference between their national vote and the number of seats they win is extravagant again, the public would compensate them for this injustice when they forced a second election, and that PR would drop like a ripe plum into their laps. But many Conservative and Labour MPs believe that, on the contrary, voters punish those who cause them to have to go to the polls more often than necessary. There can be no certainty either way.

From time to time through this Parliament, when the polls look indecisive, talk about coalition government revives. The Alliance encourages it, while each of the larger parties publicly sustains the belief that it will win outright; but there is a certain perverse pleasure in privately discussing the unsayable. Like the characters in a C. P. Snow novel, politicians enjoy dreaming of allying themselves with erstwhile enemies to ditch their Rt Hon. and Hon. Friends. Not that the words 'friends' and 'enemies' are used unambiguously at Westminster. A story is told of a new young MP who rubbed his hands in satisfaction as he glared at the Opposition benches for the first time. 'How splendid to face one's enemies across the House!' he said. The Old Hand glanced at him in sardonic disbelief. 'No, no, my boy,' he said. 'Those chaps opposite are your opponents. Your enemies are all around you.'

Throughout these years of doubt that three-party politics have created, politicians occasionally murmur that they 'could work with X', or that 'Y is a Mensch, no problem for me in being in the same Cabinet as him'. It is also wise to remember that there are Tories who can cherish no hope while Margaret Thatcher is Prime Minister. But the overwhelming mood at Westminster remained one in which Tories and Labour each intended to win an overall victory. To do that, each knew they must squeeze the Alliance further. Even John Biffen, the emollient Leader of the Commons, attacked them, declaring that 'photogenic leadership does not dissolve the unyielding reality of political choice'. As 1985 turned into 1986, his own Government was also facing painful choices.

CHAPTER 16

HOW MUCH DID THE PRIME MINISTER KNOW?

The House of Commons will excuse anyone who quickly admits a fault and says sorry. Iain Macleod once told a young Conservative that if an MP rose in his place and said: 'Mr Speaker, I regret to have to inform the House that I have murdered my mother-in-law, cut her body into small pieces, and disposed of them in the washing-machine', his final words would be drowned in a forgiving chorus of 'hear, hears' from all sides.

The Westland affair was the worst personal crisis in Margaret Thatcher's years in Downing Street. The Argentine invasion of the Falklands was more important, but Westland damaged her credibility and standing with the public as nothing else has done. To the suggestion that she might have benefited if she had been franker with the House at an earlier stage, a minister had replied: 'We're all as God made us, and he didn't make Margaret Thatcher to say "I'm wrong".'

Those who think Westland was a storm in a teacup ridicule the lavishing of so much political and journalistic attention on 'the affairs of a middle-sized West Country helicopter company', which are supposed to bore ordinary people. This rather misses the point. The Watergate affair was about the burglary of a doubtless boring Democratic Party headquarters. But the issue in Washington, as in Westminster, was standards in public life. This is an issue that does interest the public, which is already sceptical – in my view, normally far too sceptical – about the behaviour of its politicians.

Mrs Thatcher's style of running her government has always been controversial within her own Party. She suffers neither fools nor opponents gladly. What was new in the report of the Defence Select Committee which investigated Westland was the evidence of how she allowed a quarrel between two ministers, Leon Brittan and Michael Heseltine, to get quite so badly out of hand; how she was clearly on Brittan's side but allowed the battle to be fought, both publicly and clandestinely, within an ostentatious policy of 'even-handedness', in ways that risked blowing her Cabinet apart. In the process she lost two ministers, narrowly stopped her Law Officers from resigning, and left her own reputation for straight dealing open to attack by her opponents.

The Committee, which had a Conservative majority, complained that its inquiry was obstructed by the Government's refusal to allow key witnesses to appear, and by the refusal of Leon Brittan, Sir Robert Armstrong, the

Cabinet Secretary, and Sir Brian Hayes, Permanent Secretary at Brittan's Industry Department, to answer some of its questions. Despite this obstruction the Committee made damaging comments, most of them concerning the question whether Brittan and the five civil servants concerned with leaking to the Press a letter from the Solicitor-General, Sir Patrick Mayhew, thought they were acting in accordance with the Prime Minister's wishes. This letter was damaging to Michael Heseltine, so it was the old question of 'Will no one rid me of this turbulent priest?' Politicians do not come much more turbulent than Heseltine was at that time. The Prime Minister had already told Parliament why and how she caused Sir Patrick's letter to Heseltine to be written. She added that while her office did not seek her agreement to the leak, 'they considered – and they were right – that I should agree [to its contents being made public]'. She said later, 'It was to get that accurate information to the public domain that I gave my consent'. But Sir Robert Armstrong told the Committee he understood from the Prime Minister (who did not give evidence) that these words were 'a slip of the tongue'.

The report is peppered with critical and sceptical phrases directed at leading participants in the drama: 'nothing short of incendiary', 'a little strange, to say the least', 'incredulous', 'wholly improper', 'disreputable', 'flimsy, to say the least', 'cover – whatever that may mean – from Number Ten', 'bizarre reasoning', 'outrageous', 'even if the Prime Minister was content to leave the matter there . . .' The most incendiary section concerned unanswered questions. Leon Brittan had paid the political price for saying his officials acted with his full authority, but he was inexplicably reticent about his other contacts on the leaking of the letter:

> He told us that he had no discussions with anyone in Number Ten before the disclosure. We asked Mr Brittan when he was first involved in discussions about releasing the information. He refused to tell us. We also asked Mr Brittan when he first spoke to anybody in Number Ten about the publication of the Solicitor-General's letter. Mr Brittan again refused to tell us . . . We asked Mr Brittan whether or not he had any conversation with the Prime Minister about the fact that he authorised disclosure . . . before the Prime Minister received the report of the inquiry. He refused to tell us.

About the only grain of comfort for the Prime Minister in this report was its acceptance of her assurance that on the day the letter was leaked she had no knowledge of what was taking place. But it called the leak 'an improper act' and said: 'Whatever authority the five civil servants may have thought they had – whether explicit in the case of the officials at the Department of Trade and Industry, implicit in the case of officials at Number Ten . . .' Such issues were left in the air, showing a Committee that was, ultimately, divided by party, with Labour MPs willing to damage the Prime Minister, while Conservatives were not.

One of Heseltine's complaints was that he was not able to get a proper discussion in Cabinet or committee about the European consortium whose bid for Westland he espoused. He said he could not even get things recorded in the Cabinet minutes. To the public, used to more normal methods of minute-taking, this may seem astonishing, but Cabinet minutes have always been odd. In 1882 Lord Hartington's private secretary wrote to Gladstone's that two other ministers and his could not agree about what had happened at the previous day's Cabinet: 'There must have been some decision, as Bright's resignation shows. My Chief has told me to ask you what the devil was decided, for he be damned if he knows. Will you ask Mr G. in more conventional and less pungent terms?'

A Cabinet colleague summed up Heseltine's position after his resignation in this way: 'He is the mainline beneficiary of the Prime Minister's future misfortunes. He has all the money he needs, and he can therefore use all the time he needs. That time may be spent on watching and waiting. Or on guerrilla tactics. Or on frontal assaults. Of one thing you can be sure: he hasn't retired to tend his garden in Northants.'

The Thatcher–Heseltine relationship was never an easy one. He was an interventionist, she the opposite; he is a tough romantic, she a tough non-romantic. She has never taken pains to conceal her indifference, or worse, to Heseltine's triumphs at Tory conferences. Once, when men's hair was worn longer than nowadays, she passed the television set in the crowded lobby of her Blackpool hotel as a knot of Conservatives marvelled at his oratorical fireworks down the road in the Winter Gardens. The Prime Minister had only one comment as the famous golden locks collapsed in disarray under the weight of his oratory: 'What on earth has happened to Michael's hair?'

In Cabinet Heseltine found her interruptions infuriating, and his resignation provoked Sir Ian Gilmour to say, with self-conscious restraint, 'The Prime Minister has many qualities, but listening is not among the most outstanding.' Heseltine himself claimed that, as the temperature mounted during the Westland debates, he tried to get the Prime Minister to understand, through Lord Whitelaw, Norman Tebbit and the Chief Whip, John Wakeham, that he would resign if she backed him into a corner. He complained: 'She just doesn't listen.' Soon after his resignation, he told me in an interview the gravamen of his criticism: 'Collective responsibility has been removed, and the Prime Minister's will to impose her views has been put in its place. You can't accept that. That's not the way we govern this country.' There is another theory that says a strong prime minister will always prevail; it caused Shaftesbury to say despairingly: 'There seems to be no measure, no principle, no cry, to influence men's minds and determine elections; it is simply "were you or were you not, are you, or are you not, for Palmerston?"'

Margaret Thatcher finally determined that her will must prevail over that of her Defence Secretary. It was a decision they both have had to live with. Despite the envious estimate of his political opportunities reported above, Heseltine began an arid period on the back benches, free to develop alternative policies certainly, but inhibited by the approach of a general election from doing anything that might damage his Party. The Prime Minister had a period when there was some doubt whether she would be able to remain until that election. Her attempt to save Brittan was seen as a bid to stop mishap turning into disaster. Some Tories believed she was 'holed below the waterline', and that by and by a delegation of elders, led by Lord Whitelaw, might call on her with a suggestion that her last, self-sacrificing service to the Party was to lay down the burden, etc., etc.

But Margaret Thatcher is a fighter, and she set about adjusting her stance in Cabinet. Its constitution had been subtly changed, first by the promotion of Douglas Hurd, Kenneth Baker and Kenneth Clarke, and now by the post-Westland changes, with George Younger taking over Defence, and Malcolm Rifkind and Paul Channon joining it. It looked less Thatcherite, and there were some signs that the Prime Minister was allowing other ministers to have more say. It was reported that in the aftermath of Westland she was curbing her instinct to lay down the line at the outset of a Cabinet debate, leaving anyone who was brave enough to challenge her. Instead, she tended more to keep her own counsel and sum up at the end.

One minister who had always seemed conformist to a fault assured me that a new era of collective decision-taking was about to be forced upon her, that ministers would no longer accept being foisted off with discussion in *ad hoc* groups, but would insist on taking their disagreements with her to Cabinet Committee, or even to full Cabinet. But the Prime Minister retained the powerful right to hire and fire. What would any but the most irreplaceable of her ministers do if, transfixed with a stare from those steely blue eyes, he was told it would be unwise for him to challenge her authority? Little piles of whitening ministerial bones litter the trail from 1979, as a grim reminder to those contemplating revolt. It was hard to believe the atmosphere would change overnight.

Even though polls showed Mrs Thatcher's standing with the voters had been damaged, the threat to her leadership did not develop. In part this was a result of her renowned toughness; cynics said that, even if the Tory elders did call on her with the traditional (and figurative) pearl-handled pistol, she would ignore all gentlemanly precedent and use it to shoot them. Another bulwark to her position was the absence of any agreement about who should succeed her. There were a number of Tories whose 'virtues cry like angels, trumpet-tongue'd' to their own supporters, but even a long-term opponent of the Prime Minister produced this sceptical race-card of those in contention at the time, to support his belief that she would remain in office:

Norman Tebbit: 'Organ-grinder and monkey syndrome: the Party wouldn't want another eight or ten years of the same.'

Michael Heseltine: 'He started this crisis. Nuff said.'

Peter Walker: 'Lucky to get out from under his local government and agriculture reforms before his mistakes caught up with him.'

Sir Geoffrey Howe: 'The nicest and dullest man in Europe.'

Douglas Hurd (by 1986 considered a good selling-plater in this classic race): 'He has ice-water flowing through his veins. I prefer red corpuscles.'

In brief, there was a slight hiatus in the leadership stakes. Combined with the divisions and uncertainties on the Opposition side, the lack of an alternative was Margaret Thatcher's best safety belt. Some thought she had planned her Cabinet to provide it. One former minister, looking critically at her methods, said the trick of smooth government is to learn to disagree agreeably, and that in hard times a Prime Minister must make liberal use of the whisky bottle and telephone, the former to assuage bruised egos, the latter to bridge gaps. This was not Mrs Thatcher's way. She preferred to argue issues out – she is a naturally argumentative human being, and the hammering out of ideas seemed to give her real enjoyment, though not all her colleagues shared in this.

The risk of Westland for Mrs Thatcher was not just the disunity it revealed but that it put her own personality and style on the public agenda, and not in a flattering light. The charges of bossiness, of not being susceptible to rational argument, were denied by her admirers, with chapter and verse about her flexibility. But Jim Callaghan, now Father of the House, accused her of having conducted the discussions 'with all the restraint and rationality of a Saturday late-night pub dispute'. After accusing other ministers of being mice and doormats, he recalled how Clementine Churchill told Winston that Clem Attlee was right to complain about the way he ran his wartime Cabinet. Callaghan impishly suggested there might be 'a role here for some other sensible spouse'. But Denis Thatcher, who used to be a rugby referee, no doubt recognises a suicide pass when he is thrown one.

The Opposition recognised the magnitude of the chance they were offered to diminish the Prime Minister's standing. She gave a wintry smile when Roy Jenkins said in the Westland debate that he would 'count the spoons in future'. There is nothing to stiffen an Opposition's sinews like a touch of panic on the Government benches. Neil Kinnock was criticised for not pressing home the attack successfully, but his Industry spokesman, John Smith, who is a Scottish advocate, adopted a forensic style that had Conservative MPs squirming. Forensic is not the word that springs to the lips about Neil Kinnock: he has too much of the *hwyl* in him, too many echoes of Lloyd George and Aneurin Bevan, for his oratory to be encompassed by the courtroom. In the principal Westland debate he was rattled by persistent Conservative heckling and a tiff with the Speaker, but his earlier speeches and questions had rattled the Prime Minister.

David Owen was compact of menace. It was he who pushed Mrs Thatcher into her most awkward corner about when she first heard of the leaked letter. This was a delicate subject, for while Sir Robert Armstrong's report was not formally delivered until Wednesday 22 January, the day before the Prime Minister made her most anguished appearance in the House, several journalists knew its principal conclusions earlier than that. I first heard them late on the Monday night, while padding the lobbies after a Conservative revolt over rates. It took me until Tuesday evening to confirm what I had been told, and this was broadcast from nine o'clock onwards. Her opponents latched on to the hiatus between the leaking of the Mayhew letter on 6 January and the time when she learned that her private office was believed to have approved the leak. That gap was more than a fortnight.

It was a fortnight that was enveloped in mystery. What some called a Rolls-Royce performance by Sir Robert Armstrong before the Defence Committee (though other members were less flattering) did not disperse the cloud. It raised further questions: Why did he not give her a quick interim report when he discovered the leak was an inside job, authorised by her office? Why did Leon Brittan not tell her? Or the private secretary concerned? Or his chief, who sits in the same room? Or her press secretary? And why did she never ask?

The Prime Minister's veracity concerned the Opposition, but some of her supporters had other worries. One young turk took a different view from Iain Macleod on the wisdom of being frank. He criticised his elders for running round like headless chickens, damaging their own election prospects by criticising her. He detected hypocrisy among those who threw up their hands in holy horror because a little ducking and diving might have taken place. Stuff and nonsense, he cried; the public expect a degree of deviousness from politicians. What worried him was that people might see recent events as evidence of incompetence. Margaret Thatcher had been criticised by Tories for many aspects of her policy and style, but until then she had been given credit for getting things done, an ability to drive her government relentlessly in the direction she wished. What would be damaging was if the public, and especially her own supporters, concluded she had run out of luck in achieving that.

No sooner was Westland off the immediate agenda than a row broke out over British Leyland. Roy Hattersley deserved the credit on the Labour side for revealing that General Motors wanted to take over Land-Rover as a prerequisite of going ahead, as sole bidder, for the trucks division of BL. This unleashed a remarkable national feeling – call it patriotism or chauvinism, according to taste. The Prime Minister wanted Whitehall to be rid of the motor industry. But to many of the British, it seemed, Land-Rover, a potent symblol of our eroding manufacturing industry, must remain as *British* as motherhood and apple-pie. And what was good for General

Motors was not necessarily good for Britain. What gave the dispute its political edge was that privatisation of BL's commercial vehicles came just after the Westland crisis, during which Michael Heseltine had blown the whistle about American takeover of Britain's high-tech industries. Labour joined in with the suggestion that, while the taxpayer was still asked to rescue companies in trouble, when heavy public investment had made them an inviting proposition it was the shareholder rather than the taxpayer who garnered the fruits. In the end political sophistication, in the substantial forms of Lord Whitelaw and Norman Tebbit, and two Cabinet members with Midlands constituencies, Peter Walker and Norman Fowler, took over, and the Government avoided doing itself serious damage on this latest banana skin.

Beneath the adrenalin-pumping row over Union Jacks and Stars and Stripes was a debate with more political mileage. This was growing public anxiety about unemployment. Any belief among ministers that they would get unemployment much below three million by the next general election had now drained away. One used the formula common before the 1983 election: 'If we can just get the statistics turning down, even if the absolute figure remains high, the public may be satisfied.' Special job-creation measures might improve the figures at the margins, but what the Government needed to lift it out of the electoral doldrums was a more certain sign of an economic breakthrough. Some Conservatives were inclined to think that since Mrs Thatcher had increased her majority handsomely in 1983 despite high unemployment, she had nothing, politically speaking, to worry about. But Professor Anthony King, examining Gallup Poll figures, concluded that 'alarm bells should now be ringing in 10 and 11 Downing Street'. He pointed out that the proportion of voters choosing the Conservatives as the party best able to deal with unemployment had halved since the last general election.

This issue came into sharper focus in the Cabinet discussions before the Budget. Francis Pym, after his dismissal, had made his own wry comment on the Thatcher revolution: 'Conservatism and radicalism need not be incompatible, but they sensibly prefer to indulge in brief and passionate flirtations rather than a permanent relationship.' With epithets like 'prudent' and 'cautious' now slipping frequently into the speeches of even more radical ministers, observers began to think Pym was being proved right. For weeks before the Budget preliminaries, ministers had been on their exercise bicycles, attaining peak fitness for the much-previewed fights over tax cuts versus public spending. But these, it turned out, were academic questions, for on Treasury estimates there was no substantial money to give away, because lower oil prices had savagely cut the Chancellor's revenue. John Biffen, that sensitive barometer of Toryism, was relieved to have avoided a vulgar preoccupation with tax cuts when 3.4 million people were without jobs.

But the Government was in that risky area between the devil and the deep blue sea. Peter Walker wanted to raise public borrowing to tackle unemployment more directly, and spending ministers like Kenneth Baker and Norman Fowler signalled the need for more public spending in their areas. What looked like an old-fashioned Keynesian plea for pump-priming had the backing of the CBI. Margaret Thatcher and Nigel Lawson were still convinced that both economic and political salvation lay through tax-cutting, if not at once then as soon as possible. The Chancellor had reaffirmed Geoffrey Howe's 1979 aim to get the standard rate down to 25 pence. As it happened, passing through London about this time was a leading candidate for the Republican nomination for President of the United States in 1988. A number of journalists had lunch with him, and he made politely clear his belief that the difference between President Reagan's success and Mrs Thatcher's failure in making the Enterprise Culture catch on depended on the risk Reagan took by running a deficit in order to cut taxes.

Congressman Kemp came to politics through American football. He exudes vigour from every inch of his six-foot, 200-lb frame. As he crushed the effete hands of Fleet Street's Finest in greeting, we could see why (as the Embassy's CV put it) he was an outstanding quarterback, causing the Buffalo Bills to 'permanently retire his Number 15 jersey' when two broken ankles, two broken shoulders, a broken knee and eleven concussions eventually forced him to hang up his shoulder pads. Kemp, who saw the Prime Minister, Chancellor and Foreign Secretary during a whirlwind visit, presented his economic thought in footballers' terms: he saw his own proposal, in Nixon's time, to cut personal taxes by 33% as 'the number one offensive play in this country'. Mrs Thatcher, who had no desire for her number one jersey to be retired for a long time yet, showed greater caution than Congressman Kemp about her defences. She craved an Enterprise Culture, but . . .

Perhaps the decisive moment of Margaret Thatcher's premiership had come during the 1983 election when, after the Think Tank report on the future of the Welfare State had been leaked, she declared that the Health Service was safe with her and guaranteed the future value of many social benefits. However politically prudent or socially desirable this was, it did present Conservative radicals with a problem that remains unresolved: how to pay for the tax cuts that visitors like Kemp, along with many on the New Right in Britain, think necessary to launch an Enterprise Culture on the American model, if all present programmes remain substantially intact? If the Prime Minister continued to give defence, education, welfare services, the NHS and the rest even existing amounts of money, never mind the improvements which many people thought essential, it was hard to see where tax cuts were to come from.

The economic debate at Westminster was beginning to centre again on the risks to be taken to achieve economic growth. 'It is already higher,' said the Government. 'But not high enough to bring down unemployment,' replied the Opposition parties as well as Tory critics. Yet few, even among Keynesians, were now arguing for an old-fashioned 'dash for growth', such as Reginald Maudling had fathered. At the heart of the thinking of Roy Hattersley, Labour's Shadow Chancellor, was caution about Labour's old bugbear, the balance of payments, when North Sea oil began to run out. Hattersley argued that only revival of Britain's moribund manufacturing could replace oil in maintaining our surplus. The Shadow Chancellor drew an uncomfortable contrast with the United States, which, in addition to expanding service industries, created an extra million jobs in manufacturing as it emerged from recession, while Britain's factory workforce fell by 1.6 million. Labour declared 'a bias in favour of public expenditure rather than personal tax cuts' to stimulate demand; investment and jobs, rather than consumption, 'often of foreign goods'.

Many Conservatives were worried that there was a split mind at the core of the Thatcher experiment. The political and economic equations of enterprise, tax cuts and public services looked so much more difficult in our old society than to the attacking quarterbacks of Buffalo and Washington DC.

When the Budget came, it seemed a remarkable example of the conviction politics that scares the wits out of nervous Tories. Although the fall in world oil prices had drained £5 billion from the Chancellor's oil revenues, he took a penny off income tax, kept the price of drink unchanged, tried to jawbone the oil companies into holding petrol prices down, abolished the tax on gifts, and launched two controversial schemes for widening share ownership.

Many Conservatives were worried that not much was done about unemployment, and Sir Kenneth Lewis, a veteran MP from Stamford and Spalding, who is a bellwether of party opinion, tossed out the intriguing thought that 'if more money comes in from the North Sea', the Chancellor should consider a second Budget. What for? 'The old phrase "priming the pump" is not dead, though it may be forgotten,' said Sir Kenneth.

Well, it might not be dead in pragmatic shire territory like Stamford and Spalding, but it was dirty talk in the polite society of Downing Street at the time, though as Nigel Lawson's autumn statement on public expenditure was later to prove, the approach of a general election can alter the most refined political theories. But at 1986 Budget-time Thatcherite backbenchers were strongly against higher public spending. One said reprovingly: 'We must not go down that path like gabardine swine', a malapropism of genius.

A crucial by-election took place in Fulham soon after the Budget, and it illustrated again the complexities of three-party politics. Fulham was a traditional Labour seat that had gone Conservative; its eccentricity consisted in a shattering mixture of wealth and deprivation within a small area nestling on the north bank of the Thames. Knowing observers predicted, rightly, that it was not as fertile territory for the SDP as might appear, because there was less likelihood of a Conservative desertion to the SDP to stop Labour. 'If you've paid £200,000 for your house, you don't vote anything but Conservative,' said one. 'They're not so much Yuppies living here, as Young Fogeys or Blown Sloanes.' The explanation of the second term is that Chelsea has become so expensive, what with Arab millionaires buying anything between Sloane Square and the Thames, that many ex-Sloane Rangers (and Hooray Henrys, their male equivalents) have been blown into the only slighly less des. res. up the river.

The Budget received a mixed reception from Fulham's transient popu-lation. I witnessed an interesting encounter between a Conservative canvasser and a young woman who liked the Budget and much else in government policy. But when asked how she would vote she said Labour, and explained to me later that, although she preferred the Alliance, Labour seemed to have the better chance of defeating the Conservative, so she and her friends were voting Labour. This was a classic 'squeezed vote' inter-view. In the event Labour won handsomely from the Conservatives, with the SDP a poor third.

The Shadow Chancellor, Roy Hattersley, laid out the case on which Labour fought in Fulham and elsewhere. He said the Government, which was already spending £21 billion, in taxes lost and benefits paid because of unemployment, was reconciled to 3 or 3.5 million out of work for the rest of the decade. He charged the Government with attacking, not unemploy-ment, but merely the statistics. Hattersley clearly shared the Chancellor's suspicion that lower oil prices, while awkward for the Budget, might do the national economy, and therefore Conservative chances, a good turn some-time in the following year. But Roy Jenkins accused Nigel Lawson of behaving like a man who has fallen from the fiftieth floor and, as he passes the twenty-fifth, says it is 'all right so far'. The former Chancellor told the present one that his prospect was highly dangerous: he had already used most of the £51 billion he got from the North Sea in seven years to pay out £33 billion for unemployment costs. If manufacturing did not pick up before the oil ran out, unemployment would be devastating.

Labour's victory in Fulham marked for it a more cheerful beginning to the second half of the decade. From its point of view, two revolutionary factors had dominated the whole period. One was the personality of Britain's first woman Prime Minister, the other Labour's internal troubles, which created the SDP and the Alliance. Success in Fulham and in the council elections in May were a measure of how far Labour had come since its 1983 election disaster. Then it had allowed Mrs Thatcher to increase her Commons majority from 43 to 144. Its share of the vote had slumped from 36.9% to 27.6. Worse, the upstart Alliance was breathing down its neck as the Official Opposition, with 25.4% of the national vote, even if its number of MPs was not nearly in Labour's league. Worst of all, Labour had conscientiously tied a number of millstones round its neck.

The most obvious of these were compulsory reselection of MPs at least once in each Parliament, and the idle way in which Labour had allowed its constituencies to be infiltrated by zealots of the Militant Tendency, who were about as popular with many Labour voters as radioactivity in Chernobyl. To add to such self-inflicted wounds, Norman Tebbit had imposed compulsory ballots on unions with political funds. The financial base of the Labour Party seemed in danger of being undermined. There was no lack of opponents and commentators to predict that after eighty more or less glorious years, the People's and Workers' Party was going down the Swanee.

In the event it did not work out like that. In adversity, with their backs to the wall, Neil Kinnock's supporters rediscovered their vigour and common sense. Reselection was not exactly a non-event; apart from a handful of Labour MPs actually dropped, others retired, so if Labour won, the number of newcomers might be uncomfortable, both ideologically and because the Party had been more prodigal of its experience than it could afford. But although reselection might still be a negative factor in Labour's recovery, it had not wrecked the party in the way predicted.

The belief on the far Left, as among many Conservatives, was that Kinnock's bloody campaign to break Militant's power would damage the Party electorally. The scouse cliché for this was 'fighting his own comrades when he should be fighting the Tories, cuts, unemployment, etc.' But seen with the hindsight of 1986, Kinnock's speech at Bournemouth the previous October had been a turning-point. One of the most familiar political sounds of the mid-eighties, played and replayed on television and radio, was the incredulity in Kinnock's voice as he denounced Liverpool's Labour council for hiring taxis to deliver redundancy notices to their workers. This became the new Mersey Sound.

It seemed that the Labour leader might have glimpsed one of those moving clay-pipes that pop up momentarily at the funfair rifle range and, even if not demolished, disappear from view. Militant in Liverpool lined up on Kinnock's side all the key groups: the council employees, the unions, the unemployed, the great down-to-earth mass of Labour. At Bournemouth, as in accents of scorn reminiscent of Aneurin Bevan he repeated falsetto the words 'a *Labour* council' (as if it would have been quite a reasonable action for Tories or Alliance), nails went into the coffins of Derek Hatton and the other Militant leaders, even though their funerals dragged on for most of the next year.

Meanwhile, ballots on union political funds proved a useful campaigning ground for Labour's supporters in the unions, who became more firmly committed to the Party than before because they had to fight for the right to remain affiliated to it. So the predicted obstacles to Labour's recovery looked less formidable by the middle of 1986: the Party would always have a troubled internal life, and the far Left had fanatical grittiness, but it no longer seemed that the antics of Militant and others would be an insuperable hurdle if the country were otherwise in a mood to elect a Labour government.

Reaction on the Fulham doorsteps and in the opinion polls suggested that, so long as Neil Kinnock appeared to be moving in the right direction against extremism, he was exorcising the damage. What remained more problematical was the balance sheet of his own leadership. His lack of Whitehall experience was a constant preoccupation of both opponents and colleagues. His innocence of the intellectual discipline of having served in government made him less of a leader-writer's dream than previous Opposition leaders – Hugh Gaitskell, who emitted policy by the yard of carefully sculpted statements from a more docile National Executive Committee; or Harold Wilson, who established the custom of preserving the leader's freedom of action by making policy on the hoof. But Kinnock showed the virtue of his faults by being a man for his own time. Polls suggested he was winning the support of a huge slice of young voters – if Labour could only persuade them actually to vote.

The new voters of 1986 had been aged eleven when Jim Callaghan was last in Downing Street; no one under thirty voted to elect the Labour Government of 1974; no one under twenty-five was an adult during the Winter of Discontent. So Mrs Thatcher's tendency to meet every criticism of her administration by referring back to Labour's record began to seem less effective, especially since Neil Kinnock had not been in that government. The obverse of this coin was that, after Labour's seven years in Opposition, the selling of new personalities was a difficult task. For Kinnock himself to prove his high seriousness without having held public office was a herculean labour. More experienced colleagues took comfort from the determination and shrewdness he had shown in pulling his own party out of the pit it dug for itself. One shadow minister said enthusiastically: 'This is what Neil is good at, running this party.' When asked if he would be equally good at running the country, the reply was: 'That's easy by comparison.'

Three-party politics is full of ironies. While Norman Tebbit drilled into voters his message that a vote for the Alliance might return a Labour government, the Alliance had a more direct impact on Labour. If Neil Kinnock was really weaning it away from a decade of self-destructive introspection, his best argument was fear of oblivion. To that fear the growth of the Alliance massively contributed. As Alliance men after the Fulham result noted, Nick Raynsford, the Labour victor, was less interested in ideology than in jobs, housing, pensions and social welfare, and was therefore a candidate of the Labour Party they had once belonged to. It seemed possible that their departure from Labour might eventually drive it nearer to its less dogmatic roots. But if Conservative Party leaders worried most about a Labour government, it was the Alliance which troubled many Tory MPs, especially in the South where their challenge had been strongest in 1983 and looked likely to be formidable in the next election. Fulham was a disappointment, principally because the Conservative voters refused to switch to stop Labour, as they had done in Brecon the previous year.

David Steel, like previous Liberal leaders, both enjoyed and suffered from his role in a third party that had no chance of power. He had used the freedom of not expecting office to tell embarrassing truths, and that gave him a special place in public affection, although it had minuses as well as plusses. His partner, David Owen, set himself the tricky job of picking up the plusses without the minuses. He spoke with the authority of one who had held lower and higher offices but who was willing to bury the past, with a dash of the buccaneering freedom that has been Liberal leaders' strong suit. He throws off opinions like a Catherine wheel, and makes up for his Party's lack of defence-in-depth against the multi-Tebbited missiles that came its way in 1986 by offering offence-in-plenty. Journalists and media producers could always be sure of a choice of half-a-dozen stories or 'a good turn' from David Owen, and in a grey world that is not the worst thing for a politician to have on offer. But his task was essentially the same as Kinnock's, though the two men, who do not like each other, will not relish the comparison. From their widely different careers, attitudes and styles, they reached the same crossroads in 1986: Could they turn charisma into 'bottom', or gravitas?

The Alliance's vote-winning record in by-elections in this Parliament, even after Fulham, surpassed that of the two larger parties, and the same applied to council by-elections. If one swallow did not make a Labour summer, one nip of frost did not spell an Alliance winter. But Fulham was a reminder, as Michael Meadowcroft, the Yorkshire Liberal MP, remarked, that 'the Alliance cannot win seats like Fulham with sweetness and light and attacks on extremists'. There are risks in being simply a residuary legatee of political discontent. For all its hard work on policy-making, the Alliance had still to stake out its home ground, otherwise it would always be playing on the hostile pitches of its opponents.

May 8 produced the broadest electoral test since 1983, for the Government decided to hold by-elections in Conservative seats in Ryedale (Yorkshire) and West Derbyshire on the same day as they defended local council seats they had won at the height of Falklands euphoria. The result was severe reverses for them in both; a further brick in the slow rebuilding of Labour's self-confidence through its success in the local contests; and victory in Ryedale and a near-miss in Derbyshire to restore Alliance morale after Fulham.

May 8 confirmed to Conservatives that Labour was their principal opposition, because its gain of council seats had an impressive geographical spread. Low polls might counsel caution, but Labour's retreat in 1983 into its Northern, Scottish and Welsh fastnesses had now been reversed. The North, as Roy Hattersley once put it, had come further south. Labour made sizeable gains in the Midlands and it was also back into the South – not just Inner London, but with substantial progress in places as far apart as Bristol, Reading and Brighton.

So Tories warned voters who were unhappy with the Government, but not ready to move right across to Labour, that a vote for the Alliance might let Labour in. In a situation full of ironies, Alliance advocates of proportional representation would wearily point out that such results are in the nature of the present electoral system. But as Macaulay once said, timid politicians think more about the security of their seats than the security of their country. What Tory MPs with Alliance runners-up fear is not so much the Red Bogy as that the renewed publicity Liberal by-election success brings might make their own seats more vulnerable.

More optimistic Conservatives argued that these were 'mid-term blues', and that governments always gain strength before a general election. But the reverses in May produced divided views on how the Government should prepare for the election. John Biffen made himself unpopular at Downing Street by urging the Tories to present a balanced ticket – rather, by implication, than a dominant Prime Minister who was less popular than previously. The argument that 'bad presentation' was the problem seemed *démodé*. The May elections showed that, whatever statistics might say, the people believed the health service, education, council services and roads were being run down, and they preferred spending on these rather than on tax cuts. But on the morning after the voting, the Prime Minister, outside Conservative Central Office, played another stanza of 'We shall not be moved', while Norman Tebbit's view was that if voters wanted higher public spending they would vote Alliance or Labour anyhow.

Nigel Lawson retained his sceptical view of the merits of higher public spending, as compared with tax cuts. He would probably have endorsed the telegram Joe Kennedy sent to his son, the President: 'Dear Jack, Don't buy a single vote more than necessary. I'll be damned if I'm going to pay for a landslide.' Both sides in the Cabinet felt strongly that theirs was the better way to achieve a third election victory, and that the alternative might be dangerous. Yet all the ingredients were present for a fudge, a phrase which, before David Owen gave it a bad name, used to be a synonym for 'the British genius for compromise'.

So quite soon after the May mini-election the Prime Minister was signalling that there would be more money for education and health. A group of spending Ministers – Kenneth Baker, Norman Fowler, Douglas Hurd, Malcolm Rifkind, with allies like Kenneth Clarke – wanted public spending to improve services and promote employment in other fields also. One of their supporters said what was needed was 'a slush fund of a billion or a billion and a half to spend on socially worthwhile and electorally attractive schemes'. Crudely put, perhaps, but when November came Nigel Lawson's agreement to accommodate the over-run of public spending – by more than £4 billion in 1987–88 – looked not all that different from what they were seeking.

The debate about health spending is fiendishly difficult. Arguments behind the published figures – about the impact of higher rates of 'health inflation', shorter hours for nurses, an ageing population, and developments in surgery – are so complex that 'presentation' alone could not win the day for the Government. The public would only be convinced when the hospitals were given more money.

Not all of the Government's worries in 1986 were domestic. During the Suez crisis thirty years ago, Lady Eden complained that the Canal was flowing through her drawing-room. With the American bombing of Libya, as a reprisal for what President Reagan called state-controlled terrorism, the ghosts of the Middle East came stalking through British politics again. But the rush to judgement on how London's permission for the United States to use bases here would affect the next general election always seemed premature. After all, three years after the Suez débâcle Harold Macmillan won an increased majority for the Tories.

I adhere to the ancient belief that British elections nowadays are not decided by foreign affairs. The Conservatives clearly worried about the immediate damage to their popularity after the raids. These came in the middle of another remarkable week in British politics, for they were taking place while the Government was in the process of being defeated in the House of Commons on the far-distant issue of Sunday trading. Labour had cruel public relations luck, for the defeat came too late for the evening news programmes on television and for most editions of national newspapers, and by the next day it was smothered by news from Libya. Tory rebels believed the bill showed the Government had lost its political touch, and was imperilling seats at the next election by running itself into an unnecessary row over a dogma of deregulation that united churches, unions and parts of the retail trade. A Conservative MP who had voted with the Government, and therefore wanted indescribable punishments inflicted on his Party's whips for allowing the defeat, told me that he had received, amid a scream of criticism, one letter favouring the Bill. This was from the manager of his local Woolworth's. But he had written his loyal replies and cast his loyal vote, and seen his local political opponents run rings around him.

So Tory morale was shaky as MPs made their way home after the Government's defeat. Most of them had left Westminster before the raids on Libya were announced. That was the one piece of parliamentary luck for the Government amid all the gloom. The group of ministers handling the American request for use of bases – the Prime Minister, Lord Whitelaw, Sir Geoffrey Howe and George Younger – heard that the F-111s had left England at about 6 p.m. They assumed news of the attack would break long before the Commons vote on Sunday trading, which was timed for midnight. So Mrs Thatcher would have to come down to the House to make a statement on the bombing just as the debate reached its tumultuous conclusion. It was a great relief to them when the Libyan news did not break, and the statement could be deferred to the next day. One minister said: 'There's no occasion in modern times on which such a statement, made late at night, has not turned into a fair-sized disaster.'

The debate about whether Britain should have agreed to use of bases here was sharp and rumbled on for months. Ministers themselves accepted the decision with differential enthusiasm. Norman Tebbit, Nigel Lawson, John Biffen, Lord Hailsham and Douglas Hurd were among the doubters. But the conclusive argument was that, after Europe had failed to deliver much by way of diplomatic or economic help against Libya, a British refusal would have had a devastating effect on the Atlantic Alliance, the bulwark of British and European defence since 1941.

In a shower of criticism, there was one brief window of hope for the Government, thirty-six hours after the raid, when a report from Tripoli suggested a coup against Gadaffi might by under way. I was lunching with a senior minister at his club when a younger member of the Cabinet arrived in great excitement with the rumour. Briefly one was able to see what a remarkable difference it would have made to the Government's fortunes if Gadaffi had been toppled as a result of raids Mrs Thatcher made feasible. It might have been her second Falklands, the anti-banana skin for which her friends and foes constantly look, in longing or in loathing.

But a shrewd politician–tactician, Denis Healey, believed the Prime Minister could be damaged by the raids. He focussed on her failure to consult more widely, and said with ostentatious sadness that he had hoped after the Westland affair that the leopardess had changed her spots. He had even detected 'ministers who had been imprisoned in the dungeons of the Cabinet for many years emerge blinking into the sunlight, chanting the Hymn to Freedom from *Fidelio*'. But, alas, his hopes had not been fulfilled, for the Cabinet was apparently now back to admiring 'another of the manic monologues from the Prime Minister that always shed about as much light on the issue as an electric drill'.

Healey might not be the most disinterested critic of the Prime Minister's style, but even in her own Party the theory that, since the Westland affair, she was more inclined to act as *primus inter pares* was fading fast. Some ministers were indignant that she had not consulted more widely before the Libyan raids. One said that since she had commissioned Nigel Lawson to put the economy right and Norman Tebbit to win the election, and since the aftermath of Libya might be relevant to both these tasks, the two men were entitled to feel aggrieved. She was also criticised for rough handling of Sir Geoffrey Howe over earlier US–Libyan incidents in the Gulf of Sirte. One said later that the popular Howe had been abominably treated, but added that the rest of the Cabinet had 'kept our heads below the parapet, and hoped we'd soon be discussing milk quotas'. Even some of Mrs Thatcher's most loyal friends feared that the qualities which made her a vote-winner in 1983 – decisiveness, willingness to speak her mind, certitude – might be in danger of making her seem bossy. The same criticism was heard in the Commonwealth during discussions on South Africa. But Margaret Thatcher had no time for what one of her ministers called 'the Foreign Office's H.G. List' (containing hypocritical gestures on apartheid). She did not doubt that she was right.

CHAPTER 17

THE REAL REVOLUTION IN ULSTER

Throughout this revolutionary decade in British politics, the one part of the United Kingdom in which the revolution has been not political but physical is Northern Ireland. It now has Europe's most chronic terrorist problem. Most people there have no part in the terrorism, and no sympathy with it. The 'revolution' is conducted by a tiny minority of the Catholic minority, who support the IRA against the Protestant majority. A tiny minority of the Protestants respond with violence against Catholics. So it is a minority problem, but no less bloody and stubborn for that, as had been amply demonstrated during twelve years of the Troubles before this decade began.

Since 1970, soon after the beginning of the present IRA campaign, I have believed, and written, that the only basis of a probable solution to Northern Ireland's problems lies in power-sharing between politicians representing the Protestant and Catholic, Unionist and Nationalist communities. To a Belfastman who has lived away from his native city for thirty years, in still affectionate exile, this seems the most rational hope for political progress.

The concept of power-sharing *within* Northern Ireland tackles not just issues peripheral to Ulster's ancient quarrel, like relations with Dublin or London, but the kernel of that quarrel: how two peoples with conflicting national loyalties can live together in a small area and govern their lives jointly; how the Catholics can be convinced that they are getting a fair deal within that state, without the Protestants believing they are being taken out of the United Kingdom against their wishes. The best hope of peace in seventeen weary years was the power-sharing Executive of 1974, which was destroyed by a Protestant strike after only a few months' existence. The steam behind that strike was antipathy to a Council of Ireland, which seemed to many Protestants to give Dublin a voice in the North. Whether either a more resolute attitude to the strike by the British government or the earlier jettisoning of the Council of Ireland might have saved the experiment remains controversial.

The difference in atmosphere between 1974, when that experiment took place, and 1985, when the Anglo-Irish Agreement was signed, reflects the deepening bitterness of the years between. 1985 was the third of three political initiatives attempted, with dwindling hope, during Margaret Thatcher's period in office. It was conceived in near-despair. By contrast, the atmosphere in 1974 had been one of hope; an *esprit de corps* grew with remarkable speed among the Protestant and Catholic ministers who worked together, for the first time, on the Executive. Brian Faulkner, Gerry Fitt, John Hume and their colleagues wanted to prove not only that they could administer their departments but that eventually they might persuade their followers to support the new institutions of the state. It did seem that they were rising to that higher level of political leadership which does not simply pander to its own supporters, but dares to chip away at their prejudices. By 1985 the deepening bitterness of the intervening years of violence had created a different, more sour atmosphere.

The 1974 Executive fell after the British government failed to stand up to intimidation by Protestant paramilitaries. Brian Faulkner is dead. Gerry Fitt lives in London, isolated from his own followers, partly because of IRA intimidation in his West Belfast constituency and then against himself and his family, partly because his party, the Social Democratic and Labour Party, wanted more nationalist leadership than this veteran socialist thought right. It is a salutary reminder of how stony is the path of conciliators in Ulster. On the Unionist side those leaders who came to see the need for compromise – Terence O'Neill, James Chichester-Clark, Brian Faulkner – have been outflanked by harder men. On the Nationalist side, from Redmond to Fitt, the story has been the same. Yet a political solution must one day be found.

What becomes harder to believe, however, when we remember how terrorism and counter-terrorism have frustrated all political initiatives, is that any form of political progress alone will end violence. The steady drip of horror goes on through the years: teachers shot in front of their pupils, fathers in front of their children, men tortured, mutilated, or simply killed with fearful casualness, in revenge for another death, or because they are believed to be informers, or because of their religion. The suspension of disbelief required to claim that politics alone will solve the Ulster problem is no longer possible.

There now exists, in tiny segments of both Catholic and Protestant communities, a great stench of evil. Nothing will end this except security measures sustained by an act of communal will, in Ireland North and South, and in Britain, that says this evil will not triumph. Most politicians pay some kind of lip-service to that proposition, but the political will does not seem to exist.

Apart from Britain's economic malaise, Northern Ireland has been the most persistent problem in British politics during the eighties, and for long before that. What makes the issue both fascinating and infuriating is that its politics is conducted in a three-ring circus, in London, Dublin and Belfast. Some performers move from one ring to another with confusing grace – and variable acts – but no circus master controls the whole performance, and the result is chaotic. The root cause of much mutual incomprehension between English and Irish politicians is what might be called their 'differential interest' in this subject. This is not a novel political phenomenon. Mr Pickwick was confronted, during the Eatanswill by-election, by the editors of rival local newspapers demanding to know what 'they' were saying in London about leading articles, written by each editor, savaging the opposing candidates. Pickwick, ever polite, assured each impartially that his squibs were making a great impression in the metropolis.

The English now suffer from an ancient Irish disease: telling people what they want to hear. So they behave like Pickwick and leave the factions in Ireland believing that their views, indeed their problem, is more ever-present in the national consciousness than it is. This compounds the many ambiguities that are the problem in Ireland itself. As Albert Camus wrote: 'Lying is not only saying what is not true. It is also, and especially, saying more than is true, and, as far as the human heart is concerned, saying more than one feels.' Or as the British Cabinet Secretary, Sir Robert Armstrong, one of the architects of the Anglo-Irish Agreement, might put it, being economical with the truth.

Three sets of events dominated the Northern Ireland issue during the Thatcher years. The murder of her friend Airey Neave, who was to have been Northern Ireland Secretary, at the beginning of the 1979 election was followed by the murder of Lord Mountbatten and others, and by the slaughter of eighteen soldiers at Warrenpoint near the Republic's border. This caused the Prime Minister to demand a political initiative from Humphrey Atkins, her first Secretary of State. He produced it, against the advice of his department, and it failed.

The hunger strikes of 1981, in which ten Republican prisoners starved themselves to death, led to another initiative by his successor, Jim Prior. This produced an Assembly that was supposed to lead to 'rolling devolution', but the SDLP, principal representative of the Nationalist community, boycotted it, and that initiative foundered also. But the hunger strikes and the continuing violence generated demands, from the United States, Europe and elsewhere, for another political effort. These demands coincided with a report of the New Ireland Forum, representing the Nationalist parties in Ireland, North and South. The two pressures came together in the Anglo-Irish negotiations, and these culminated in November 1985 in the signing of an agreement by Mrs Thatcher and Garret Fitzgerald, the Irish Prime Minister.

But the Unionists had not been consulted and this caused all of them, fifteen of the seventeen MPs from Northern Ireland, to resign their seats and fight by-elections on a single issue – rejection of the agreement. All but one of the fifteen were re-elected and they proceeded to boycott Westminster. The revolution had come full circle and ended in a cul-de-sac.

What has made the Ulster question resistant to political solution is the ability of the Provisional IRA to sustain their terrorist campaign from 1969 until the present. They have survived and prospered under a succession of regimes and differing security policies. For more than fourteen of the seventeen years of violence London has ruled Northern Ireland directly; Stormont has no longer been available as whipping-boy. Responsibility for everything from discrimination to violence resides in Whitehall, and violence remains the poisoned element that makes normal politics impossible.

When British politicians discuss the legitimate purposes of government, there are few enough propositions on which Margaret Thatcher, Neil Kinnock, David Steel and David Owen would all agree. Privatisation or public ownership? More or less spending on health, education? Public subsidy for industrial development? Higher or lower taxation? But nearly everyone in public life would accept that protection of the citizen from violence and death is a primary duty of any government. In that primary duty successive British governments since 1972, for understandable reasons, have nevertheless notoriously failed. Many soldiers and policemen have died in the process; so have an appalling number of Ulster civilians, both Protestant and Catholic. The support they have had from governments in Dublin may best be described as fitful. The fact that nobody believes either an all-Ireland government or that of an independent Ulster would reduce the level of slaughter does not diminish the sense among ordinary people, in both communities in Northern Ireland, that they have been let down by the only government they have, that at Westminster.

No one has produced an intellectually convincing way of dealing with the IRA. The choice appears to lie in three directions: surrender, which would lead to civil war; draconian security measures, for which the British public has no appetite; and leaving the issue to be decided on the streets, by small numbers of Republican and Protestant terrorists, producing, at best, what Reginald Maudling in the early seventies called 'an acceptable level of violence'.

When London took over from Stormont in 1972, it inherited a system of internment without trial which had begun in 1971. In previous IRA campaigns, during the second world war and in the fifties, internment proved effective in both North and South. But this time the IRA made its existence a potent propaganda weapon, and British and Irish politicians, many of whom had advocated internment, either publicly or privately, resiled and demanded that it should be phased out.

Detention without trial is an odious procedure, which has been barbarously misused round the world too often in this century for politicians willingly to defend it. Politically its abolition became inevitable, but in a series of investigations into how terrorism should be tackled a succession of distinguished jurists failed to find an alternative they believed in. Both Lord Diplock and Lord Gardiner, commissioned by Conservative and Labour governments respectively, declined to recommend immediate abandonment of internment. Diplock delivered the classic statement about the intractability of the IRA problem, and why action through normal courts would not work. After detailed analysis, he wrote:

> The dilemma is complete. The only hope of restoring the ability of criminal courts of law in Northern Ireland to deal with terrorist crimes is by using an extra-judicial process to deprive of their ability to operate in Northern Ireland those terrorists whose activities result in the intimidation of witnesses. With an easily penetrable border to the south and west, the only way of doing this is to put them in detention by an executive act, and to keep them confined until they can be released without danger to public safety and the administration of criminal justice.

The Government adopted Diplock's proposal for terrorist cases to be tried by a High Court judge sitting without a jury, because jurors had been intimidated, just as witnesses had been threatened and in one case murdered. As security allowed, or politics demanded, successive governments continued to 'phase out' internment. Lord Gardiner, in his report two years after Lord Diplock's, acknowledged that internment was providing 'a recruiting agency and a school for terrorists, with all expenses paid,' and that it also created 'a myth of repression which is becoming part of the terrorist legend'. But he also declined to say when it should be abandoned: violence was widespread, and the future unpredictable, so politicians must make up their own minds.

Merlyn Rees ended internment in 1975, announced that terrorists would be dealt with through the courts, and said there would be no 'special category' in prisons for those convicted. Previously both Republic and Loyalist terrorists, whether convicted or detained, had run their own sections of the prisons, rather like prisoner-of-war camps. But the propaganda campaign continued, since neither IRA nor Loyalist terrorists, nor the apologists of either, are concerned with civil liberties, but with victory for their own sides.

Abolition of 'special category' became the excuse for IRA hunger strikes. As for the courts, no civilian witnesses were willing to risk murder or maiming, which were the IRA punishments for informers, so the police had to rely on confessions to obtain convictions. But soon allegations were made of ill-treatment of suspects to obtain these confessions. An inquiry found some cases were manufactured but others true. The result was stricter interrogation procedures and the confessions began to dry up. Campaigns since then have been against the evidence of supergrasses and the form of the Diplock Courts. Through all these events and years the IRA campaign has waxed or waned, but never showed signs of stopping.

Just before Mrs Thatcher took office a British army report, which leaked to the press, gave a gloomy prognostication: it declared that victory against the IRA was impossible while the Republic provided 'the classic safe haven so essential to any successful terrorist movement', and pointed especially to freedom from extradition for crimes committed in the North. The new Prime Minister, faced with this unpromising prospect and dismayed by a summer of slaughter, called for a fresh initiative. She also wanted to have something to tell President Carter, who was under pressure from prominent Irish–American Democrats, Senators Kennedy and Moynihan, Speaker Tip O'Neill and Governor Carey of New York, who had issued a statement calling for Irish unity. But it was on this subject that Humphrey Atkins' initiative hit a predictable roadblock. The SDLP was now rejecting any settlement which did not pay more attention to Irish unity, but the Ulster majority remained as firm for the Union with Britain as for the previous century. Atkins' consultative assembly failed.

The hunger strike deaths dominated politics in 1981. Garret Fitzgerald, by then Prime Minister in the Republic for the first time, was critical of Mrs Thatcher when she stuck to her determination not to grant political status in prison to hunger strikers who had been convicted of terrorist crimes. Ten men died, and the hunger strike was then effectively abandoned. But the deaths further polarised opinion.

Just before Jim Prior became Margaret Thatcher's second – and reluctant – Northern Ireland Secretary in the autumn of that year, an opinion poll set the context in which he had to seek a solution. It showed that the only option enjoying majority support among both Protestants and Catholics was power-sharing. Full integration in the United Kingdom was mathematically more popular, but this was principally because 91% of Protestants backed it, though a large minority of Catholics, 39%, also did so. Prior sought to cater for this public preference by introducing an assembly in which there would be 'rolling devolution' – that is, Unionist and Nationalist politicians would have power devolved to them over subjects on which they could agree to co operate. It never had much hope, but with the killing continuing, as the economic lifeblood of a once prosperous province ebbed away, anything seemed worth trying.

If the plan was ingenious, so were the methods used to frustrate it. The SDLP announced it would stand for election but abstain from attendance. The IRA entered elective politics in the guise of Sinn Fein, and the combination of armalite rifle and ballot-paper was begun. Most of the Unionists – men who had helped bring down the 1974 power-sharing Executive – made clear they were only interested in returning to the majority rule which had made the old Stormont Parliament so inadequate to deal with Ulster's crisis. Prior's assembly lingered on for a time after he resigned, but it never had a chance.

By the time this initiative began to run into the sand a new one had begun in Dublin, and has dominated Anglo–Irish relations ever since. This was the gathering in a New Ireland Forum of four Nationalist parties – Garret Fitzgerald's Fine Gael and Dick Spring's Labour, which formed the Coalition Government in Dublin; Charles Haughey's Fianna Fail opposition; and John Hume's SDLP from the North. Their report, in 1984, suggested several variations of a Nationalist solution in Ireland: a unitary state; federalism or confederalism; or joint authority over Northern Ireland by London and Dublin.

The 'differential interest' in Irish affairs in the two capitals showed itself again. On a famous occasion when Mrs Thatcher denounced these three proposals as being impractical, the row that her 'out, out, out' remark began was to reverberate in Dublin for months, even years. Yet within half an hour of ending her meeting with Fitzgerald, the British Prime Minister was busy with the Cyprus question, followed by issues that would gain or lose her more votes: the pit strike, picketing, benefits for miners' families, Tory revolts about overseas aid.

But Garret Fitzgerald suffered a mauling in the Dail after his meeting with Mrs Thatcher. People in the Republic had been able to see both Prime Ministers' London news conferences live on Irish Television. Indeed, as journalists waited for the Taoiseach's delayed news conference, an RTE man murmured in despair: 'We'll be playing music by now.' It would have been a rash BBC man who suggested to Bill Cotton that he should tear up his schedules to broadcast live what most British viewers would have regarded as of little interest.

The incident is a parable of Anglo–Irish relations. Throughout 1984 Irish politics had been buzzing about the three options in the New Ireland Forum report; yet long before Mrs Thatcher delivered what Dublin saw as her brutal rejection of these options, Jim Prior had made clear what a missed opportunity he thought the whole business had been: 'There is one overriding and abiding reality from which we cannot escape,' he told Parliament. 'That is that consent is simply not forthcoming for any formulation that denies the Unionists their right not only to belong to the United Kingdom, but to be apart from the Republic.' He added that it was 'a dangerous fallacy' to think a British government could 'engineer' such consent.

The eighties has been a decade of gathering ambiguity on this subject. As the Anglo–Irish deal emerged, even those few Unionist politicians – as distinct from voters – who would have liked an *internal* deal with Northern Nationalists were inhibited by a suggestion from the Irish Foreign Minister, Peter Barry, that the deal was a step on the road to Irish unity. They might think this was only said to ditch Charles Haughey, and they did not believe Barry, but they could not afford to ignore him, which achieved the worst of both worlds.

At the same time, John Hume's task in seeking any internal compromise in Northern Ireland was made no easier by Haughey's insistence that only a unitary Ireland could bring peace, and that the North was 'a failed entity'. The SDLP might ask: 'If it has failed, why try to make it work?' And the IRA might conclude, with deadlier logic: 'If it has failed, why not destroy it?' But in Dublin the politicking was fierce. Whatever emerged from the negotiations with London, Fitzgerald was certain to acclaim it as an historic breakthrough and Haughey to denounce it as a humiliating sell-out which he would renegotiate.

The intellectual confusion over the doctrine of democratic 'consent' bedevils the Irish question. A minister in Dublin once told me: 'Yes, unity can come only with Unionist consent, but that consent cannot for ever be unreasonably withheld.' To Unionists this seemed to leave a democratic choice not noticeably more attractive than that offered by Henry Ford in his early days: 'You can have a car of any colour, so long as it's black.' Nearly every politician in Dublin expressed his wish to 'respect the legitimate traditions and aspirations of the Northern Unionists', but few of them seem to perceive that the *legitimate* aspiration of Unionists is to remain united with Britain, rather than such *illegitimate* traditions as coat-trailing Orange marches or anti-Catholic bigotry.

It has been against this ambiguous background that Ireland's two leading politicians of the eighties, Garret Fitzgerald and Charles Haughey, have faced each other. Irish voters might put the North some leagues behind the economy in their list of concerns, but neither leader could afford to be outsmarted on 'the national issue'. The two men's styles are far apart.

Garret Fitzgerald's political epitaph might be 'He meant well'. His manner exudes conviction in his own reasonableness and calm, but the style is staccato, and he is prodigal with new ideas. His eyes flash, he smiles shyly, his flyaway hair evokes a memory of those old *Toytown* characters from *Children's Hour* – the Inventor, with a new contraption every hour, or the Magician, semi-permanently wrapped in green smoke.

There is no hint of *Toytown* about Charlie Haughey, although his political enemies – of whom there are many in Ireland – might detect sulphur among the green smoke. As a political operator Haughey stands head and shoulders over anyone else in Ireland. At news conferences he not only answers the questions asked, but has that quality which awes journalists of anticipating what they will ask next. He has a hooded charm which won Mrs Thatcher's admiration until he blotted his copybook with her by opposing the Falklands campaign. Yet he shares with her an inner core of toughness, which explains his durability in a political career that has twice seemed certain to be extinguished. Haughey remains the epitome of irredentist Irish Nationalism, impassioned, convinced, unyielding, the mirror-image of the Ulster Unionists with their slogan 'not an inch'. Sceptics believe this is simply the game he needs to play to lead Ireland's most traditional party. It scarcely matters which is right. Both Fitzgerald's and Haughey's versions of the New Ireland were far distant from Northern Unionist perceptions. After fourteen years of killing, they evoked again Yeats' cry of pain:

> We had fed the heart on fantasies,
> The heart's grown brutal from the fare;
> More substance in our enmities
> Than in our love.

By the time Mrs Thatcher delivered her rejection of the Forum report, Jim Prior had given way to Douglas Hurd. Prior perceived that no political progress was feasible in a time-span which interested him. But that pessimism did not dissipate the great expectations in Dublin. The media hype continued: no subject attracts more prescriptive reporting than Northern Ireland, with *Cogito, ergo sum* converted into *Cogito, ergo est*. Just as the Forum had been convinced by the persuasiveness of its arguments into thinking that London and Belfast would accept the conclusions, so many journalists, in London as well as Dublin, are persuaded by their own faith in Irish unity as the inevitable solution. There is no subject on which usually rational observers prefer the harmonies in their own heads to sad reality.

By the end of 1984, under the influence of Hurd, who was a diplomat before coming into politics, and Geoffrey Howe, the Foreign Secretary, events were moving towards some kind of Anglo–Irish accord. British ministers felt that, after the Forum report, international opinion, and especially that in America, made some agreement necessary. Enoch Powell, the former Conservative minister, now an Ulster Unionist MP, described this as 'humbugging the Americans'. The long drawn-out negotiations by civil servants, led for Britain by the increasingly controversial Cabinet Secretary, Sir Robert Armstrong, were viewed with tremulous excitement in Dublin, with weary hope of only a little progress in London, and against a background of cold disapproval from Unionists in Belfast.

The treatment of Unionist politicians during a year of negotiations was botched. Even Ulster-born civil servants were not included in Sir Robert's team. Dublin regularly briefed the SDLP on the negotiations, but the Unionists, partly because of their own noisy disapproval of the whole process, were given cold-shoulder treatment by their 'sovereign government' – to adopt the phrase Nationalists favoured, rubbing the Unionists' noses in the weakness of their position.

By coincidence a book was published towards the end of the London–Dublin talks in 1985 that produced a sense of *déjà vu*. Merlyn Rees, Labour's Northern Ireland Secretary at the time of the power-sharing experiment in 1974, wrote about the Sunningdale agreement between Edward Heath and the Irish government of Liam Cosgrave (whose Foreign Minister was Garret Fitzgerald). Several Sunningdale participants have since criticised Heath for taking Brian Faulkner further along the road of an 'Irish Dimension' than political prudence allowed. In the middle of the strike that destroyed the Executive, the SDLP agreed to postpone this part of the deal, but this came too late to save the Executive. Rees wrote that Sunningdale 'had been a London–Dublin solution that had ignored the reality of the situation in the North of Ireland'. His book had two persistent themes. One, bleakly expressed by the Executive in its death throes, was that 'the new [political] arrangements are bound to be judged by the contribution which they make to peace and security'. A truism perhaps, but it is often forgotten. The persistent rage in both communities in Northern Ireland derives directly from the death and destruction of the past seventeen years. Any political initiative appears relevant to ordinary people there only if they believe it has some hope of ending terrorism.

In the Anglo–Irish negotiations the British government might have won grudging assent from the Unionist population, if not from their political leaders, if they had revealed what they were asking from Dublin as well as allowing Dublin to reveal what it was asking of London. The ending of violence has a political dimension, but it also has a – pre-eminent – security dimension, as the Provisionals' contempt for the whole Anglo–Irish process made clear. Sceptics refused from the start to invest too much of their slender capital of hope in an agreement which both the Unionists and Haughey opposed, and which did not begin to interest the IRA.

Rees's second point was even more relevant to the current negotiations. He was the first Secretary of State to reveal what his predecessors and successors, as well as army and police chiefs down the years, have hinted privately: that while Britain was grateful to Dublin for such security co-operation as it received, this was never adequate to the crisis. Rees complained about Dublin's 'all-pervading carping' about the British Army; and its habit of 'apparently not giving a thought to the deaths of British soldiers'. In his final minute to the Prime Minister, James Callaghan, he wrote that 'what was lacking was day-to-day co-operation, due to the anti-British feeling which still existed widely in the South'.

Privately, Conservative ministers monitoring the Anglo–Irish negotiations in 1985 shared Merlyn Rees's doubts about how effective security co-operation would ever be. On no subject are public and private opinions so different. Their intelligence experts told them many OTRs (On-the-Run terrorists) were in the Republic still, but the Gardai seemed unable to arrest them. Dublin had encouraged the hope that it could rescue Whitehall from the political aftermath of the embarrassing mass escape from the Maze Prison (which had almost cost Jim Prior or his junior minister, Nicholas Scott, their jobs), by recapturing most of the eighteen fugitives who had gone South. But the results were disappointing and most of the IRA men remained free, some to kill again.

Before the British Cabinet dispersed for its summer break in 1985 it held a sober discussion on the forthcoming agreement with Dublin. It was a world-weary occasion. Lord Whitelaw, Westminster's most successful

Ulster veteran, remained sceptical about what the talks had achieved. John Biffen, one of the few Conservative ministers who still speaks with affection about 'the Province', was nervous. The Lord Chancellor, Lord Hailsham, poured cold water on proposals for mixed North–South courts. The Prime Minister herself, while sharing the scepticism, agreed that it was better to go ahead than to abandon the talks. She wanted to be able to indicate to a sympathetic President Reagan that Britain was trying to co-operate with Dublin. American opinion might be ill-informed, but British ministers believed they needed all the help they could get from Washington to fight gun-running and promote extradition of IRA men from across the Atlantic.

London was also doubtful whether a permanent Anglo–Irish conference would cure Nationalist alienation in the North. Indeed, there was scepticism about the alienation itself, for there was some empathy with J. K. Galbraith's sardonic comment on the Boston Irish, the master race of Massachusetts: 'They would remain a bruised and exploited people, nature's under-dogs, as an ample and sometimes excellent literature can confirm. No other race withstands success so well.'

Neither Protestants nor Catholics in Ulster have had much success in the past decade. What the new agreement needed was some early sign that it would bring nearer the defeat of terrorism and the return of peace. For the anomaly about the agreement was that it was greeted with almost unanimous enthusiasm in London, Dublin (except for Fianna Fail), Washington and Brussels, but not in Northern Ireland, which was where it mattered. The agreement had been conceived in an ambiguity that its parents, the Prime Minister and the Taoiseach, did not bother to conceal. They have different aspirations for Northern Ireland, and one of them could not afford, while the other did not care to pretend, otherwise. So Garret Fitzgerald asserted he was as good an Irish Nationalist as Charles Haughey, and Margaret Thatcher proclaimed herself – several times at the signing ceremony – to be a Unionist and a Loyalist.

After the agreement the IRA continued, even stepped up, its campaign of killing. Unionist leaders competed with each other in threatening, boycotts, and the open or tacit encouragement of demonstrations and marches that often turned violent. The unfortunate RUC were caught between two fires. Catholics praised them when they used the hated plastic bullets against Protestant mobs. But when the Irish Foreign Minister, Peter Barry, suggested that Northern Catholics might soon be able to join the police, the SDLP responded with the deflating view that this was unlikely during the remainder of the present century. Clearly the revolution in attitudes would not be swift, if it ever took place at all.

The birth of the new era was greeted in Northern Ireland itself by hostility in all sections of the Protestant community, and widespread scepticism among Catholics about the benefits. Yet it never seemed likely that the sound and fury from Ian Paisley and other Unionist politicians would persuade Margaret Thatcher to retreat from an agreement on which she had gambled even a little of her prestige. The useful life of the agreement is less likely to be shortened by Unionist violence, boycotts or strikes than by simple inanition and what a Marxist would call 'its internal contradictions'. There was only one apparent hope: if the agreement began to reduce the level of violence, ordinary Protestants might stop listening to Paisley and his ilk and start listening to the British government.

But Whitehall was not hopeful after seeing the agreement in operation for a year. One minister wrote in exasperation on the latest schedule of demands from Dublin: 'All take and no give.' Irish ministers were also disappointed at lack of progress in the North. The central paradox remained: what pleased one side would offend the other. As Seamus Heaney wrote, in an even-handed guying of Ireland's rival bigotries:

> As the man said when Celtic won, 'the Pope of Rome
> 's a happy man this night.' His flock suspect
> In their deepest heart of hearts the heretic
> Has come at last to heel and to the stake.
> We tremble near the flames, but want no truck
> With the actual firing.

Not just the simple people of Belfast or Derry, Catholic or Protestant, suffer such intellectual confusion and moral ambiguity. The revolutionary decade continues, without evident hope of happy resolution.

CHAPTER 18

THE BITTEREST ELECTION

The unpredictable nature of British politics in this revolutionary decade was illustrated again in the summer of 1986, when the Conservatives received an unexpected bonus from the disarray in both opposition parties over defence. The first clouds of the gathering storm appeared in June, when David Owen publicly disowned an Alliance joint commission report that left open the question whether Polaris, Britain's nuclear deterrent, should be replaced.

The issue is fundamental for Owen. Its roots go back to Labour's earlier quarrel over unilateral nuclear disarmament in Hugh Gaitskell's time. Owen reminded doubting colleagues that it was because a later Labour generation was indulging in 'fudge and mudge' over defence and other issues that he and they had departed to found the SDP. Why should he now bend to Liberal demands for compromise on the same issue?

Yet there was an element of *hubris* in it all. Since the birth of the Alliance, its stock-in-trade has been to contrast its harmony with discord in Conservative and Labour parties. So their opponents felt for the two Davids what Robert Burns felt for the unco' guid. If you want to major politically in the merits of compromise, you must never, ever, fail to get your own act together. The Alliance had gained much of its support, in an angry political period, because by contrast it was led by people who manifestly liked each other, who could agree on most things, and who were not going to tear themselves apart when they disagreed. They were thought of by the non-political public as Nice People Who Don't Quarrel.

So defence faced Owen with a genuine intellectual problem. He frequently asserted his belief that the British electorate, bored by party strife, was attracted by the idea of co-operation by different parties – in the first instance Liberals and Social Democrats, but with the possibility of a wider coalition if the post-election arithmetic so decreed. This does assume the voters must be willing to leave a certain amount to be decided by politicians after the election. But if the Polaris successor was a matter of conviction for David Owen and apparently non-negotiable, what about the poor voter who also thought this decision a matter of life and death, one way or the other? Was he to vote Conservative if he wanted a British deterrent; and Labour if he didn't; but against anyone (like Owen) who advocated proportional representation, because that would make coalition more likely and therefore compromise on an issue that, for him, was non-negotiable?

The public is often uncharitable about the politician's most difficult dilemma: whether to do what he believes to be right or what he believes will win him support and votes. This is not as black and white a question as may appear, for in a democratic system those who aspire to govern their country must face the possibility of – they hope honourable – compromise. But the nuclear-defence issue has disturbed the British Left for more than forty years, and as scientists' and voters' knowledge of nuclear winter and the consequences of nuclear accident grew, the choice became more anguished.

Within the Alliance David Steel increasingly looked like the balancing point between a Liberal Party with a strong Leftward instinct on defence and an SDP that touches base with its Gaitskellite origins, although some of its leaders suspect that after seven years of Mrs Thatcher's government the politics of unbending conviction may be less fashionable. By the autumn conferences David Owen had been convinced of the magnitude of the political problem. His instincts, however, are combative. Just before I left for Harrogate a Tory minister enlivened lunchtime with a comparison of the two Alliance leaders:

> David Owen is like a subaltern in the Great War, switching his boot impatiently with his riding-crop, determined to get his men over the top before any other unit. That's the way VCs are won, but you do tend to get a lot of soldiers killed. David Steel, on the other hand, is a steady brigade major, who won't look so glorious, but won't get so many of his men killed: they'll still be on the battlefield at the end.

Although Owen behaved more emolliently at both his own and the Liberal seaside conferences, he repeated his belief that it would be impossible for the Alliance to rubbish Labour on defence, as the Conservatives undoubtedly would, unless the Alliance itself had a clear line. But the Liberal Assembly – though by only 27 votes out of 1300 – exploded any hope that this could be easily achieved, for it came out in favour of non-nuclear defence. After the conferences were over, both parties saw the damage being done to their standing in the polls and a compromise, favouring Owen's line, was patched up in London.

This quarrel epitomised a wider difference in political attitudes between Liberals and Social Democrats. David Steel, during ten years as Liberal leader, had frequently urged his followers to avoid becoming 'the political equivalent of jogging', 'an academic think-tank', or 'an occasional safety valve in the political system', and to fight for a share in power. But some Liberals are not averse to political jogging. They bear the honourable stigmata of their years in the wilderness, and some seem averse to becoming spotted by the Whitehall world. By contrast, Social Democrats who had power once in Labour governments have no doubt that it is their job to win it again.

The defence row was a tragedy for the Alliance, which relies more than the larger parties on media exposure at its conferences. Alliance leaders feel they suffer a third-party squeeze in publicity, although Michael Foot has mischievously written that 'the idea of the two Davids being unfairly treated by the media is the most monstrous display of ingratitude since Goneril and Regan turned on their father'. Perhaps the most damaging blow during the defence squabble was to the Alliance's high standing with commentators. In an attempt to bridge the internal gap the two leaders undertook an extensive series of visits in Europe in the summer of 1986, and developed a policy based on Anglo–French co-operation on nuclear weapons. But alarmingly for them this produced widespread criticism that their initiative itself lacked the 'intellectual consistency and integrity' that David Steel belaboured Liberal delegates for not displaying.

The charge made was that talks in Paris and elsewhere were only a little French dressing to drown the taste of an independent British deterrent for those Liberals who found that distasteful. David Owen had always admitted that the fingers on buttons would have to be those of British Prime Minister and French President. A letter to *The Times* from the chairman of the French parliamentary commission on foreign affairs, Jean de Lipowski, dispelled any hope among the more naive Liberal peaceniks that their leaders might be able to woo the French away from a nuclear future. He declared that 'France has never wavered in her resolve to build and maintain an independent nuclear deterrent', and cited the decision, backed by all French parties, to instal by 1990 M4 missiles – 'these more powerful nuclear weapons' – as parallel to Britain's switch from Polaris to Trident, of which he apparently approved. Not much help seemed to be available to any of the Opposition parties from across the Channel.

The other great issue facing the Alliance in the run-up to the election was David Owen's determination to go for broke on the tax and benefits plan that formed the SDP attack on poverty. David Steel was also quite radical on redistribution, but Liberalism has a more complex history than social democracy on this subject. Its highly individualistic creed in the pre-industrial era turned into a market economic philosophy in the nineteenth century, with social Liberalism appearing only in Gladstone's later governments, and the welfare state with Lloyd George.

Asquith was also committed to Lloyd George's crusade against the grinding poverty of the early twentieth century. He must be the last British Prime Minister to do a breakfast-time stint on the front bench, after his Chancellor had been up all night fighting his Finance Bill through the Commons. But Asquith's own instinct was for what his biographer, Roy Jenkins, calls 'the maximum of radical result while arousing the minimum of conservative opposition'. David Steel's attitude is not dissimilar. Modern Liberals rely for their electoral support on getting the deserting Conservative vote; in recent years they have usually done well after a long period of Tory government. So although Steel found himself to the Left of David Owen on many issues, he had to be careful not to drive away Tory deserters by too radical economic and social policies. 'The maximum of radical result while arousing the minimum of conservative opposition' was his motto too.

When Labour assembled in Blackpool the week after the Liberal row over defence, it took natural comfort from its rivals' troubles. But Labour was soon to learn that it had been done no favours. First, if Alliance voters defected because they did not like a non-nuclear defence policy it would be to the Conservatives, and not to Labour. Second, the whole subject was now at the top of political agendas again, and since opinion polls showed that two out of three voters favoured British nuclear weapons, that would not help Labour either. Some Labour leaders hope that, as defence re-emerges as a major issue in the election, their policy will seem less ambiguous and more appealing to the young than in 1983, when it was a final nail in the coffin of a preordained defeat. Before and during Labour's 1986 conference American Defence Department officials signalled their unhappiness with Labour policy, and at the conference itself the American ambassador gave television interviews that made clear the policy is likely to be subject to searching international examination.

There is a tricky anti-American card that Labour leaders will hesitate to play. Labour is committed to support NATO, but because President Reagan is more unpopular on this side of the Atlantic than most American presidents, there may be a public reaction to anything that appears like intervention in British internal politics.

Neil Kinnock, a life-long unilateralist, hopes he can turn defence into an electoral asset. Already informal contacts with the American administration aim at producing at least a *modus vivendi*, which will reduce the damage to Labour during the election. Denis Healey, who believes the best Labour can hope for is that defence will not lose it votes, also appears determined that his party will not suffer next time from the internal divisions that appeared during the election campaign of 1983.

But once again defence looked like the most difficult election issue for Labour. In November, in the debate on the Queen's Speech, the Prime Minister embarked on what was to be a sustained attack, with liberal quotations from Denis Healey's and Roy Hattersley's past opposition to unilateral nuclear disarmament. In vain did they argue that the international context since Reykjavik had changed, that it was Mrs Thatcher whose views were anachronistic. The Conservative attack on this subject was relentless, and interest centred on how much further Neil Kinnock could bring himself to move in negotiation with Washington on the withdrawal of nuclear weapons from British soil. By November he was acknowledging that this might take 'more than a year'. With Labour's standing in the opinion polls at the start of the winter varying between 36 and 41%, the number of people in a Gallup poll who opposed Labour's defence policy was 62%. This seemed to suggest that defence might be a major factor in preventing support moving up above 40, which Neil Kinnock's strategists thought was the launching pad for election victory.

There is no doubt which subject Labour would like to dominate the election: unemployment. Neil Kinnock has deliberately set out to establish Labour in the public mind as the party of production, and specifically of manufacturing industry. The Conservatives, recognising from the opinion polls that unemployment may influence many votes, have responded to Labour's plans with one of the best-known forms of attack in the political lexicon: How would you pay for your programme?

The Shadow Chancellor, Roy Hattersley, was the target of much abuse from Treasury ministers, who claimed that Labour would have to raise income tax and VAT to astronomic levels. Unfortunately for Hattersley, a former Labour Cabinet colleague, Lord Barnett, had left some notable hostages to fortune in a frank book which became Margaret Thatcher's favourite bedtime reading. Barnett, who as Chief Secretary to the Treasury had responsibility for public spending, wrote: 'Expenditure priorities were generally decided on often outdated and ill-considered plans made in Opposition, barely thought through as to their real value, and never as to their relative priority in social, socialist, industrial or economic terms.' For good measure, he quotes Roy Hattersley as paraphrasing Bernard Shaw thus: 'The Labour Party is always wanting to bake plum-pies before we have picked the plums.'

It was in this fruitful orchard that Nigel Lawson's men were now harvesting. But Roy Hattersley had remained consistent in his attitude. Since Labour's programme began to take shape, he has reminded colleagues that they must not get committed to spending without regard to priorities. He also gave a brave – some said rash – commitment to reverse any further tax cuts. This is an issue that will be hard fought, and after the Shadow Cabinet elections in November elevated Bryan Gould, one of Labour's brightest young men, to the front rank, he was appointed to shadow the Chief Secretary, John MacGregor, and engage him in combat on both Conservative and Labour spending plans.

During the summer the opinion polls looked sufficiently good for Labour people to think they might become not just the largest party, but even have an overall majority. These rising expectations were due to the remarkable revolution that had taken place under Neil Kinnock's leadership. The launching of his latest campaign, 'Freedom and Fairness', was another sign of his single-minded determination to turn his party away from the ideologically sterile path that nearly led it to destruction in 1983. His decisive tactic has been simultaneously to gain control of the National Executive Committee and to erode its importance. The Parliamentary Party now has more influence on policy and the NEC less. Labour concentrates public attention on a small group of its most attractive front-bench spokesmen, including Kinnock, Hattersley, Healey, John Smith and Jack Cunningham. The counter-revolution against the dominance of party conference and the Left-wing executive in the seventies and early eighties rolls on.

Much of the change derived from Kinnock's own personality. His personal advantages are that he is amusing, likeable, with an attractive accent and a touch of poetry in his speech, a lilt of Welsh song in his oratory. Above all, perhaps, the most uncovenanted blessing to a nation feeling tired, he represents a new generation of politicians, with a handsome wife and a young family to underline the point. What surprises some Labour people is Kinnock's fascination with organisation and presentation, con-trasted with his apparent lack of the intellectual curiosity that is the driving force of many politicians. It may be that he is accepting for himself the same self-denying ordinance he tries to impose on others: don't endlessly con-template your political navel, but get on with convincing the public your policies are sensible.

Doubts about Neil Kinnock's experience will not be stilled before the election, probably never could be until he had been in Downing Street for several months, when the mysterious and slightly spurious cloak of authority, and even omniscience, with which civil servants clothe all their political masters would envelop him also. But Labour people were content that the new star in their political firmament was a man so devoted to the modernisation of their party, and to an unrelenting search for policies that would make it seem relevant to the times. The Bournemouth speech against Militant and the campaign that followed had changed the minds of those who thought him only a laughing lightweight.

Kinnock still faces his most difficult political task of all: to win from the trade unions the kind of understanding on wages that will make Labour's economic expansion plans appear credible to voters. But the thrust of his economic appeal is already clear, the same appeal that Harold Wilson made in 1964, after thirteen years of Conservative rule, and John F. Kennedy made in America four years earlier, after Eisenhower had been President for eight years. It is the almost invariable pitch of a challenger from the Left after a long period of government by the Right: an appeal to all who are bored or offended by the status quo, a claim to be able to get the country 'moving' after a period of inertia. Kennedy said it in the tones of upper-crust Boston, Wilson in the accents of Yorkshire, Kinnock with Welsh passion; but it is the same, the inevitable message.

At Labour's Blackpool conference it became clear that the new public relations team planned to play *fortissimo* the age gap between Margaret Thatcher and Neil Kinnock. The Neil-and-Glenys show moved smoothly from platform to crèche, from Red Review to Welsh Night to travel-by-landau, along a path strewn with the roses of youth, or – even better – of young middle-age, for that age-group votes while the really young are too busy about their own more exciting lives. She smiles at everyone, he enjoys himself much of the time, and they both understand the political advantage of emphasising the age difference, to counter the experience difference which the Tories emphasise.

The Prime Minister's age and possible retirement date inevitably became an issue. After Westland she faced the most insidious threat to any politician: the dry rot that can undermine a reputation beyond repair, the disease that brought Macmillan down after the scandals and rows of 1962. She also suffered from an ailment that did not afflict Gladstone or Disraeli in their media-free era: public boredom because of over-exposure. No modern politician quite measures up to Shakespeare's praise of Cleopatra: 'Age cannot wither, nor custom stale her infinite variety.' In politics 'infinite variety' is called inconsistency.

Margaret Thatcher's style is not varied. The single adjective that describes her strength and weakness is 'unrelenting'. This is a great asset in winning a war, or driving through an economic policy of whose rightness she remains convinced. But it is a quality of which voters can tire. Her second problem was that by 1985 some Tories assumed she would not want to risk a third election, and indulged in their ever-popular sport of king-making. The Prime Minister put paid to that, making clear she wanted to continue well into the new Parliament if she won, and that although she had bought a house at Dulwich, there was no undertone to Deux Eglises. 'The nineties' kept being mentioned. While I was writing this book she asked me about its nature. I said it covered the period of her governments but was not a biography. 'Oh, no!' she replied. '*Far* too soon for that.'

So the Government will go into the election with the undoubted advantage of Mrs Thatcher's experience; with the benefits and handicaps that any prime minister accumulates over seven or eight years; and with the double-edged factor of public reaction to her personality. For her personality does divide the nation more than would that of a more tentative leader, more than a member of the less visible sex who used to have a monopoly of national leadership; more, perhaps, than any prime minister since Lloyd George in the early twenties. Attitudes to her range from the 'Good ole Maggie' of her admirers to the 'Ditch the Bitch' of her most virulent detractors. They either love her or hate her.

Her personal decision on whether to fight another election must have been a difficult one, though little sign of this appeared in public. Once, at a reception at Mrs Gandhi's funeral, Jim Callaghan, who had been travelling in the Far East, described to Denis Thatcher how pleasant his travels are nowadays. He is still treated with the consideration shown to heads of government, but no longer endures the remorseless flow of Red Boxes containing official papers to be dealt with at the end of exhausting days. Denis Thatcher murmured: 'I can't wait.' That is not the Prime Minister's attitude. Yet she would be more than human if she had not noticed that her election record is good. In fact, in a league table of Prime Ministers she is well placed in Division One:

	Played	Won	Lost
Attlee	5	2	3
Churchill	3	1	2
Eden	1	1	0
Macmillan	1	1	0
Douglas-Home	1	0	1
Wilson	5	4	1
Heath	4	1	3
Callaghan	1	0	1
Thatcher	2	2	0

Mrs Thatcher has what football goalkeepers call a clean sheet, and she will want to keep it that way, to go into history as one political leader in this century who has been in charge for a long time, yet has never been defeated. Her strengths as Prime Minister and party leader have been an ability to win votes; an unremitting appetite for hard work; a mind and instinct for political decisions and pitfalls that have usually been as sharp as razors; a shell like a tortoise, into which she can withdraw as the missiles fly around her; an ability not to be bored by her own habit of repetition, of hammering out, again and again, the arguments that suit her – higher production, lower inflation, more home-owners, more shareholders, and so on.

The general view of Mrs Thatcher is as a kind of Boadicea, quite free from self-doubt. But a mandarin who has worked closely with her, though not wholly an admirer, once told me that he considered her a deeply self-questioning politician, who was much less sure of herself than she appeared. If this is true, the Prime Minister faces a difficult period, both in the choice of the election date and in her knowledge that she will be defeated, not just if Labour gets more seats, but even if she is head of the largest party but with no overall majority. For although the Alliance might be able to do a deal with a minority Conservative Government, they could not, on present intentions, accept a Prime Minister who had just been deprived by the voters of a majority of 140.

So the final stage of her leadership before the election makes even greater demands on her. So far, she has relied on those Grantham-based qualities of industry and cleverness that are summed up in the German word *fleissig*. They have made her the best single vote-winner since Harold Wilson. But after the buffeting of the year since Westland, to regain her unique position in politics and ensure supremacy over opponents, she needed more than cleverness and hard work. What she needed to show was political wisdom of the highest order, which does not come cheap. As the

Prophet Job observed: 'The price of wisdom is above rubies.'

Margaret Thatcher's Cabinet reshuffles remained throughout the two Parliaments a subject of baffled speculation. Her sackings seemed to show determination to weed, gradually but relentlessly, the team she had inherited from Edward Heath. But even before she had fully achieved that objective, helped by the political casualties of such events as the Falklands and Westland, she promoted new men from the same Left wing of her Party – Douglas Hurd, Kenneth Baker, Kenneth Clarke and Malcolm Rifkind among them. She has usually, though not invariably, contrived to put Right-wingers in the economic departments and Left-wingers in spending departments.

But the Prime Minister's aversion to the quiet life did not wither with the years. Nicholas Ridley was the first fully paid-up member of the Dry Tendency she dared to put in the Environment Department, which has long been regarded as the embassy in London of local councils – just as the old Ministry of Labour was the embassy of the TUC. We had seen what happened to Labour (now Employment) when Norman Tebbit took over, and councillors, particularly in Labour-controlled authorities, believed that Ridley's appointment was an indication of another Thatcher election theme: that central government has an obligation to control zany local councils.

The Prime Minister's selection of her driest minister to undertake the most difficult privatisation, water, seemed a shrewd choice. But Ridley showed an appreciation of the unwisdom of walking under ladders just before a general election, and discovering that the Water Bill would probably become controversial and damaging to the Government, he postponed it. The measure was unpopular with some Tories, in both Lords and Commons, would be bitterly opposed by environmental groups as well as the unions, and was fraught with legal complications. In fact, just the kind of Bill to keep Parliament sitting through long, sticky June and July nights in the period immediately before an election. The consumption of water would give way to Pym's No. 1 on the Terrace, and Dr John Cunningham, one of Labour's best debaters, would have the chance to send his oratorical *Water Music* trilling out over the Thames and into the campaign. So Ridley dropped it.

On the other wing of the Cabinet, Kenneth Baker was a minister who seemed able to walk on eggshells without damage either to them or his shoes. His fascination with technological advance coincided with a matching prime ministerial enthusiasm, and overrode any doubts she had about promoting such a notorious friend of Edward Heath to the glamorous job of Mr Infotec. Baker was moved on from that post, smelling of roses and computer printouts, leaving Geoffrey Pattie to wrestle with the gathering gremlins. Baker switched to Environment to help pick up the shattered pieces after Patrick Jenkin's run-in with the GLC and metropolitan counties. Jenkin had got the odium and the sack, while Baker was promoted and stayed just long enough in the senior Environment job to demonstrate that he had skills in presentation that the Government desperately needed in one of its troubled areas, Education.

When Baker succeeded Sir Keith Joseph (who had announced that he would be retiring at the next election), one Tory said: 'Thank heaven we have one chap on the front bench who looks happy, pleased with what he's doing, who just smiles a lot.' Baker, spectacles agleam, eminently competent and self-confident, smiled on into the future. He had a standing ovation at the party conference, and he looked what he is, one of the most cheerful and amusing personalities in politics, manifestly enjoying what was happening to him. It was about then that he began to be mentioned as a possible future leader.

For almost imperceptibly discussion of future Conservative leadership had changed since Mrs Thatcher appeared certain to fight another election. The qualities and weaknesses of the longer-standing candidates – Sir Geoffrey Howe, Norman Tebbit, Peter Walker, Michael Heseltine – have been mentioned earlier. But by the likely time of her departure – in the middle of the next Parliament if she won; after the election if she lost – Conservative MPs might to looking at a new generation. One advised: 'Start from Baker's age [51] and work downwards.'

That seemed too drastic. Taking January 1989 as an arbitrary guess at when a victorious Margaret Thatcher might retire, the ages of present (and one former) Cabinet members in the Commons would be: Geoffrey Howe 62, Nicholas Ridley 59, Douglas Hurd, John Biffen and Michael Jopling 58, Norman Tebbit and George Younger 57, Peter Walker and Nigel Lawson 56, Michael Heseltine and Tom King 55, Kenneth Baker and Nicholas Edwards 54, Paul Channon 53, John MacGregor and John Moore 51, Norman Fowler 50, Kenneth Clarke 48, and Malcolm Rifkind 42.

Now Churchill, Attlee, Macmillan, Home and Callaghan all became prime minister in their sixties, but most recent choices have been younger. Wilson, Heath and Thatcher all reached leadership before they were fifty, and Kinnock, Owen and Steel were even younger. So many prominent Tories are left wondering whether they have missed their chance of reaching the top of Disraeli's greasy pole. Some might extract wry comfort from a story told when Curzon suffered the disappointment of being pipped for the Conservative leadership by Baldwin, who, he assured the King's secretary, was a man 'of the utmost insignificance'. Curzon's second wife, Grace Duggan, was very rich, and when a lady at a house-party said to Balfour that 'dear George' would be terribly disappointed, he replied: 'Oh, I don't know. After all, even if he has lost the hope of glory, he still possesses the means of Grace.' Sixty years ago, politicians were both wittier and more thoroughly versed in the cadences of the Book of Common Prayer.

Hurd and Younger were other candidates among the recent promotions whose names began to be canvassed in 1986. But what was still lacking was a credible candidate of the Right, the wing of the Conservative Party which had, after all, produced the Thatcherite revolution of the eighties. Until 1986 Nigel Lawson had been thought of as almost non-political, so little effort did he make to master the arts of glad-handing, so insensitive did some nervous MPs believe him to be about their wish to be re-elected. But at the party conference Lawson had a triumph, and suddenly the Thatcherites, if they decided that Norman Tebbit could no longer be elevated, had a philosopher of the Right as their champion. The Opposition parties also began to keep a warier eye on Lawson. Even before the autumn statement, in which he suddenly found it necessary to yield to the tide of overspending, David Steel had pictured him as ringmaster of an election circus in which assets are sold, investment depressed, money printed, consumption boosted and taxes cut, not to help Britain but to buy votes. Labour also shuddered to think the Tories might run an old-fashioned pre-election boom to avert voters' eyes from the dole queues, and they conjured up memories of R. A. Butler's pre-election and post-election budgets in 1955.

It would, indeed, be an odd election if Opposition politicians, who for years have berated Margaret Thatcher for the stiffness of the whalebone in her economic corsets, were suddenly to see her cast them aside, and do a quick can-can for the delight of the electorate. Nothing, they feared, could more quickly draw away the crowds from the economic attractions of the Neil-and-Roy Dream Boat or the David-and-David European Revels further down the pier.

The Chancellor's own instinct was for the Conservatives to choose the role of prudent managers: since they had come to power as zealots for controlling state profligacy, there was not much political mileage in trying to outbid the Opposition in public spending. But the Treasury, in that inelegant phrase from American defence jargon, seemed willing to spend if it could have 'a bigger bang for its buck' – i.e. more votes for each pound spent. Yet to see Lawson's autumn statement, in which he agreed to overshoot previous spending targets by about £10 billion over two years, as a planned U-turn was to give too little weight to the cock-up theory of history. In future Lawson will probably be seen neither as Iron Chancellor nor as Artful Dodger of Great George Street, but more as Micawber, trusting that something will turn up.

What turned up in the autumn of 1986 was an irresistible force – in the form of overspending on health and social security, local councils and, prospectively, education. At least, if not irresistible it could not be resisted without great pain and strife. The Cabinet might have allowed the Chancellor to dig in his heels and insist on cuts, but not without a furious row. The alternative was to make a virtue of necessity, alter the planning totals which the Treasury elevates as the totem poles of economic propriety, and swear till hell freezes that borrowing will be controlled, and that tax cuts must therefore come out of (fortunately buoyant) revenue. As one minister put it, mixing his metaphors between the marriage and bastardy laws: 'We have made a virtuous woman out of the overspend; we gave it legitimacy.'

Lawson dismissed suggestions of an old-fashioned pre-election boom. When confronted on television with the remarks of a former Treasury colleague, Lord Bruce-Gardyne, who urged a spring election so that the consumer boom could be reined in as quickly as possible after victory, because of renewed risks of inflation, the Chancellor said sadly that 'Jock has always been of an apprehensive temperament'. Such crticism could not be levelled at Nigel Lawson. He is one of the bounciest of a bouncy trade, taking a sanguine view of any enterprise in which he engages.

If this makes the Chancellor seem like a gambling man, the theory that he gambled with the British economy just to get the Conservatives re-elected, though widely believed even by pro-Conservative experts, especially of monetarist views, is an oversimplification. He gambled on what he regarded as a racing certainty, his own sagacity. Disraeli, when prime minister, recommended a little known candidate for the Treasury to Queen Victoria by commenting on his great stature, 6 ft 4 in.: 'He has the sagacity of the elephant, as well as its form.' Leaving aside the present Chancellor's physical form, his past form includes a self-confidence that critics fear shades into a deficiency of sensible self-doubt.

Lawson had been criticised in the past by Conservatives for being insufficiently political, too much of an economic *apparatchik*. That is a misreading, derived from his facility in economic ideas and jargon, and his deficiency in political tact. His strength and weakness were simultaneously illustrated when, after the autumn statement, he was asked about its effect on demand management, and he replied, with austere wit, that he could not understand such neo-Keynesian concepts. But after his conference triumph; after his flexibility over spending, which is less the U-turn of a juggernaut, more the subtle, jinking run of an ambitious fly-half; after Norman Tebbit's bumpy year which has left the Right with no obvious candidate to succeed Margaret Thatcher, the Chancellor, who has never been a humble man, has raised his sights. As Disraeli said when helping the aged John Bright into his overcoat: 'After all, Mr Bright, we both know very well what brings you and me here: ambition.'

But as the election approached the question of a next leader, fascinating as it always is to politicians and journalists, was a matter for the future. Margaret Thatcher, who had given the Tories two remarkable victories, was looking for a third. Her win in 1979 was in part by courtesy of the unions, who created the Winter of Discontent; and General Galtieri helped her with the second. But even most of those Conservatives who did not like her version of their creed acknowledged that she was the right person in the right place so far as winning was concerned. Those who still believed their Party would one day need a counter-revolution against Thatcherism (née monetarism) were watching the election with fascinated ambiguity.

Tory MPs wanted to hold their own seats, of course, and most would regard a Labour government as somewhere on the horror scale between the South Sea Bubble and the Black Death. But this did not mean they all loved what Mrs Thatcher stood for. Ian Gilmour, writing after she dismissed him in 1981, had compared Thatcherism with the early Christian heresy of Arianism. Though condemned by the Council of Nicaea in AD 325, this was eventually accepted by both Eastern and Western Churches thirty-seven years later, causing St Jerome to complain: 'The whole world groaned in astonishment in finding itself Arian.' But Sir Ian cheerfully recalled that the adoption and apparent triumph of Arianism were the beginning of its downfall, for both East and West soon returned to orthodoxy. 'As with Arianism and Catholicism, so, let us hope, with monetarism and Conservatism,' he devoutly concluded.

Margaret Thatcher's place in Conservative history is already secure. Despite all their criticisms most Tories believe she took necessary steps to curb trade union power, reverse the inexorable march of the State, and reassert in the Falklands Britain's unwillingness to be pushed aside. If she won a third election, this would turn her into a Conservative figure to be compared only with Churchill in this century. The stakes were higher than usual, for if she lost the election, the subsequent battle for the soul of Toryism would be bitter and bloody.

Even among Tories she produces strong reactions, negative as well as positive. For some, time had made her more a mother of the nation, in the Golda Meir or Indira Gandhi mould. For others, familiarity has bred, or increased, contempt. Opposition MPs vacillated in their attitudes. A senior shadow minister, who has been gloomy for years, emerged from his conference believing that Labour could, perhaps even would, have an overall majority. He admitted to a lingering doubt that victory could yet be frustrated by the Thatcher Factor, which he had converted into the Prometheus Factor. Because he was hurrying back to the platform at Blackpool and I to a television studio when he produced this pearl, I remain uncertain whether the Prime Minister was meant to hurl fire at the Labour Party, turn the more clay-like figures on the Tory benches into a fighting army, or be chained to a mountain for eternal punishment by Arthur Scargill. But his point seemed to be that she was the kind of soldier, like David, who could turn a battle single-handed, or a sportsman like Botham or Dalglish who could do the same in a match. On the other hand, my Labour acquaintance also believed that she could lose the election, by public reaction to her personality.

Opposition politicians find it hard to believe that the public will not eventually turn against Margaret Thatcher more decisively than the polls have ever suggested. The battle between her and Neil Kinnock is titanic, because behind their differences of party, political belief and ideology, lies an older, deeper division. It is between people who neither like nor respect each other, and each of whom will use every kind of weapon and stratagem to bring the other down. Life at the top in 1987 and 1988 was not to be the most charitable period in Our Island Story. Not that there is much love lost with the Alliance leaders either. Kinnock and David Steel get on well enough, but the Prime Minister regards the Liberal leader as a kind of dishonorary 'wet'; and though David Owen has occasionally expressed guarded admiration for Mrs Thatcher's determination, he and she are both too personally abrasive to become chums. As for Kinnock and Owen, the bad blood there runs deep, right back to Labour's split in 1981.

Margaret Thatcher and Neil Kinnock glare at each other across the despatch boxes each Tuesday and Thursday with the same mutual incomprehension that made Harold Macmillan and Hugh Gaitskell the least congenial sparring partners in recent British history. Their tones became so acerbic that Rab Butler believed they were adversely affecting public life. He claimed to be trying to pour oil on the troubled water, though whether that deeply complex man really meant to is difficult to say. No one would even think of trying to bring Thatcher and Kinnock together.

Oddly, one physical problem does unite them. Each has a tendency to throat infection or hoarseness. Just as gardeners suffer from lumbago, journalists from cynicism and ulcers, newspaper proprietors from megalomania, and brewers' draymen from lipomas, this is the occupational disease of politicians, caused by too vigorous and frequent exercise of the larynx. Incurable, of course, but if you're sufficiently single-minded you scarcely notice the inconvenience.

So as this remarkable political decade reaches its electoral climax, Margaret Thatcher and Neil Kinnock, David Owen and David Steel are locked in an unbreakable embrace of antagonism. One leading politician told me he expected this to be the bitterest general election since the war, because it was a real fight for power between opponents who genuinely dislike each others' personalities and policies.

Special reasons for bitterness are present this time: a government which has been in power for a long and turbulent period, and with many controversial episodes behind it; a Prime Minister loathed by her opponents, seeking a third term; Labour and Social Democratic politicians who once served in the same Cabinet, and who now hate each other with the enmity unique to civil wars; a country whose spirit may have gone a little sour. The febrile nature of the polls suggests that the voters are reluctant to make up their minds.

After the revolutions that have engulfed all three political parties since the seventies, the pattern of politics is difficult to discern. The key to this is Labour. Neil Kinnock's reputation with Labour people ranges from hero-worship to grudging respect because he has pulled his party from the abyss of 1983, when it seemed that the Alliance's breaking of the mould might leave it as an unwanted fragment. Labour people still think they have a hope of winning, although sceptics still wonder whether the Age of Kinnock is one of convalescence for his party, or merely a remission in the disease that struck it earlier in the decade.

Yet something odd is happening. When a government has been in office for seven years, the electorate might be expected to divide between those who want to keep it in and those who want rid of it. In a three-party situation, there would be a Conservative vote of finite size, and an Opposition vote which might swing between Labour and the Alliance, depending on (1) how well each is doing; and (2) how much the Government is disliked, and therefore how much people are prepared to plump for whichever party is likely to displace it. According to 59% of Gallup respondents in the autumn of 1986, that party would be Labour. But instead of this scenario, what appears to exist is a Labour and an anti-Labour vote. For while Labour support in the polls has remained in the high thirties, with occasional figures in the low forties, the remaining votes have moved back and forth between Conservative and Alliance. In 1986, once the Alliance moved into the doldrums, the Conservatives caught up with, and passed, Labour. The degree to which the Alliance revived was therefore certain to have a significant, perhaps decisive, but certainly unpredictable effect on the fortunes of the two older parties.

The decade has been a bottomless pit of political surprise. Consider events since 1980. Labour's hijacking by the Left, followed by the split that created the SDP, and then the Alliance. The blitzkrieg take-over of Conservatism by Margaret Thatcher and her free-market allies. The end of full employment. The Falklands victory, which made the Prime Minister invincible in the 1983 election. Since then: The Brighton bomb. Neil Kinnock's counter-revolution in the Labour Party. The Westland crisis, with its air of obfuscation. The Alliance row and reconciliation over defence. Kinnock's long civil war with his local-government Left in Liverpool and London. The Parkinson and Archer affairs. MI5.

Margaret Thatcher could be forgiven if she murmured, with Macbeth: 'I have supped full with horrors.' But politicians, all of them, are made of sterner stuff. The battle goes on.

SOME KEY DATES

1975	May	Margaret Thatcher elected leader of the Conservative Party.
1976	April	James Callaghan succeeds Harold Wilson as Labour Prime Minister.
1978–9		Winter of Discontent: strikes damage Labour government.
1979	May (3)	General Election: Conservatives win majority of 43.
	August	IRA murder Lord Mountbatten in Irish Republic, and 18 soldiers in County Down.
	October	Labour's constitutional changes begin.
1980	October	Callaghan resigns as Labour leader.
	November	Michael Foot defeats Denis Healey for Labour leadership.
1981	January	Labour's Wembley conference establishes electoral college.
		Council for Social Democracy formed.
		Norman St John-Stevas dismissed from Government – the first wet.
	March	SDP launched.
		Sir Geoffrey Howe's deflationary budget angers Tory wets.
	Spring	Ten Irish Republican prisoners die on hunger strike.
	September	Three more wets – Sir Ian Gilmour, Lord Soames and Mark Carlisle – dismissed; Norman Tebbit, Nigel Lawson and Leon Brittan enter Cabinet; Jim Prior moved to Northern Ireland.
	November	Shirley Williams wins Crosby from Conservatives.
1982	March	Roy Jenkins wins Glasgow Hillhead from Conservatives.
	April–June	Falklands war.
	June	Jenkins defeats David Owen to become first SDP leader.
1983	February	Liberal Simon Hughes wins Bermondsey from Labour.
	March	Labour hold Darlington.
	June (9)	General Election: Conservatives win majority of 144; Francis Pym dismissed; Howe becomes Foreign Secretary, Lawson Chancellor, Brittan Home Secretary.
		Own replaces Jenkins as SDP leader.
	September	Neil Kinnock elected Labour leader to succeed Foot; Roy Hattersley elected deputy leader.
1984–5		Miners' strike.
1984	October	IRA bomb at Conservative conference in Brighton.
1985	June	Liberals win Brecon and Radnor from Conservatives.
	October	Kinnock launches attack on Militant Tendency.
	November	Anglo-Irish Agreement signed.
1986	January	Westland affair: Michael Heseltine and Brittan resign.
		Fifteen Ulster Unionist MPs fight by-elections; 14 retain seats.
	March	Labour gains Fulham from Conservatives.
	May	Alliance gains Ryedale from Conservatives.
	September	Alliance divided on defence; rift healed by end of the year.
	December	MI5 man's book in Australian court-case.

SELECT BIBLIOGRAPHY

Robert Blake, *The Conservative Party from Peel to Thatcher* (Fontana).
William Keegan, *Mrs Thatcher's Economic Experiment* (Allen Lane).
Peter Riddell, *The Thatcher Government* (Martin Robertson).
Hugo Young and Anne Sloman, *The Thatcher Phenomenon* (BBC).
Francis Pym, *The Politics of Consent* (Hamish Hamilton).
Ian Gilmour, *Britain Can Work* (Martin Robertson).
James Prior, *A Balance of Power* (Hamish Hamilton).
Michael Foot, *Aneurin Bevan* (Davis-Poynter h/b; Paladin p/b).
Anthony Crosland, *The Future of Socialism* (Cape).
Harold Wilson, *The Governance of Britain* (Weidenfeld & Nicolson/Michael
   Joseph).
David Lipsey and Dick Leonard (ed.), *The Socialists Agenda – Crosland's Legacy*
   (Cape).
Susan Crosland, *Tony Crosland* (Cape).
Roy Hattersley, *Choose Freedom* (Michael Joseph).
Joel Barnett, *Inside the Treasury* (Deutsch).
Robert Jenkins, *Tony Benn* (Writers and Readers Co-operative).
Robert Harris, *The Making of Neil Kinnock* (Faber).
David and Maurice Kogan, *The Battle for the Labour Party* (Kogan Page).
Michael Crick, *The March of Militant* (Faber).
Roy Jenkins, *Partnership of Principle* (Radical Centre/Secker & Warburg).
David Steel, *The Decade of Realignment* (Hebden Royd).
David Owen, *Face the Future* (Cape).

INDEX